The Power of Diversity

Also available from Network Continuum

Pocket PAL: Learning Styles and Personalized Teaching – Barbara Prashnig
Learning Styles in Action – Barbara Prashnig
Personalizing Learning – John West Burnham and Max Coates

THE
POWER
OF
diversity

New Ways of Learning
and Teaching through
Learning Styles

Barbara Prashnig

continuum

Continuum International Publishing Group

Network Continuum

The Tower Building

11 York Road

SE1 7NX

80 Maiden Lane, Suite 704

New York, NY 10038

www.networkcontinuum.co.uk

www.continuumbooks.com

British Library Cataloguing-in-Publication Data

A catalogue record for this book is available from the British Library.

ISBN: 9781855394414 (paperback)

Library of Congress Cataloging-in-Publication Data

A catalog record for this book is available from the Library of Congress.

Typeset by Fakenham Photosetting Limited, Fakenham, Norfolk

Printed and bound in Great Britain by Cromwell Press, Wiltshire

5. Too Many Provocations?

6. Don't Teach Me – Let Me Learn!

7. The New Look of Learning and Teaching

8. Staff Training in Style – Effective Preparation for Student Diversity

9. Learning Styles are Life Styles

If you find errors in this book,
please keep in mind that they are
there for a purpose.

I wrote something for everyone,
and some people are always
looking for mistakes.

All uncredited photographs are
the author's own, taken with
permission at various international
training sessions and visits
to schools.

Ten years have gone by since this book was first published in New Zealand and I observe with gratitude and amazement the impact this book is still having on people around the world. It has been ten years of hard work of developing the Learning Style Analysis (LSA) instruments for students and the Teaching Style Analysis (TSA) for educators; ten years of travelling the world and spreading the message. But it has also been ten years of immense enjoyment and pride about having created something people can accept, put to good use and pass on to others.

When I am travelling, I still observe style differences. Watching people still shows me how different and yet how similar human beings are; how difficult it often is to interact, communicate, and to understand one another. How much easier it would be if we all knew more about ourselves, our style differences and how we could get on with each other.

During the past ten years I conducted hundreds of training seminars and worked with thousands of educators in many different cultures – from the Arabic World to European countries, from the United States and Canada to Australia, South America and China. Learning Styles projects are underway in many countries and it seems that educators everywhere are more willing than ever to accommodate learning diversity in their classrooms. I discovered that certain style features are universal and that the 'Diversity Concept' is understood and applicable anywhere because it deals with human beings.

In the meantime this book has been translated into Swedish, Finnish, Norwegian and Indonesian. Our assessment instruments are available in English, Finnish, Swedish, Norwegian, Danish, German, Turkish and Spanish. I have realized it is a truly universal concept and I am grateful that modern technology as well as long-distance travel have made it possible to reach so many people around the globe. The biggest impact on 'spreading the word' was undoubtedly the expansion and greater reliability of the internet which has made a huge difference in delivering our assessment instruments via our website to anyone anywhere in the world.

I feel honoured that you, the reader, have chosen to read, skim, or browse through this book and I hope you can find plenty of interesting ideas which will excite you so much that you want to share them with others. I also hope that you are keen to continue learning about yourself, your family members, partners, friends, superiors, and about human diversity in general.

As with any book of this kind (semi-scientific, based on professional experience) it would have been impossible for me to put all the information together without the professional knowledge, advice, support, friendship and love of the many people I have met and learned from along the way.

I want to express my gratitude to the many professionals, peers, colleagues and friends who influenced me most over the years and I would like to thank them sincerely for what they did for me, even if they might not be aware of it.

On a professional level I would like to thank:

Jim Houghton of NEP for being an inspiring publisher and the team at Continuum for their support and expert advice;

Dr Rita Dunn for opening my eyes to Learning Styles all those years ago;

Dr Kenneth Dunn for accepting me as the co-author for our new LSA and WSA Models;

Dr Georgi Lozanov, Tony Stockwell and Charlotte Le Hecka for teaching me the art of Suggestopedia;

Alan Cooper for his courage to be the first principal in New Zealand (NZ) to fully introduce learning styles into his school and trusting my professional advice;

The many principals and deputy principals particularly in NZ, Australia and the UK for accepting my training, for allowing the introduction of learning styles into their schools and for doing pioneering work;

Janice Tofia, principal at Forbury Primary School in Dunedin and staff members for being courageous enough to apply the learning styles concept under extremely difficult conditions and succeeding against all the odds;

Graduates of my teacher training programme 'Diploma in Holistic Education' and participants at my learning style seminars around the world for their open-mindedness and their never-ending efforts in putting my suggestions into practice – often against all odds;

The new pioneers in Austria who have taken great interest in this concept during a time when educational standards are slipping and new ways of teaching must be applied;

Past and present staff at Creative Learning in Auckland for giving me all the back-up I need for my upfront work and for keeping the office going when I am away;

Mikhail Diatchenko for being such a great programmer, webmaster and team member;

Dr Yvonne Walus for her tremendous skills in supporting our international partners, for being my wonderful assistant and for her loyalty during difficult times;

Our team of national and international facilitators for sharing the same vision for students, teachers and schools, and for being such good team players.

And on a more personal level I'd like to thank:

My late husband, Armin Prashnig, for believing in me and for having always been there for me when I needed him – I miss him dearly.

My daughter Siggy for giving me support and without her tremendous computer skills I would not have been able to complete the first edition of this book;

My late parents Maria and Peter Stastny for instilling in me the love for learning;

My new home country for over 20 years, New Zealand, for giving me the freedom to do what I love and to give me the inspiration and creativity I need for bringing positive change to so many people;

My native Austria – my old and new home country – for giving me a solid education, excellent teacher training, a profound respect for human society, and more recently a wonderful place to live in Vienna while I'm doing my work in the northern hemisphere.

By Professor Dr Michael Schratz, Dean of Education, University of Innsbruck

This is not a conventional book about how to inspire and teach people of all ages to learn better. It is a much more ambitious work that challenges conventional beliefs about good teaching. On a first skim through the book you will be hooked up by such provocations as 'Underachievement – the unnecessary disease in our schools', 'Don't teach me – Let me learn!', 'Learners – an endangered species', 'There are no learning disabilities – only teaching disabilities', 'To learn without doing is like making love without touching'.

Beware: these central messages might hurt the professional pride of teachers, but the author, who went through similar experiences herself, addresses a view on education which I believe is growing around the world: Although educators have the vision that all children can learn, schools treat most students as if they can learn the same way. This misconception has led to what some regard as the longest distance in the world, namely the distance from a policy paper to the student in the classroom.

Both as an international researcher and a policy adviser in several countries I experienced that educational structures often run counter to the idea that all students can learn. Classes are organized in year cohorts, content is fragmented into curricular units, meaning is derived from content, classroom interaction is constructed by didactic orientation with little space for individuality. This dilemma has lead to a crisis in educational outcome which many countries try to answer by introducing or intensifying testing students' achievement.

Barbara Prashnig does not believe in such solutions of uniform outcome. She envisages a crisis of learning and encourages us to look closer at the individual student and learn to recognize his or her uniqueness as a starting point for further educational measures. The great number of schools and countries around the world she visited seem to concede a point to her, when she suggests that the key to addressing the crisis of educational outcome in our time lies in a new way of looking at learning.

Claus Otto Scharmer, the founder of the Society of Organizational Learning at the MIT, shows that we can look at the work of an artist at least three ways: We can focus on the *thing* that results from the creative process, say, a painting. We can focus on the *process* of painting. Or we can observe the artist as she stands in front of a *blank* canvas.

If we apply this artist analogy to learning, we can look at the learner's work from three different angles: First, we can look at *what* learners (have to) do. Tons of (text) books have been written from the point of what students have to learn. Second, we can look at the *how*, the learning process. That's the perspective we have used in enhancing teaching methods hoping that students would learn better. Yet we have rarely looked at the learner from the third, or blank-canvas, perspective. The question we have left unasked is the unique style of learning, thinking and working of an individual. Barbara Prashnig's learning style theory embodies this third view.

For Heinz von Förster, a key figure in constructivism, 'Learning is the most personal thing in the world. It is as peculiar as a face or like a fingerprint, even more individual than love life.' Barbara Prashnig unfolds the message that everyone of us has a thinking style, learning style and working style as unique as our fingerprints.

In conventional educational settings, very few people learn or work in a way which is best for them and the way in which their brain works. The resulting fallacy of teaching and learning which still dominates many classrooms around the world has caused thousands of students to repeat classes, fail schools and drop out altogether. In the long run, such failures might put society at risk or, as the author states, might 'lead from missing (social) skills to social ills'.

Some chapters of the book let the reader assume that a quiet revolution took place at the schools the author worked with, when we read how learning disabilities have disappeared, discipline problems have ceased and underachievers (both 'slow learners' and 'gifted students') suddenly have accelerated in their learning and can exceed their limits.

What is the secret force behind Barbara Prashnig's books, which have meanwhile sold well over 250,000 copies in several languages? It is a simple but effective approach. With her pioneering concept of learning and working styles she offers an instrument which explores each individual's unique style of thinking and learning. Its application not only opens up the great diversity of multiple biographies in a classroom, but, with the help of a teaching style analysis, also demonstrates the possible mismatch between teaching and learning (styles).

In several case studies from different parts of the world she presents stories about the importance of these styles and reflects on the impact they have had on disruptive classes and failing schools. I love the pictures of classrooms depicting students at work, which grasp learning in its whole complexity. They show how interconnected places and rooms are with feelings and emotions, whereas conventional teaching is usually based on cognitive aspects of the curriculum.

Not all her findings are new. Among others, she draws on the original work of Rita and Ken Dunn, builds on the multiple intelligences of Howard Gardner and uses Georgi Lozanov's findings in suggestopedia for the layout of her book. Weaving together the various (re)sources into an impressive knowledge base to personalize learning, she shares with the reader her collective wisdom from very diverse settings.

The *Power of Diversity* offers valuable tools, resources and practical applications that help teachers, trainers, parents and students to reach their full potential. Moreover, it will contribute to realizing what the famous philosopher Aristotle stated 2400 years ago: 'The greatest inequality is the equalization of unequals.'

Innsbruck, August 2007

A Vital Message of Hope by Gordon Dryden, co-author of *The Learning Revolution*

I love this book. It delivers a vital message of hope that is desperately needed by millions of students and parents around the world. Those are the millions who are stupidly and wrongly condemned to fail at school when they can just as easily succeed. This book shows how to achieve such results.

At its simplest, Barbara Prashnig's message is disarmingly clear:

- Everyone of us has a learning style, thinking style and working style as unique as our fingerprints.
- We each take in information, store knowledge and retrieve it in different ways.
- Parents and schools can now easily identify those individual styles, and so can businesses for their employees.
- It is imperative for schools, parents and organizations to cater to those individual differences.
- Unless that happens, millions more will be wrongly classed as school failures or learning disabled students and become dropouts because their learning style is not suited to their school's teaching style.

In some ways those dropouts are in illustrious company:

- Winston Churchill did poorly at schoolwork. He talked with a stutter and a lisp. Yet he became one of the greatest leaders and orators of the twentieth century.
- Albert Einstein was a daydreamer. He even failed mathematics early in high school. Yet he went on to become the greatest scientist of his age.
- Thomas Alva Edison was beaten at school because his teacher considered him 'addled' for asking so many questions.
- Beethoven's tutor said he was hopeless as a composer. He never learned to multiply or divide.
- Louisa May Alcott's teacher complained that she drew instead of doing addition.
- Emile Zola scored zero in his final literature examination.
- United States president Woodrow Wilson couldn't read until he was eleven.

And all had something in common. They had individual learning styles that were not suited to the style in which they were taught. Fortunately each seemed to have the temperament and drive to succeed by themselves – or with the help of loving parents and/ or understanding mentors. For millions of others the same mismatch continues today. It is probably the biggest cause of school failure. And it need not be.

For most of the last three centuries, many school systems have been geared to teaching every child in one or two main ways – mathematically and linguistically. Even worse, today, so-called 'intelligence' tests have been devised to label those two main ways as the only forms of intelligence – as if brilliant sporting achievers, musicians, painters, mathematicians, top sales people, orators, golf course designers, writers, accountants, lawyers, politicians, jewellers, architects, cooks, doctors and computer programmers all had the same talents.

For well over a century most schools have succeeded in graduating about 20 per cent of their students fully qualified for careers in management and the professions. Some schools have done a reasonably good job of schooling another 30-odd per cent to become craftsmen, tradesmen, clerks and typists. The other 50 per cent of so-called 'low achievers' have traditionally gone on to become manual or unskilled workers.

Today most of those unskilled jobs have gone. And we know that most of those school dropouts are youngsters whose learning styles do not suit most school teaching styles. The amazing thing is how professionals in our education systems have perpetuated the myth that all learn in roughly the same way.

In my own case, I am very comfortable as a 'print-oriented visual' learner. I can happily skim-read book after book. At one stage, for seven years as a talk-show host, I averaged 15 new books a week. I am also a morning person and I prefer to read stretched out on a bed or a sofa – before breakfast. I find great difficulty reading while sitting at a desk or table. Little wonder that I dropped out of school at the age of fourteen – and started learning.

I also store information in a different way: tactile/visually – by marking books with a highlighter and particularly by typing summaries. And I retrieve information by 'internal visualization' – by recalling images in my mind's eye, or presenting it from visual slides.

As a youngster I flew through primary school. Fortunately a great headmaster identified my self-learning ability and introduced me to the wonders of the public library and its gifted librarians. Yet for me high school was a disaster. At the age of 13 I was reading four mystery novels a *week*. But the teacher wanted me and every other third-former to read only one book a *year*: Shakespeare's *The Merchant of Venice*. Stagger through it over several months, regurgitate some of it in an examination – and you passed.

Every person reading this page would have collections of school students with different learning traits – not always with the same outcome. Over the last ten years at least 20 different methods have emerged to identify those learning styles.

Harvard professor Howard Gardner has argued extensively that we each have at least seven different 'intelligences'. More recently he has argued for an eighth: the naturalist intelligence. I would personally argue that visual and spatial abilities can be separate, and the love of nature is more a preferred learning style than a different form of intelligence. Amazingly, Professor Gardner leaves out one of the most important of all: the ability to create new ideas by recombining existing elements in new ways. But the overall logic of his argument is obvious from straight observation. Some children in the same family love playing the piano, others detest it. Some are almost magical in their ball-handling ability and can play table tennis, basketball and other sports almost instinctively. Yet others score highly in logic, while others are brilliant at painting.

Richard Bandler, John Grinder and Michael Grinder, in their pioneering work on Neuro-Linguistic Programming (NLP), present strong proof that generally we each have one dominant learning trait: visual, auditory or kinesthetic. They and others conclude, quite rightly, that it is the 'mainly kinesthetic', or physical learner, who misses out in most schooling systems – wrongly labelled 'hyperactive' or with a 'learning deficit disorder' when the real difference is in learning style. Despite strong research findings, it still amazes me that many NLP practitioners still make the ludicrous claim that 93 per cent of all learning is subconscious. Having proved that we all learn differently, they repeat, in a new way, that we are all the same! They also do not differentiate sufficiently between kinesthetic and tactile learning preferences, and Barbara Prashnig's field study findings are particularly valuable.

The husband and wife team of Ken Dunn, professor and chair at Queen's College, City University of New York, and Rita Dunn, professor at St John's University, New York, have isolated five different factors in their pioneering work on learning styles: environmental, emotional, sociological, physiological and psychological. These determine how human beings take in information, store and retrieve it. Together with Dr Ken Dunn, Barbara Prashnig has redeveloped the learning style model and also extended it into a working style model for people in the workplace.

But there are five major factors which, in my view, set Barbara Prashnig's work apart:

- While others rely largely on 'book research', Barbara has travelled the world to study with many of the leading researchers at first hand. She has studied learning styles, multiple intelligences, NLP, brain research and accelerated learning.
- She has then applied and tested their findings thoroughly in her new homeland of New Zealand: in primary/elementary schools, high schools, universities and in business settings.
- She has not taken one isolated aspect or method of learning and turned it into a new Holy Grail. Nor should she. If a child learns better through music, movement and touching, then Barbara's quest has been simple: find out how best to use music, movement and touch to enhance the learning process.
- Better still, she has used this multiplicity of experiences to fashion new ways to cater for the great diversity in students, teachers and workers alike.
- She also travels extensively to introduce her methods and test them in action in different cultures and to improve them continually.

Some of her findings were presented in an earlier book. I was honoured to be asked to contribute the preface. But this extended book is even more thorough, even more exciting, even more practical, even more essential.

I recommend it to teachers, trainers, parents and students alike. The world needs its message and the results it demonstrates and celebrates.

This workbook is an introduction to diversity, different learning and working styles, new teaching methods and creative, accelerated learning techniques. It explains how to develop your learning potential in any environment. It can be read in a conventional manner or be used as a workbook for a self-study programme during which you will experience how these methods can be applied and find out how they work for you. If you are an educator or parent you can try out the recommendations or act upon your newly gained insights to help your students or children to have more fun and experience more success during the learning process.

If you decide to use this as a workbook, the following steps are recommended:

1. You will have noticed that the **layout** of the book is rather unusual. On all the left-hand pages you will find **visuals**, **thoughts** and **graphs**, while the text on the right-hand pages has been written in **suggestopedic format** to speed up your reading and help you with your recall. If you want to find out more about suggestopedic methods go to page 169. You are also invited to **complete** the various **exercises and mind maps** throughout the book and use the empty spaces for your **own notes**.

2. Do one most important thing first: get your own personal Learning Style Analysis profile (**LSA**) to make the best possible use of your own **learning ability**. Please see **Appendix I** for obtaining your personal **Style Analysis**. If you also want to know how you teach, you can also obtain your Teaching Style Analysis (TSA-Ed). It will be of great help to understand better how you come across as a teacher and how different or similar your teaching is from your learning style – you might be surprised!

3. If you want to find out about your students' or children's learning ability and discover their true **learning potential**, you can download LSA questionnaires and obtain their personal profiles via the internet from the CLS website: www.creative. learningcentre.com. The result – their **Learning Style Analysis** – will give you a detailed overview of their true learning needs, their **personal preferences**, their **dislikes** and their **flexibilities**. By knowing their strengths and weaknesses and by following the detailed **recommendations** given in the LSA Report they will considerably enhance their information intake skills, their study habits and their long-term memory. You will also be able to enhance your communication with them by understanding their style much better.

4. Decide where you want to work through this book – check your **physical environment** – is it arranged in a way that you feel **comfortable**?

5. Consider if you need absolute **quiet** or if you want to put on **background music** while you are going through this book. If so, refer to Chapter 6 (pages 171–181) to select the most appropriate **learning music** to keep your brain alert and your concentration high as long as you like. You can use the learning music recommended on pages 172 and 174 or choose your own music and switch it on **NOW**!

6. Prepare a **note pad**, a pen, several **sheets of blank paper** (A4 format or bigger) and at least five **coloured felt pens** or **highlighters** for your own note taking. As all the chapter overview mind maps are in black and white, you might like to colour them in after you have read the chapter to personalize them and to jog your memory.

7. Before you start working through the book, go to pages 166–167 and read about a very useful note-taking technique – **Mind Mapping®**; create a **mind map** as a **summary** of these instructions and use this technique for summarizing each chapter you have read.

8. Browse through the whole book, look at the **mind maps** on the left-hand pages, particularly those with chapter overviews, or read the table of contents to gain an overview, the big picture, of the new learning content. This will especially help visual learners to remember.

9. To improve your **memory** and maximize your **retention**, make sure you read the book at a **time** when you are most alert and when you can concentrate easily. As **motivation** and **interest** are excellent learning enhancers, keep your **curiosity** high and reward yourself if you have discovered something new and exciting and when you can remember it!

10. However, if you are tired and still want to be **mentally alert** to read the book, do some **Brain Gym®** exercises as described on pages 164–165. They will help you to get energized, more alert and better focused. But if you feel you are too wound up, too uptight and stressed out to be able to concentrate, maybe some of the **relaxation/visualization** or **centring exercises**, as suggested on pages 158–165, might help you. Whatever it takes, help your body and brain to take in the information contained in this book with enjoyment and ease.

11. Now begin working through the book, learn a lot, remember it well, and most importantly – **ENJOY IT** and **HAVE FUN!**

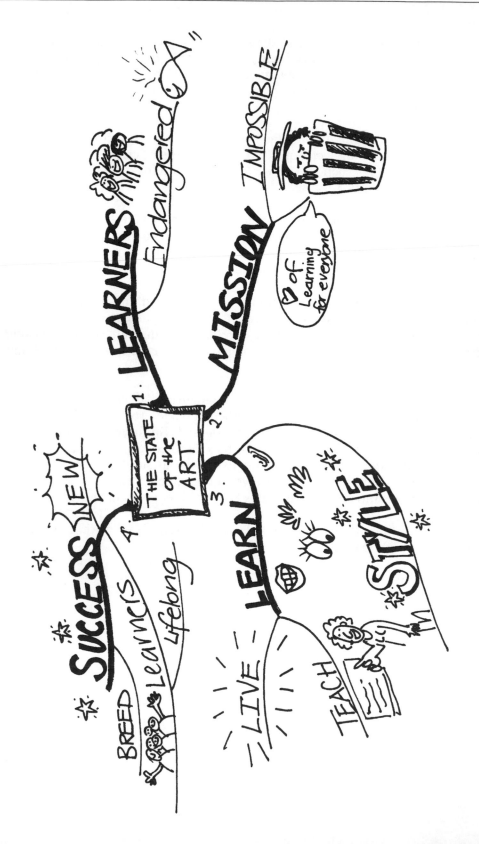

1. Learners – an endangered species

Over the past 10–20 years many species,
like whales, have been exposed to an <u>environment</u>   **environment**
which is no longer safe, which no longer supplies
what their <u>basic needs</u> require for survival, and is   **basic needs**
threatening their livelihood. The results of such
conditions are devastating not only for the species
itself but also for the entire environment. Whenever
a <u>species is decimated</u> or, worse, becomes extinct,   **species is decimated**
there is always a <u>major upset in the balance</u> of   **upsets the balance**
any ecosystem.

As we well know, this is presently happening
on a huge scale worldwide. However, we tend
to ignore it or prefer to believe that such events
won't have the predicted negative impact.

If we compare the example from the animal
kingdom with the situation learners find themselves
in these days (especially in secondary and tertiary
education), it is obvious that such learning
environments are really <u>no longer conducive</u>   **no longer conducive**
<u>to successful and satisfactory learning</u>.   **to successful learning**

Traditional education practices with a strong
emphasis on mathematical and linguistic skills
and formal delivery, using mainly <u>analytical,</u>   **analytical, left-brain**
<u>left-brain</u> teaching methods (as described on
page 6), do not allow many students to develop
life skills and learning abilities which would enable
them to survive easily in our fast-changing world.

Students can neither understand themselves
as learners or what is happening to them, or
why they cannot produce adequate results
during their years of schooling. As a consequence,
their <u>self-esteem</u> and <u>motivation</u> are <u>reduced</u>   **self-esteem and motivation**
<u>dramatically</u> and finally their minds are lost for   **dramatically reduced**
lifelong learning – they are literally <u>extinct</u>   **extinct**
as a <u>learning species</u>.   **as learning species**

The results are dangerous for any human society
and manifest themselves in climbing figures
for crime rates, drug abuse, unemployment,
alcoholism, divorce, child abuse, violence,

There Are Three Categories Of People:

The Ones That Make Things Happen,

The Ones That Watch Things Happen,

And The Ones That Wonder

What The Hell Is Happening.

economic recession, environmental problems, poverty, social unrest, perhaps even war.

It might not be obvious but the <u>social ills</u> every developed society is stricken with today seem to have their roots in <u>poor education</u>, dropoutism, underachievement and <u>low self-esteem</u> which can often be traced back to the parent generation.

social ills

poor education
low self-esteem

So, what can be done to <u>break the vicious cycle</u>, to prevent these developments continuing?

break the vicious cycle

2. No more mission impossible – love of learning for everyone?

The claims that everyone can learn, that mass education is mental mass destruction and that this creates learning disabilities, are not new but sound like <u>provocations</u> because the generally held view, at least here in New Zealand, is that we have one of the best educational systems in the world – including our high school system.

provocations

Reality, however, seems to support the opposite: the number of underachievers in schools is on the rise; learning disabilities have become a fact of life; learning motivation goes down the longer students are in the educational system; nearly everyone is glad when school is finally over; and even many of those who successfully finish a degree find studying hard and frustrating.

As fond memories of school learning are rare, and in most people's minds knowledge acquisition seems to stop when they leave school, it is no surprise that <u>lifelong learning</u> is usually not part of our mindset. Yet most people appreciate the learning they experience in 'real' life; in fact over the years they usually get better at it and even enjoy it! However, as soon as they have to go back to <u>traditional training</u> situations or, even worse, to <u>formal learning</u> or <u>studying</u>, they immediately develop negative feelings – the same feelings they experienced through their school learning: anxiety, frustration, boredom, stress, decreased motivation.

lifelong learning

traditional training
formal learning/studying

And yet – considering the <u>human brain</u>,

human brain

HOW I FEEL ABOUT LEARNING
Pre-test

Please respond to these statements by ticking the appropriate box –
do it fast, without analysing.

	True	**False**
1. If I really want to learn something, I have to do a lot of studying and repetition.	☐	☐
2. Learning is something very interesting and pleasant for me.	☐	☐
3. I think I have a good memory.	☐	☐
4. Learning is hard work most of the time.	☐	☐
5. I think I've always been a good learner.	☐	☐
6. I wish I could concentrate better.	☐	☐
7. I don't think I'm very intelligent.	☐	☐
8. Often I think 'If only I didn't forget everything so quickly'.	☐	☐
9. If I can learn something new, I get the feeling of deep satisfaction and contentment.	☐	☐
10. If I think back to my time at school, I think 'Oh no! I'm glad that's over!'	☐	☐
11. I think learning is very hard for me.	☐	☐
12. I know I learn quickly.	☐	☐
13. Learning has hardly ever been fun for me.	☐	☐
14. Learning gives me satisfaction, happiness and contentment.	☐	☐
15. I can't imagine that I'll ever be able to master a difficult subject (for example, a foreign language, mathematics) easily.	☐	☐
16. Foreign languages have always been my favourite subject	☐	☐

Scoring, see page 352

it is quite clear that its <u>main function</u> is to learn, and that human beings can <u>increase</u> their <u>skills</u> and <u>knowledge</u>.

main function
increase skills/knowledge

Furthermore, given the amazing brain power every human being has, <u>learning</u> as well as studying and information intake <u>should actually be fun</u>, very <u>easy</u>, always <u>without stress</u> and should have <u>long-lasting effects</u>.

learning
should be
fun, easy, stress-free,
have long-lasting effects

If all that is really true, why do so many people have learning difficulties, a poor memory, concentration problems, and find information intake and skills acquisition often very stressful?

The answer is very simple and the reality behind it all is nearly too good to be true: the <u>key</u> to successful learning and working is knowing one's unique personal <u>learning</u> or <u>working style</u>, accepting one's strengths as well as one's weaknesses, and <u>matching personal preferences</u> as much as possible in any learning, study or work situation.

key
learning/working style

matching personal
preferences

The short pre-test on the opposite page can be used as a quick way of finding out your true <u>attitudes to learning</u>, which often go back to your early childhood.

learning attitudes

3. Learn, teach and live in style

People of all ages can learn virtually anything if allowed to do it through their own <u>unique styles</u>, through their own <u>personal strengths</u>. They are more capable of consistent performance if their working conditions suit their individual style preferences. Research over the past 25 years, mainly coming from St John's University in New York, has shown that human beings can learn any subject matter successfully when the <u>instructional methods</u> used are <u>matched</u> with their individual learning <u>preferences</u>. When <u>human diversity</u> is taken into account and <u>respected</u> in the learning process, in training situations or in skills acquisition, the <u>results are always positive</u>: the <u>learner</u> experiences

unique styles
personal strengths

instructional methods
matched with preferences
human diversity
respected

positive results for learner

Elements of Traditional Teaching

disciplined, ordered, logical, analytical
low emotional impact
meaning derived from content
strong emphasis on 3 Rs
sitting at desks – limited activities
stress on auditory mode
'chalk – talk – handouts'
lecture/didactic oriented
suppressing energy
little brain stimulation
belief that learning is difficult
mistakes recognized/corrected directly
strong association with failure
create tension and stress in student and teacher
low learning motivation
acceptance of students' mental state
content is fragmented/no big picture
finish when time is up
emphasis on quiet class
institutional rituals
school uniform
mass instruction/little room for individuality

Based on experience and handouts by Eric Jensen and Jeannette Vos

pleasure, gains a sense of accomplishment
without frustration and stress, experiences
increased motivation and is always <u>in control</u>
<u>of the learning process</u>.

in control of learning

Before you will be able to gain an insight
into the complexity of a person's style elements,
it is necessary to define what learning style is
and, as an extension of that, what working style is.

According to Drs Rita and Kenneth Dunn,
two of the leading researchers in this field,
'<u>learning style</u> is the way in which human beings
begin to <u>concentrate on</u>, <u>absorb</u>, <u>process</u> and
<u>retain new and difficult information</u>.' (1)

**learning style: how to
concentrate, absorb,
process, retain new and
difficult information**

Similarly, <u>working style</u> can be defined as
the way people in the workforce usually <u>absorb</u>
and <u>retain new and difficult information</u>, <u>think</u>
or <u>concentrate</u>, generally do their daily work
and effectively <u>solve problems</u>.

**working style: how to
absorb and retain new
and difficult information
think, concentrate,
solve problems**

4. A promising new species – lifelong learners in their own style

After having investigated why students do have
learning problems and why many people find it
so difficult to keep up their work performance,
it is obvious that the secret to success in learning
and teaching lies in knowing oneself, one's style,
one's potential and the resulting consequences.
The enormous benefit from all the aspects of
<u>self-knowledge</u> will be noticeable not only in
areas of learning, teaching and studying, but
also in one's personal and professional life.

self-knowledge

If people are allowed to learn and work through
their own styles and find suitable environments
for their activities, there is no limit to what
human beings can achieve, and they can actually
do it with much <u>less stress</u> and much <u>more joy</u>.

less stress and more joy

Teachers will be more understanding of their
students' <u>true learning needs</u> and more aware of
their own teaching style and the resulting style
matches or mismatches.

true learning needs

Ms Barbara M Prashnig
Director – Training and Research
Creative Learning Company Ltd
PO Box 5422, Wellesley Street
Auckland 1
NEW ZEALAND

Friday, 7th March 1997

Dear Barbara

I have just finished not simply reading, but also interacting (actually, it's the same thing for me), with your book 'Diversity is our Strength' and feel impassioned to write you a note of genuine, volcanically ardent appreciation. You have poured in your warmth, sincerity, and erudition onto the pages of the book, and anyone not interested in such material WILL be suitably 'metamorphosed'. (Your book was lent to me by a friend, can't find it in the shops here in Singapore.)

Your passionate spirituality, in the purest sense of the word, will prove to be an inspiration to humanity. I am certain that your presence in the learning ecosystem is as vital as oxygen is for our planet.

How wonderful that another terrific human being, Gordon Dryden, wrote the preface to your book. What a guy!

I believe your message needs to sweep across all continents. We seem to have largely lost touch with our essence. In truth, we see with our eyes, but observe with our brains. We hear with our ears, but listen with our minds. We touch with our hands, but feel with our hearts. We utter with our lips, but speak from our souls. We need to sense all by observing, listening, feeling, speaking, doing! For we sense with our spirit, and then, we embrace life! All this we were born with. What happened along the way? This is my question to us all, ergo your work has total relevance. Very well done, Barbara.

May I present you with a small token of my appreciation. It accompanies this letter and the title 'Superbrain' could just as easily apply to you!

Take care and God Bless

Dilip Mukerjea
Spiritual Entrepreneur (author of *Brainfinity* and *Superbrain*)

This will lead to better attitudes towards learning in a large group of students who cannot learn well with traditional teaching methods, who come to believe they are stupid and who are often lost for lifelong learning. If, however, they are encouraged to learn in their own way, utilizing their unique style preferences, they usually get very excited about learning tasks and can actually become lifelong learners.

utilizing unique style preferences

Everyone will also be more effective in their interpersonal relationships because understanding human diversity gives them new and better tools for interacting much more successfully.

understanding human diversity

When human beings know their potential, their unique style and how to go about effective information intake, they will naturally become what they are meant to be as a species: successful lifelong learners in their own style.

know potential

lifelong learners

5. Individualized learning and student-centred teaching

Around 1990, the emphasis in pedagogical theory shifted from the long-overused 'curriculum-centred' teaching to 'student-centred' teaching with the idea that teachers should focus more on students' learning needs. This sounded great! Many teachers – especially in primary schools – embraced this idea wholeheartedly, mainly in Scandinavia because education systems there seem to leave teachers more freedom in class. In the rest of the world however, and particularly in secondary education, it remained a catch phrase because nobody really knew or could imagine how to accommodate diverse learning needs in mass education. And so, teachers continued with their traditional, but well-known frontal methods to the detriment of many of their students who couldn't learn this way.

'curriculum-centred'

focus more on students' learning needs

Scandinavia

catch phrase

mass education

Then, more technology was introduced to classwork and dutifully, teachers got trained how to use the internet and electronic whiteboards, all in the hope of reaching students more effectively. This was helpful to a certain extent, but was hugely labour intensive, and again, in high schools impossible to implement on a larger scale with hundreds of students per teacher. The dream of reaching EVERY student remained a dream – until Learning Styles (LS) came along as we will see.

more technology

reaching students

**impossible to implement
hundreds of students**

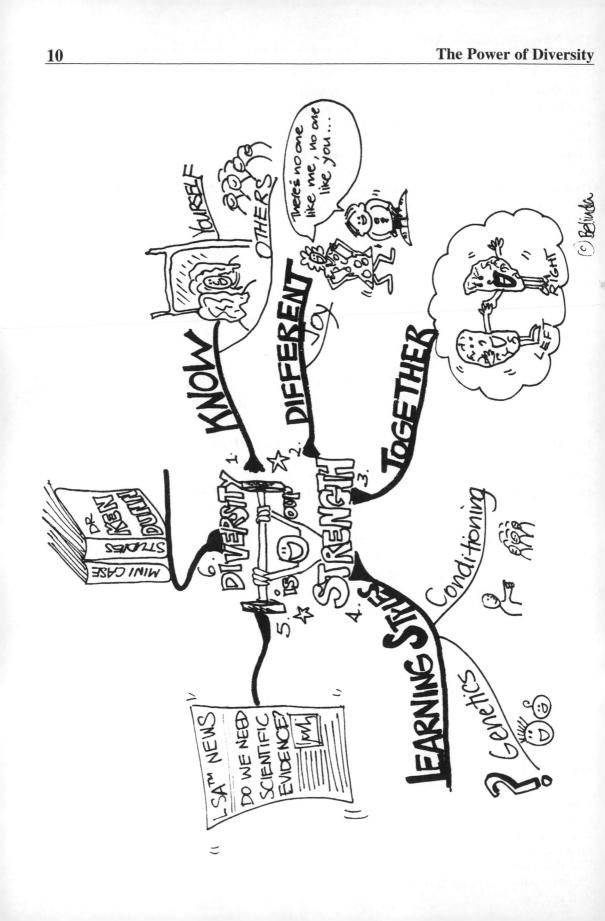

1. Getting to know yourself and others

Considering rapid developments in technology,
information overload, change in educational
and social systems in all modern societies, and
breaking down of traditional business structures,
it is more important than ever that human beings
know what makes them tick, why they do things
they do or simply 'who they are' as a person.
This self-knowledge is not only vital for coping **self-knowledge vital**
with our fast-changing world as we find it
at the start of the twenty-first century,
it is also immensely helpful as a tool which **helpful as tool to**
facilitates understanding of people we have to **understand people**
or choose to interact with in our private and
professional lives.

Only by knowing ourselves first will we ever be
capable of really understanding others and
less prone to misinterpret their communication **less misinterpretation,**
or actions and misjudge their behaviour. **misjudgement**

With better insights into our own and other people's **insights into**
brain processes (and we are only at the beginning **brain processes**
of a most exciting journey to this true last frontier)
it might be possible to utilize our brain power **utilize brain power**
much better, have more fun doing so and ultimately
live in greater harmony, not only with ourselves **live in harmony**
but, more importantly, with the people around us.

There are scientific tools available for finding out **scientific tools**
style differences, and psychological tests have
been in use for a long time. They all give detailed
insight into various aspects of human behaviour,
thinking and personal preferences. Two of the
newest and most comprehensive instruments in
this area are the Working Style Analysis see Notes **Working Style Analysis**
(WSA) for people in the workplace, and for students
of all ages, the Learning Style Analysis (LSA), **Learning Style Analysis**
combining cognitive, biological, psychological and
social style aspects. The result is a very detailed
description of a student's preferences,

Listen teacher,
listen to me.
Don't look away.
See my eyes, they hold messages
that can make you understand me.
Hold my hand and your heart
will warm towards me.
Let me dance and sing you
my own songs which you don't know,
and you might smile as you have
never smiled before.
Hear me tell you a story
of my ancient past
and then, maybe, you can see
another person in me.

Emma Kruse Va'ai

flexibilities and non-preferences during the
learning process, as fully described and explained
in more detail in Chapter 4.

Alongside these researched tools there are also
a great number of non-scientific tools available.   **non-scientific tools**
Although they might not hold up to scientific
scrutiny, they are usually a lot of fun and can be
a light-hearted but nevertheless insightful
introduction to the notion of human diversity.   **introduction to**
human diversity

One of the most astonishingly accurate and short
tests about human diversity is from a very clever
and entertaining book by Susan Dellinger,
Psycho-Geometrics (1), which I like to use in my
seminars because it is a lot of fun and people
love to discover in a non-threatening way how
different we all really are and that there is nothing
wrong with being different. On the contrary,
without diversity life would be very boring.

2. There is no one like me, no one like you – the joy of being different

As you begin to understand yourself and human
diversity a bit more, the idea of *equal but different*
might take on deeper meaning, and it is possible
to appreciate some of the many advantages a new   **advantages**
understanding of differences will bring:

* We can finally stop puzzling about ourselves
  and cherish our own individuality, understanding
  more who we are and the characteristics we have.   **understanding ourselves**

* We can help create unity through diversity in   **unity through diversity**
  our private and professional lives by recognizing
  that different styles are needed in any group
  to make it work effectively.

* We are able to celebrate diversity when we   **celebrate diversity**
  understand why children are often so different
  from their parents and why opposites attract
  (see Chapters 10 and 11).

Job Description of the Brain

Each brain hemisphere seems to be specialized in different ways of processing information

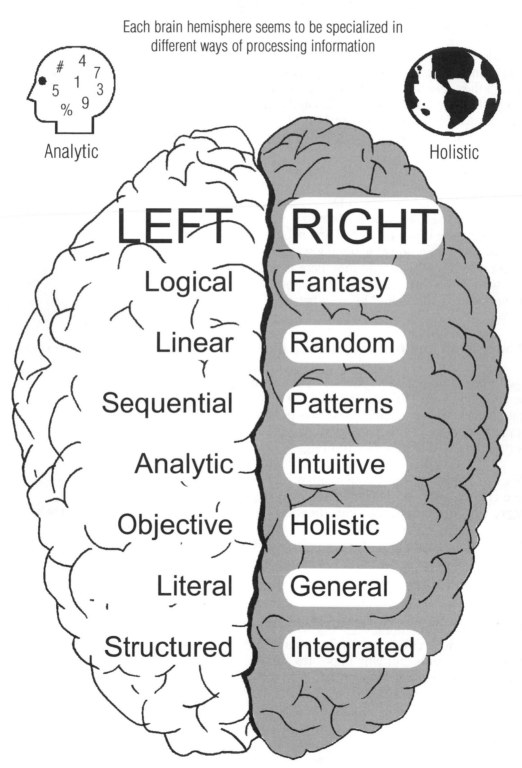

Analytic

Holistic

LEFT	RIGHT
Logical	Fantasy
Linear	Random
Sequential	Patterns
Analytic	Intuitive
Objective	Holistic
Literal	General
Structured	Integrated

3. Left brain–right brain: get your head together

Not all people <u>process information</u> the same way; therefore it is very important to know how different thinking styles translate into different learning and working styles. A good understanding of these basic <u>style differences</u> is vitally important for anyone who deals with people in all sorts of situations, not only in learning and training.

information processed differently

style differences

Over the past few years a considerable amount of information has become available about the differences between <u>left-brain</u> or <u>analytical</u> processing styles and <u>right-brain</u> or <u>holistic</u> styles. Although different authors have given these two different brain processing styles <u>various names</u> – as the list on the opposite page shows – they all fit the original terminology used by the Dunns. However, for our new instrument, the Learning Style Analysis, we have chosen a different term for <u>right-brain processing</u> because we believe 'holistic' describes this brain processing style more accurately.

left-brain – analytical right-brain – holistic

various names

right-brain processing holistic

Among the numerous examples of how these two <u>distinctly different</u> brain processing styles manifest themselves or how <u>flexibility</u> (when using both hemispheres equally) <u>integrates both styles,</u> the following descriptions are characteristic:

distinctly different flexibility integrates both styles

a) How do you find your way around a new city? Do you immediately purchase a street map and trace your route from point A to point B each time you leave your hotel, or do you 'feel' your way around, sensing where each place should be? Or do you alternate between map reading and following your nose, and intersperse visual clues with exact distances?

b) Consider these two people whom I know well. Both are successful; neither ever seems to change. One person does everything quickly in a set order all the time; his desk is neat; his briefcase has tidy compartments for office papers and house documents; and his clothes match and are well organized. Another is forever losing his keys; his clothes, while expensive, are always somehow mismatched; and he finds all sorts of weird things in his pockets.

BASIC FUNCTIONS

LEFT HEMISPHERE	RIGHT HEMISPHERE
ANALYTIC Breaks down into details and component parts. No concern or interest for the whole.	**OVERVIEW** Sees the whole big picture. Correlates entire situation. Does not look at details. Synthesizes.
FOCUSES Focuses attention on fine detail. Zeros in on a small area of activity.	**DIFFUSE** Spreads out over a large area. Not concentrated in one place.
SERIAL Piece by piece, sequential. Auditory. Logic. Language. Mathematics.	**SIMULTANEOUS** Spatial relations. Visual. Rhythm and flow. Music. Managerial. Multi-operational.
TRY Conscious control and effort. Ego. Expressive. Struggle.	**REFLEX** Survival instinct. Impulse. Unconscious. Receptive.
BREAKING DOWN Figuring things out step-by-step and part by part.	**SYNTHETIC** Putting things together to form wholes.
TEMPORAL Keeping track of time, sequencing one thing after another.	**NON-TEMPORAL** Without a sense of time.
LOGICAL Drawing conclusions based on logic: one thing following another in logical order – for example, a mathematical theorem or well-stated article.	**INTUITIVE** Making leaps of insight, often based on incomplete patterns, hunches, feelings or visual images.

From: *The Children's Song Book*, by B. O'Hara

Brendan O'Hara (1991)

c) When I remember holiday preparations in our family, I always see my father planning every detail weeks in advance, every route and detour we might take, distances and places for sightseeing, with my mother making long lists of what to take and laying out everything at least one week before departure; the final packing was always done exactly two days before we set off! Although I realized that many preparations were necessary, it always bothered me that everything was done in such a precise way. My style of packing – until out of necessity I learned to get much more organized – was the following: leaving everything to the last minute, then grabbing what was available and throwing it into the suitcase which, of course, never closed properly. So either I had to sit on it and force its locking or I would take pieces out, only to realize at my holiday destination that I needed exactly the things I had left behind. More than once I had to buy those missing items!

d) It's no accident that we learn the words of popular songs very easily – you don't have to make any effort to do that. You learn very quickly and remember for a long time because the left brain and the right brain are both involved. The left brain is processing the words and the right brain is processing the music.

Can you relate to these descriptions? Do they make sense to you? Then it's time to investigate how left- and right-brain dominance influences certain aspects of a person's learning and working style.

left/right-brain dominance influences learning and working style

Research on the Dunn & Dunn Learning Style Model has shown that typical left-brain processors prefer a learning or work environment that is:
quiet, brightly lit and formally designed.
They don't need snacking, and learn or work best alone or with an authority figure present.

left-brain processors

In contrast, most typical right-brain processors prefer so-called 'distractors':
noise or music, dim light, informal design, snacking, mobility and peer interaction at work or while learning or concentrating.

right-brain processors

It is quite obvious that traditional classrooms and workplaces were designed with left-brain processors in mind (by left-oriented designers, of course) and it is necessary, therefore, to adjust workplaces or classroom environments for people with right-brain preferences. And there are many more out there than we might like to think, particularly among younger students!

traditional classrooms designed for left-brain processors adjust workplaces, classroom environments

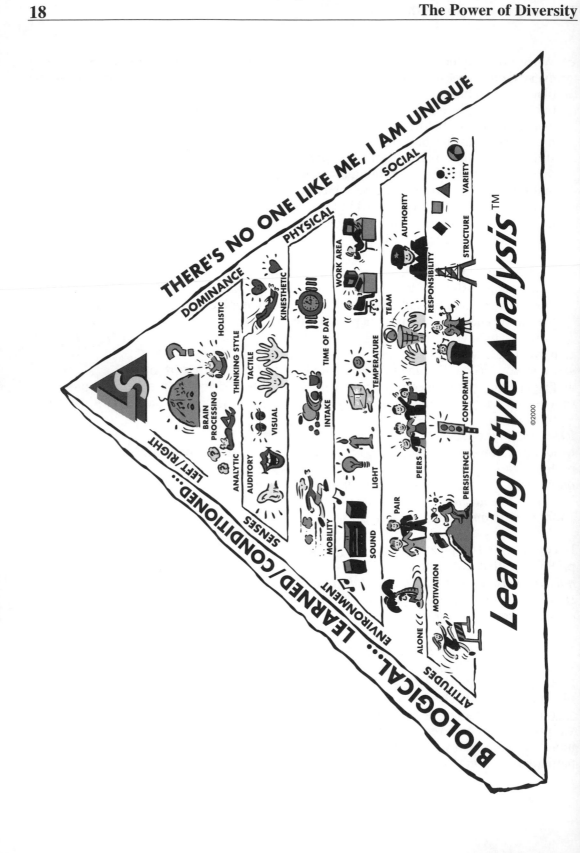

However, people who can integrate the use of both hemispheres are obviously better off because they can use their flexibility to adjust to any situation, whether it requires logical, analytical and sequential thinking skills, or holistic, simultaneous and intuitive approaches. Techniques for increasing flexibility are explained in more detail in Chapter 12. How these differences in brain processing styles can even affect relationships and communication between males and females we'll explore in Chapter 10. Knowing and accepting diversity is the first step, yet the true mastery in learning and teaching is developing and applying methods which draw out every learner's full potential.

integrate
both hemispheres
flexibility
analytical – sequential
holistic – simultaneous,
intuitive

affect relationships
between males and females

developing, applying
methods draw out
full potential

4. Learning Styles (LS) – genetics or conditioning?

Why are we all so different and similar at the same time? What happens to our styles when we grow up? Do our styles change or do they remain the same throughout life?

style changes

The search for explanations of human diversity goes back centuries. Scientists have always been eager to find keys to unravel the mysteries of male and female differences, of character features or personality types. Although there is an ever-increasing amount of literature available in this field (see section on Recommended Reading) and research is continually going on in many institutions around the world, no one has so far come up with a reliable conclusion.

search for explanations
of human diversity

no reliable conclusion

To the best of my knowledge, the Dunn & Dunn Learning Style Model, from which both the LSA and the WSA are derived, is the only instrument containing scientifically researched style elements which are clearly biological and remain fairly stable over a lifetime. Research dating back to 1979 reveals 'that three-fifths of learning style is genetic; the remainder, apart from persistence, develops through experience'. (2)

style elements
biological, remain stable

Overview of Learning Style Models

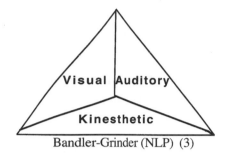

Bandler-Grinder (NLP) (3)

The VAK Model is the basis for Neuro-Linguistic Programming (NLP – the study of 'words and nerves'), taking into account through which modalities (senses) people process and store information. Created in the 1970s, it is now widely used for counselling, learning and communication training.

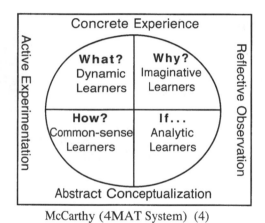

McCarthy (4MAT System) (4)

The 4Mat System Model was developed in the early 1980s and is based on right- and left-brain dominance, giving insight into how human beings first perceive and then process information. It functions as a model for teaching and is used in schools for enhancing instructional techniques.

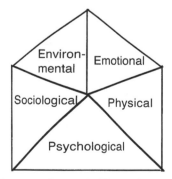

Dunn and Dunn (LSI, PEPS) (5)

The Dunn and Dunn Model was developed to help 'educationally disadvantaged' children. Research began in the late 1960s to identify individual preferences in students during the learning process. It is the most comprehensive and best researched learning style model and is available in two versions: LSI (Learning Styles Inventory) for school children and PEPS (Productivity Environmental Preference Survey) for adults.

When we developed the new, extended versions of
the WSA and LSA models (see pages 64 and 72),
we, of course, constructed the pyramids based on
these findings, and for many years the <u>division</u>
<u>between biological and learned elements</u> of the
new models seemed to hold well. Over the past
few years, however, more and more discussions
with educators and users of these assessment
instruments revealed that the divide might <u>not</u> be
<u>so clear-cut</u>, particularly in adults.

**division between
biological/learned
elements**

not so clear-cut

Several <u>new insights</u> are now emerging that even
some of the <u>learned/conditioned style elements</u> of
the model (see page 76) seem to have <u>biological</u>
(maybe even genetic?) <u>underpinnings</u>. Anecdotal
evidence seems to confirm that some learners are
much better off learning by themselves, can't be
with others when they need to concentrate, are
highly motivated from an early age on and show
high persistence with learning tasks. Where does
this come from when children have not been
conditioned in this area? Is it possible that they
have been born with these features?

**new insights
learned/conditioned
style elements =
biological underpinnings**

Taking these considerations into account, we have
now added these two significant words to the <u>new</u>
<u>LSA Adult pyramid model</u> as can be seen on
page 18.

**new LSA Adult pyramid
model**

On the other hand, how much DOES <u>conditioning</u>
<u>alter our style features</u> in the <u>biological areas</u> (see
page 74) of the model? Can students change their
preferences for sound, light, study area and physical
needs during the learning process after years
of exposure to certain classroom environments
with certain rules, or do they just <u>become more</u>
<u>flexible</u>? Many students seem to <u>adjust</u> quite well,
get on with their studies and achieve good results,
but many others just can't, they don't fit in and
can't learn like some of their classmates, as every
teacher can confirm.

**can conditioning alter
biological style features?**

**become more flexible
adjust**

When these <u>biological needs are matched</u> in learning
or work situations, human beings can <u>concentrate</u>
<u>much better</u> and for longer periods, are able to
<u>improve their performance</u> and enjoy what they
are doing.

**biological needs are
matched
concentrate much better
improve their performance**

Overview of Learning Style Models

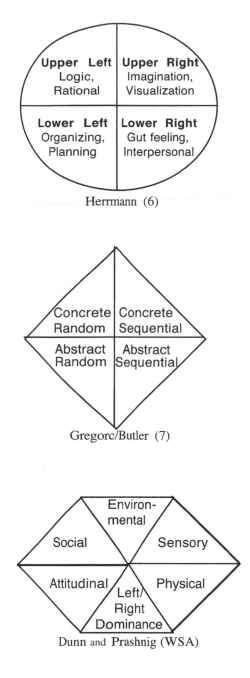

The Brain Quadrants of the Herrmann Brain Dominance Model describe preferences for mental functioning and brain dominance. Based on brain-related research, it was created in the late 1970s and is being used in management training to enhance creativity and productivity of people.

The Gregorc Energic Model of Mindstyles, created in the mid-1970s, provides an organized way to consider how the mind works. It identifies four qualities found within four basic mediation channels. Butler refined it, and it is used for instructional strategies to enhance classroom teaching.

The Working Style Analysis is based on the original Dunn and Dunn Model but has been extended in two areas: sensory and left/right brain dominance. It was co-created in 1993, computerized in New Zealand in 1994, and is particularly applicable for people in the workforce and for career planning.

5. When conditioning plays havoc with our learning ability

Many discussions with teachers and observations of successful and unsuccessful students during the learning process has led to the realization that becoming flexible in biological areas is mostly helpful, particularly in adverse situations. Yet being conditioned into a style which is not your own, is damaging in many ways. It can lead to learning problems, frustration and low self-esteem.

conditioned into a style
damaging

Nevertheless, the way human beings tend to take in information, process and store it, seems to depend more on preferences which are inherent rather than acquired and, despite conditioning in school or work environments, these preferences don't seem to change. We often don't know why we have them and when or where we acquired them; we only know they usually stay with us. They can often disappear for a while or might be suppressed due to particular circumstances but tend to surface time and again during the course of life.

preferences

don't seem to change

tend to surface

Let's take preferences for time of day: if students can concentrate well in the morning, they will have no problem with participating in academic subjects which are generally scheduled for the morning hours in timetables. However, if their natural preference is for the evening hours, they will have to adjust to the school requirements and for many years they will have to stretch their flexibilities, wake up early, show up early and be ready for learning. Despite strong efforts, this doesn't work for everyone and when other mismatched factors come into play, over time, students will physically suffer and their learning ability will be greatly reduced. I can now hear many educators protest and say that it is impossible to accommodate such time preferences because school is in the morning and that's that! Agreed, it is probably not possible to change time tables but teachers can COMPENSATE for this mismatch by using teaching strategies which accommodate as many other natural style needs of this student. And there won't be only one, there will be many of that kind, particularly among high school students.

natural preference

stretch their flexibilities

physically suffer
learning ability
greatly reduced
impossible to accomodate

COMPENSATE for
mismatch
accomodate
other
style needs

Graph 3. Learning Style Tendencies

Compare this result with your Left/Right Brain Dominance in Graph 1

ANALYTIC ("Left")	HOLISTIC ("Right")
quiet //////////	—————— sound/noise/music
bright light //////////	—————— low light
formal study area //////////	—————— informal study area
high persistence ???????	??????? low persistence
no/low intake ???????	??????? intake needed

Three or more of the following elements: preferring quiet, bright light, formal design/study area, high persistence (to complete tasks without interruptions) and low need for intake tend to suggest an ANALYTICAL (sequential) learning style. On the other hand, preferring sound, soft lighting, informal design, low persistence (completing tasks in bursts while working on multiple tasks simultaneously) and need for intake suggests a HOLISTIC/ GLOBAL (simultaneous) learning style (Bruno, 1988; Dunn, Cavanaugh, Eberle, and Zenhausern, 1982).

The more **QUESTION MARKS** are visible in a personal profile, the more it is likely that this student:
    a) is under stress,
    b) is currently experiencing confusion or is undergoing change in these areas,
    c) has reading problems, or was confused about the questionnaire (occurs very rarely).
This can lead to behaviour problems, loss of motivation, learning difficulties, underachievement, and ultimately dropping out of formal education. It is important that teachers and parents talk to the student about these areas in their LSA profile and attempt to find out the reasons for these inconsistencies. It is also recommended to redo the profile in 2-3 months' time when the situation has settled down.

Graph 1. Natural / Biological Elements

ANALYTIC ("Left")	HOLISTIC ("Right")

BRAIN DOMINANCE

INFORMATION PROCESSING
sequential ——————— ////////// simultaneous

THINKING STYLE
reflective ——————— ⬤ impulsive

It is similar with the need for sound: this generally misunderstood phenomenon, particularly among male teenagers, causes unnecessary stress for teachers and students alike. It leads to discipline problems which cannot be resolved traditionally with punishment because the need for sound is biologically determined and most students with this preference are not even aware that they have it – they just like a lot of noise and loud music. And here is the problem: if such students have to concentrate in quiet classrooms, they find it extremely difficult, even threatening, as their brains need sound stimulation. Therefore they will always try to make some noise, but that of course is not acceptable. Instead of constantly requesting 'Quiet, please!' teachers should learn to use music as a learning enhancer and will be surprised how the right learning music in the background reduces noise in the classroom and helps these students to concentrate and learn better. For more information on that subject see Chapter 6, Part 7.

misunderstood phenomenon

discipline problems

need for sound
biologically

concentrate in quiet classrooms

make some noise

music as a learning enhancer

6. Do we need scientific evidence?

One might think that most people would know their style elements but in my work with thousands of people I have experienced that comparatively few are certain about their real preferences, their true style and how they can function best.

few know
their true style

That's why we need scientific evidence – not only to help individuals come to terms with their own strengths and weaknesses, to convince them to utilize their real abilities much more confidently, but also to make it obvious to educators, trainers, teachers, parents and students themselves that there is no one 'best' way, no one single style for guaranteeing successful learning or studying, for information intake, problem solving and accomplishing tasks. Because when science 'proves' something, people are more inclined to believe it.

scientific evidence

helps utilize real abilities

no one single style for successful learning

The old saying 'Do as I do' or 'Do as I say', often used by parents for their children, and between teachers and students, instructors and trainees, employers and employees, is definitely not

LEARNING

is a matter of

ATTITUDE

not

Aptitude.

Dr Georgi Lozanov

Research tells us:

Learning about learning has more impact than study skills.
One programme used material from the history curriculum making it the
object of reflection; another used generic learning skills materials.

The students in the first group developed more advanced conceptions of
learning, got better grades on essays and achieved better examination results.

Chris Watkins, London Institute of Education

the best approach in drawing out people's
abilities because it <u>does not take into account
human diversity</u>. On the contrary, such a
'one fits all' attitude is very unjust to everyone
and does <u>a lot of harm to the development
of human potential</u>, resulting in low self-esteem,
decreased motivation, high stress, anxiety and
inconsistent performance. Disregarding diversity
is <u>probably at the core of most social ills</u> today.

**disregarding
human diversity**

**harms development of
human potential**

at core of social ills

However, many people, particularly in education
or in authority positions, are not yet ready
to accept that <u>diversity has great advantages</u>
and that there is always more than one way
of accomplishing anything. They can only be
convinced by <u>scientific evidence</u>, by hard
statistical <u>facts and data</u> or by written reports
as in personal profiles. They need time to reflect
and reconsider, judge and evaluate. Then,
armed with research results, the accumulated
information and guidelines for implementation,
they are ready to act upon these findings
recognizing, finally, that the majority of people
do need an <u>individualistic approach</u> rather than
commonly practised mass instruction.

diversity has advantages

**scientific evidence
facts and data**

individualistic approach

People never like being treated as numbers,
neither in education nor in their daily work.
Therefore it is crucial that we not only accept
differences but begin to acknowledge and
appreciate them.

7. Dr Ken Dunn – how to release your personal power

Thousands of students and adults have used our
<u>important research</u> over a period of 30 years to
release personal learning power. Research in more
than 100 colleges and universities and responses
from more than three million children and adults with
nearly 20 national and international awards provide
the base of validated <u>reliable results</u>. Success style
is not only directly related to individual personal
strengths important for the learning process, it is
also a natural, <u>common-sense approach</u> to self-
confidence, productivity and heightened motivation.

important research

reliable results

common-sense approach

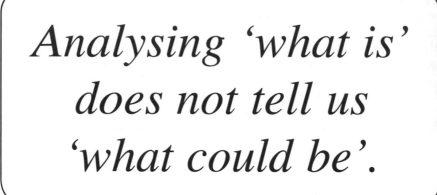

Analysing 'what is' does not tell us 'what could be'.

There ain't no rules around here! We're trying to accomplish something.

Thomas Edison

Mini case study one

A young high school girl in California struggled to achieve a B average. Her parents and older brothers and sisters all received honours in high school and college. This obviously intelligent student was very unhappy with the manner in which her parents required her to study. When the parents asked me to help I interviewed the frustrated young lady to determine what was wrong with the rules of study established by her parents. With tears in her eyes she described her every evening torture. 'I have to go to my room, turn on the lights, sit up tall at my desk, shut the radio and TV off, and get rid of all the food and drinks until I finish. Then I get 78 or 82 on my tests and my parents say I should try harder.' Now the tears flowed uncontrollably. I asked her to tell me what her preferences were and to take a success style instrument. Then I reassured her that I would relate the results to her parents and that they would abide by her scores and follow my recommendations, at least for a trial period of one semester. She calmed down immediately and couldn't wait to answer the success style questions.

In checking the results and listening to her preferences it was easy to prescribe a new pattern of studying and learning at home. The young student preferred an informal setting – on the floor. She liked to nibble on fruit while working, and did not do well in bright light which caused her to squint and feel tired. During the interview she neatly packaged her success style preferences. 'I love my parents and I really want to BE with them when I'm studying. They watch television news and shows after dinner, and talk to my brothers or sisters when they visit. All I want to do is lie on the floor and study in the living room and have them all around while I work.'

It took some convincing but the parents had agreed to try the new study pattern based on the results of the questionnaire.

Six months later they called to thank me. 'The transformation is remarkable! Our daughter is scoring in the high nineties and smiles all the time now.' These well-intentioned parents had prescribed the right study patterns for the young student's siblings but they were absolutely wrong for her.

Mini case study two:

Jimmy was an 11-year-old who was labelled LD – Learning Disabled – because he couldn't seem to learn the multiplication tables. His mother had tried everything: a personal tutor, computer software designed to teach the tables, his friends, daily practice and so forth. The youngster was a B+ student in all subjects except maths, which he was failing. Jimmy's mother was a teacher who had just taken a workshop with me and agreed to test him for learning and success style preferences.

AUTOBIOGRAPHY
IN FIVE SHORT
CHAPTERS
by
Bertia Nelson (1994)

Chapter One

I walk down the street.
There is a deep hole in the sidewalk.
I fall in.
I am lost ... I am helpless.
It isn't my fault.
It takes forever to find a way out.

Chapter Two

I walk down the same street.
There is a deep hole in the sidewalk.
I pretend I don't see it.
I fall in again.
I can't believe I'm in the same place.
But it isn't my fault.
It still takes a long time to get out.

Chapter Three

I walk down the same street.
There is a deep hole in the sidewalk.
I see it is still there.
I still fall in ... it's a habit.
My eyes are open.
I know where I am.
It is my fault.
I get out immediately.

Chapter Four

I walk down the same street.
There is a deep hole in the sidewalk.
I walk around it.

Chapter Five

I walk down another street.

He clearly was tactile and learned with his hands. He liked projects and building things. He liked puzzles and putting things together. Indeed, he could look at packaged devices and put them together correctly without spending much time on the manual of directions. 'I wonder if Jimmy could learn the multiplication tables with the flip chutes you taught us to make during the workshop?' asked his mom. 'I don't see why not!' I replied. Then I suggested that she place her decorated flip chute and a full set of multiplication tables flip chute cards on a food preparation table near the refrigerator because that's what an 11-year-old usually visits first when he gets home from school. Then I suggested that she just stand there and not say anything.

Jimmy came running in at 3.30pm, reached for the refrigerator after hugging his mom hello and stopped when he saw the half gallon decorated flip chute labelled the Green Learning Machine. 'Mom, what's that?' 'What's what, Jimmy?' 'This box. What does it do?' 'Oh, the flip chute! It has two slots and when you put a question in the top, the answer falls out the bottom,' said mom. He became very quiet and forgot about what was in the refrigerator. Finally he said 'I wonder if I could learn the multiplication tables with this flip chute thing?' 'I don't see why not,' she echoed my words and 'I just happen to have a whole set of multiplication cards that fit this green machine.'

Jimmy forgot about eating and ran upstairs to his room and placed the flip chute and cards on his bed – he was an informal 'horizontal learner'. At 6pm his dad came home and his mother called 'Jimmy, dinner's ready!' 'I'm not hungry, Mom. Is it OK if I keep playing with the flip chute? I like it!' His mother brought him a turkey sandwich and some milk on a tray but he kept putting the cards in with little time out for eating. Mom stayed up to see how long Jimmy would persist.

At 2am his lights finally went out. In the morning Jimmy came down with eyes a bit sleepy but flashing triumphantly. 'I know them! I know them! And I'm getting faster and faster. I'm using the stopwatch you gave me because our teacher wants us to do them in record time this year. I'm always last but not anymore. I'm going to be champ this Friday!' 'Now wait a minute, Jimmy. You didn't get 11 x 11 and 12 x 9 right away. You always had trouble with those ones.' '121 and 108.' 'How did you do it? That's wonderful! But why didn't you learn it with the tutor or with the computer?' 'Oh the tutor tried but she did the same things our teacher did and I couldn't remember them. And I hate the computer. Every time I got the wrong answer it made a buzz and everyone could hear I didn't get it right, <u>again</u>.'

'Well, why does the flip chute work?' 'It's great, I put the question in and then I see the answer right away. And when I was wrong I just put the card on the bottom and when it came up again I could see the answer in my head and I could get it right!' Jimmy was champ on Friday – two days after he started out using the tactile teaching machine. The flip chute held the key to his personal success style.

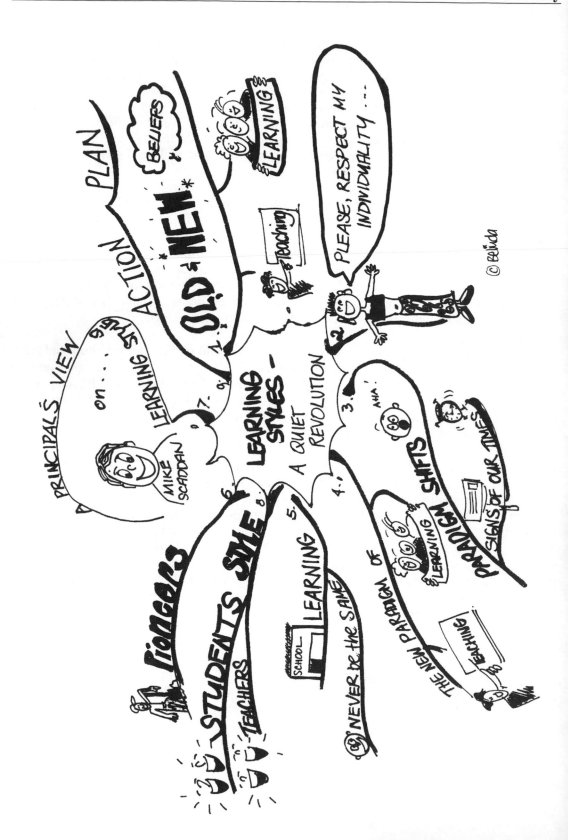

1. Visionary principals and their views on learning styles

First from New Zealand, where Mike Scaddan reports from Te Puna, the country's largest rural primary school:

'My interest in alternative learning came about after reading research as to how ineffective the majority of schools' in-service training was in bringing about <u>long-term change</u>.

long-term change

When I arrived at Te Puna in 1995, I instigated an in-service programme which included a series of 26 staff meetings dealing with principles in the "Learning Revolution" book by Dryden and Vos, and the introduction of a <u>Thinking Programme</u>. All staff meetings included <u>games and activities</u> to reinforce learning about <u>brain functions</u>. What we did in effect with adults was use good junior teaching practice. We worked for an extended period of time on this development, constantly reinforcing and supporting <u>new classroom practice</u>.

Thinking Programme
games and activities
brain functions

new classroom practice

This, however, was only the beginning. I was lucky enough to attend a two-day Principals' Seminar conducted by Barbara Prashnig, and there I made the commitment that our next step was to enrol the whole school in the "Diploma of Holistic Education" course. We began at the end of 1995 and the course was run during weekends and holidays, and I want to acknowledge the staff for agreeing to this <u>huge time commitment</u>. All teaching staff, teacher aides, some parents and even our secretary participated.

huge time commitment

The value of Barbara's course was that it reinforced much of what we had already covered, and she was also seen as an <u>outside expert</u> in the field and therefore "must know what she is doing". The diploma course modules followed similar lines to our staff meetings, involving learning games and activities to reinforce ideas. The courses were also extremely well planned and organized with a good flow.

outside expert

What have the <u>changes</u> been <u>in the classroom</u>? Staff <u>awareness</u> of their own and their pupils' <u>individual learning styles</u> has led to the use of a raft of games and activities to reinforce learning. New ideas and learning tools are regularly shared and ideas exchanged during

changes in the classroom
awareness of individual
learning styles

Classroom 2000 Considerations

**Some factors that should make us think about
the future of teaching:**

- 80 per cent of the children in their first year of primary school will enter careers that don't exist now, involving technology that hasn't yet been invented.

- Employees will change professions, not just jobs, four or five times during their working lifetime.

- 90 per cent of the workforce will work for companies employing less than 200 people.

- The amount of information in the world is doubling every 2.5 years.

- When Year 2 students in the USA complete Year 12, the body of knowledge will have doubled four times since 1988.

- Today, engineers find that half their knowledge is obsolete in five years.

- Children in the year 2000 will live to 81 years old on average compared with 75 for children born in 1986.

- Graduates will have been exposed to more information in one year than their grandparents were in a lifetime.

- 90 per cent of information and knowledge required in the year 2000 has yet to be invented.

Handout during a course on 'Classroom Strategies'

interval and lunchtime discussions. We have now
employed a full-time resource manager whose sole   **resource manager**
job it is to make learning materials to support our
programme. Lately we have also developed a
specialization in producing learning tools especially
for immersion Maori pupils. Learning tools are used in
varying forms and curriculum areas from Year 1 to
Year 8.

All pupils ages six and above have completed the
Learning Style Analysis survey, to find out their   **Learning Style Analysis**
preferred learning styles and the conditions most
favourable for their learning. Results have been shared
and discussed with parents. Classroom layout has   **Classroom layout has**
changed to include groups, pairs and single-unit   **changed**
seating, with a variety of high and low furniture,
enabling children to choose an environment which
suits their learning needs. By removing light bulbs we
have created conditions of varying light, and our   **varying light**
pupils who require low noise levels have found a use
for broken headphones – they make great earmuffs.

All class teachers have multiple copies of music   **music**
designed to assist learning, and manual or taped   **to assist learning**
sound effects are also popular. We are now entering
the phase of trying suggestopedic learning concerts.   **suggestopedic learning**
Games to reinforce learning are an everyday part of   **concerts**
class programmes. These mainly involve cross-over   **Games**
exercises, thinking skills or alternative methods to   **cross-over exercises**
share information. The use of Koosh ball circles or   **Koosh ball circles**
similar exercises to start the day have become an
integral part of our new Self-Esteem Programme.
Children often need to be "warmed up" for the school
day and this is proving to be a successful method.

Junior staff have noticed no significant changes in
class with the new programme as children's individual
learning needs have been already accommodated but
the newly introduced learning music seems to   **learning music**
be popular.

Middle and senior class teachers' comments include:
"Koosh ball circles are really popular. A huge range
of issues are now being discussed. Pupils are expressing
their inner thoughts more and are less afraid to share
opinions with others. There is more celebration of the
positives. Pupils are enthusiastic about making and
using learning tools. They love to manipulate them   **learning tools**
and share them with others. Knowledge retention appears **Knowledge retention**

The incurable ACADEMIC,

watching a teacher successfully

using creative teaching methods:

'But would it work in

THEORY??'

BAD EDUCATION = SLAVERY

It enslaves people for life

to be <u>improved</u>. Whether this is the tools, the learning concepts or a combination, we are unsure. Learning is now being reinforced in many ways, like with raps, tools, mind maps and kinesthetic activities. Older children have become more selective about participating in learning activities, e.g. a group of visual learners chose not to take part in a kinesthetic maths tables activity. Children are settling more quickly after activity breaks and <u>concentration appears to be better</u>. They prefer baroque and classical music to no music at all. One child wrote that her teacher plays 'soothing' music. The tools have a real value as multi-testers. I feel <u>more relaxed</u> because pupils are in charge of their own learning."

improved

concentration appears to be better

more relaxed

Our Board of Trustees were keen to <u>involve parents</u> in these developments, so I have begun a series of night classes which run for 10 hours. These have been so popular – 29 enrolments for the first series – that we are offering a rerun next term. Other schools have heard of our programmes and I have been <u>sharing our ideas</u> with them on a regular basis.'

involve parents

sharing our ideas

How schools in other countries with similar visionary principals have implemented LS is described later in this chapter, and in greater detail in my book *Learning Styles in Action*, where their individual contributions are testimony of a pioneering spirit literally sweeping the world and changing the way we teach.

2. Please respect my individuality

Everyone who is a parent or works in education these days has to be aware of <u>human diversity</u> and has to do more than just acknowledge differences among family members and students in class. Teachers and educators alike must know about learning style differences among human beings, young or old. In our age of mass education the old adages often heard by high school teachers 'We know what's good for our students' and 'Our methods have worked successfully for the past one hundred and fifty years' have kept educators from learning more about <u>individual learning needs</u>. If teachers want to be successful in reaching all their students, they will have to take into account style differences, not only in their daily teaching strategies but also in their preparations.

human diversity

individual learning needs

ABOUT SCHOOL

Anonymous

He always wanted to say things. But no one understood.
He always wanted to explain things. But no one cared. So he drew.
Sometimes he would just draw and it wasn't anything.
He wanted to carve it in stone or write it in the sky.
He would lie out on the grass and look up in the sky and it would be
      only him
and the sky and the things inside that needed saying.
And it was after that, that he drew the picture. It was a beautiful picture.
He kept it under the pillow and would let no one see it.
And he would look at it every night and think about it.
And when it was dark, and his eyes were closed, he could still see it.
And it was all of him. And he loved it.
When he started school he brought it with him.
Not to show to anyone, but just to have it with him like a friend.
It was funny about school. He sat in a square, brown desk
like all the other square, brown desks, and he thought it should be red.
And his room was a square, brown room.
Like all the other rooms. And it was tight and close. And stiff.
He hated to hold the pencil and the chalk, with his arm stiff and his feet
flat on the floor, stiff, with the teacher watching and watching.
And then he had to write numbers. And they weren't anything.
They were worse than the letters that could be something if you put
      them together.
And the numbers were tight and square and he hated the whole thing.
The teacher came and spoke to him. She told him to wear a tie like all the
      other boys.
He said he didn't like it and she said it didn't matter.
After that they drew. And he drew all yellow and it was the way he felt
      about morning.
And it was beautiful. The teacher came and smiled at him.
'What's this?' she said. 'Why don't you draw something like Ken's drawing?
Isn't that beautiful?' It was all questions.
After that his mother bought him a tie and he always drew airplanes and
      rocket ships
like everyone else.
And he threw the old picture away.
And when he lay out alone looking at the sky, it was big and blue and all
      of everything,
but he wasn't anymore.
He was square inside and brown, and his hands were stiff,
and he was like anyone else.
And the thing inside him that needed saying didn't need saying anymore.
It had stopped pushing. It was crushed. Stiff.
Like everything else.

It is believed that the teenage student who wrote this poem committed suicide two weeks later.

When students in class can experience that their
individuality is accepted and they are allowed and
encouraged to learn 'their way', motivation goes up,
their schoolwork becomes more enjoyable, study
skills improve, and with these positive developments
their self-esteem increases.

individuality accepted

self-esteem increases

For parents it is similarly important to accept that
their children do have different learning styles and
that their learning needs might vary wildly from
their own. As we will see in Chapter 11, once
parents begin to understand and support their
children's individuality when it comes to learning,
school and homework, family life, communication
and interactions between parents and children can
profoundly change for the better, particularly during
teenage years. Beyond that, for everyone's peace
of mind, it is also necessary that children understand
their parents' styles and that their brains might
function very differently when it comes to learning
and information intake. This is particularly
important when family tensions are high and
understanding of each other is at a low point. I wish
I had understood the importance of style differences
and individuality years ago; it would have helped
me to avoid many family conflicts.

parents understand
children's individuality

parents' styles

During the past few years, since I have made
diversity the core idea behind any training session,
be it with teachers, trainers, parents, managers
or business executives, I have realized that it is
always the little things which make a big difference
to people. (See also Chapter 13, Part 8.)

diversity as core idea

little things/big difference

Around the world I have seen people in tears
after discovering their true style, when they finally
have the proof that they are not dumb and useless
at learning. I have experienced teachers in seminars
standing up and apologizing publicly to the audience
for the injustices they have done to their past
students. I have heard parents apologizing to their
children for not understanding their uniqueness
and trying to mould them into something they
will never be. And many people have shared their
experiences with me that when they began to work
or study through their strengths, they were much
more effective, and less stressed and frustrated.

The Paradigm Shift Question:

What is impossible

to do in your business (field, discipline,

department, division, technology etc.),

but if it could be done,

would fundamentally change it?

Joel Arthur Barker

Even their private lives benefited from truly understanding diversity and acting upon it. So the power of new insights can influence behaviour, and even reshape people's values and beliefs.

power of new insights

3. Paradigm shifts – happening faster than ever

Many new trends in education have made headlines over the years but most of them were not here to stay; they were merely preparing us for coming changes or the high turbulence associated with times of crises.

new trends in education

Most of the turbulence in education these days is caused by two factors:

turbulence in education

1. The failure of old education paradigms, as well as unsuccessful attempts to prop up those outmoded systems. According to Joel Barker (1), paradigms are sets of rules and regulations that do two things: they establish or define boundaries, and tell us how to behave inside these boundaries so as to be successful.

education paradigms

sets of rules
define boundaries
how to behave

2. The creation and introduction of new paradigms. In times of crisis, people expect, often demand, great change. This willingness to accept great change produces two results crucial to any future development in education:
   a) more people, responding to the demand for great change, try to find new ways, in other words, new paradigms which will resolve the crisis and increase the likelihood of paradigm shifts;
   b) more people are willing to accept fundamentally new approaches to resolve the crisis and, by doing that, increase the opportunity to change paradigms. This mechanism sets the stage for radical change.

new paradigms

great change

new ways

new approaches
change paradigms

Joel Barker's general cycle of paradigm shifts (2) can easily be related to the cycle of shifting educational paradigms which has already begun and is continuing to work in New Zealand (some educational institutions and communities are already going through Step 9!):

general cycle
shifting
educational paradigms
New Zealand

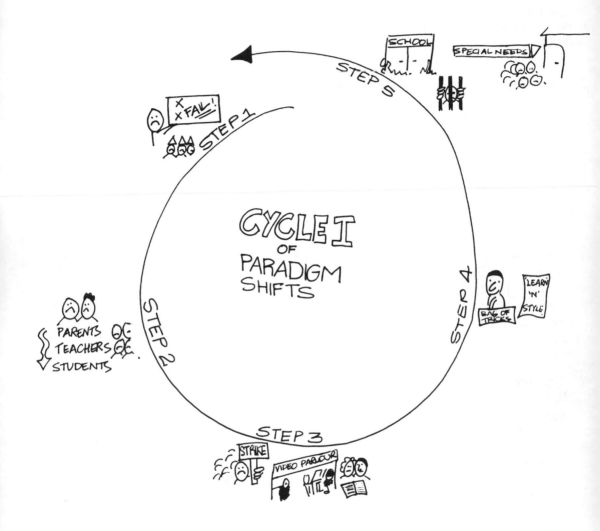

Step 1 *The established paradigm begins to be less effective*: traditional education methods fail and their general application to all students in New Zealand is no longer effective.

established paradigm less effective

Step 2 *The affected community senses the situation, begins to lose trust in the old rules*: parents are dissatisfied, teachers stressed out, students frustrated; there is more and more academic failure.

affected community begins to lose trust

Step 3 *Turbulence grows as trust is reduced – the sense of crisis increases*: teacher strikes become more frequent, underachievement and truancy increase, parents begin to look for new alternatives to traditional schooling.

turbulence grows crisis increases

Step 4 *Creators or identifiers of a new paradigm step forward to offer their solutions*: many of these solutions (like Suggestopedia, Brain Gym®, creative accelerated learning, matched instructions based on learning styles, etc.) have been around for a long time, yet generally disregarded by mainstream education.

paradigm creators offer solutions

Step 5 *Turbulence increases even more as paradigm conflict becomes apparent*: there are higher dropout rates, more and more so-called 'special needs' and 'learning disabled' or ADD (Attention Deficit Disorder) students, increased unemployment, domestic violence, drug abuse, gang activities and crime.

turbulence increases paradigm conflict

Step 6 *Affected communities are extremely upset and demand clear solutions*: economic downturn leads to reduction of government spending, ruling parties lose elections, alternative political groupings occur; there is breakdown of social and educational structures, social tension and unrest.

community upset demands clear solutions

Step 7 *One of the suggested new paradigms demonstrates the ability to solve a small set of significant problems that the old paradigm could not*: accepting new approaches to teaching and learning like '**everyone** can learn when taught with matched instructions based on their individual learning styles'.

new paradigm demonstrates ability to solve problems

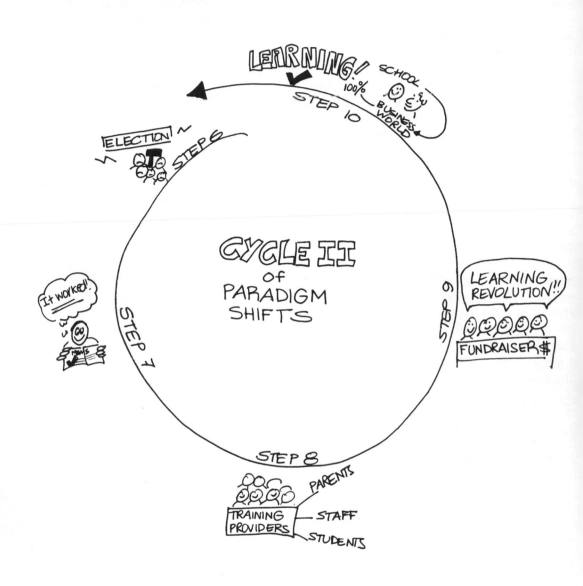

Step 8 *Some of the affected community accepts the new paradigm as an act of faith mainly out of desperation*: private training providers offer their services to groups of interested teachers who then successfully implement new holistic methods; individual, progressive schools join new and progressive change programmes, train their staff, assess their students' learning styles and begin to teach for diversity; at the same time they re-educate parents about these new methods. Very rapidly, sometimes after a few months, these schools experience dramatic changes for the positive in their students, teachers and their community.

**community accepts
new paradigm
out of desperation**

Step 9 *With stronger support and more funding, the new paradigm gains momentum*: more schools want to be part of the 'Learning Revolution'; they apply for funding from government and/or find new ways of co-operating with the business community to raise funds. The successful change process is monitored and documented, results are publicized widely. Finally, legislation makes it possible for every student in the country to have their learning styles assessed and be taught according to their individual preferences.

**stronger support
new paradigm
gains momentum**

Step 10 *Turbulence begins to wane as the new paradigm starts solving problems*: educators realize that these methods are not a fad or gimmick but help learners to develop their true strengths, their untapped potential; the affected community has a new way to deal with educational problems; the new learning methods seem successful and are transferred over into the business community which is pleased about the qualities and attitudes of students having gone through a successful education process.

**turbulence wanes
paradigm solves problems**

At this point, a combination of holistic education, learning styles and creative, accelerated learning methods has become the new standard in schools across the country and serves as a model for successful teaching strategies in other countries. With the affected community increasingly comfortable with the new prevailing paradigm, the level of tolerance for more new ideas drops dramatically and the cycle is complete. Now

**comfortable with
new paradigm
cycle is complete**

If you can come

through the snow and the rain

and the sleet,

you know you can

make it easily

when the sun is out

and everything is all right.

Malcolm X

society must wait for the next round of
significant problems in education (that this
newly accepted paradigm cannot solve)
to trigger a <u>new cycle</u>.

new cycle

If you think the described process does not apply
to your educational system, your society or your
country, and the proposed <u>solutions</u> seem
far <u>too simplistic</u>, <u>unworkable</u> and idealistic
because you believe the whole problem is much
more complex, just sit back and reflect on
these <u>possibilities of change</u>. Where does any
change begin? Who can and will instigate it?
What does it take to bring changes about? What
might be your own role in this change process?
Are you actively involved or are you trying to
avoid or even resist changes?

solutions
too simplistic, unworkable

possibilities of change

If, after answering these questions honestly,
all that business of change still seems too utopian,
too 'way out' for you, maybe you yourself are
locked into so-called '<u>paradigm paralysis</u>' –
<u>a mindset that is very limiting</u> because it tells you
only logically what's possible and what's not.
Be aware that that terminal disease, as Joel Barker
calls this 'paradigm paralysis', might <u>prevent you</u>
from <u>recognizing</u> future developments
or <u>possibilities</u>.

paradigm paralysis
limiting mindset

prevents
recognition of
possibilities

It is time to <u>look beyond</u> what we are used to, what
is familiar to us and <u>what has worked in the past</u>.
Only then will we be able to cope with the demands
of the future and actually <u>enjoy the change process</u>.

look beyond
what worked in the past

enjoy change process

4. The new paradigm of teaching and learning

As we have seen before, paradigms are sets of rules
which define boundaries and help us to behave so
that we are successful. Within these frameworks
we virtually do everything: learn, work, teach,
choose our partners, bring up our children; in short,
run our lives. As long as <u>paradigms are useful</u> and
really help us to perform better, feel better and
achieve what we want, <u>they are good for us</u>. But,
when existing frameworks do the opposite for us,
or <u>are even damaging</u>, particularly in education,

useful paradigms

are good for us

but when damaging

There can be no significant innovation
in education that does not
have at its centre
the attitudes of the teachers.
The beliefs, assumptions, feelings
of teachers are the air of
the learning environment; they determine the
quality of life with it.

Postman and Weingartner (1977)

Belief (Webster):
1) An acceptance of something true
2) Trust, confidence – (I have belief in her ability)
3) An opinion, expectation, judgement

we have to look for new ones which serve us better. So, what are the new paradigms for teaching and learning? They are really very simple but they also contain provocations for traditionalists and those who have a very limiting mindset.

we need new ones

contain provocations

For teaching, the new paradigm is: 'When students cannot learn the way we teach them, we must learn to teach them the way they CAN learn.' For human learning the new paradigm is: 'Everyone CAN learn but everyone learns in a different way.'

new paradigms for teaching and learning

This whole notion of human diversity and learning ability has its roots in recent brain research findings about learning. The question everyone is asking is if any of that will help us create better schools where students will achieve more and better learning. The answer has to be a sound 'Yes!' Why, might we then ask, haven't we known about all that before? There is a good reason: most of our present understanding of the human brain dates back only 30 to 35 years, and most of it much less than that. Neuroscientists have made great progress but much helpful work has also been done by other disciplines, such as cognitive science, biopsychology, brain evolution, anthropology and computer science. Only recently have facts, findings and concepts from these fields come together and thrown some light on what is considered the most complex structure in the known universe.

create better schools

understanding the brain

most complex structure

Knowledge about the brain will change teaching and learning for ever, and brain research applied to the school environment is not a fad and is here to stay. There is a simple reason for that: the brain is the organ for learning because all learning occurs in the brain and seems to be stored there. The brain not only controls all body functions, it controls all emotions, and as the 'executive' organ makes all the decisions about our behaviour.

brain research applied to school environment

For teachers it means that understanding learning processes in the brain, accepting human diversity and different learning needs will lead to better teaching practices, to the use of new learning tools and to new classroom management techniques.

understanding learning

leads to better teaching practices

Five similarities how *Homo Zappiens** learn in the new global economy:

>> Students work in times slots of four hours instead of 50 minutes

>> Students work in groups of 90 to 150 but *act* in basic groups of 12

>> Learning is research based, authentic and has relevance to children

>> Content is communicated through interdisciplinary themes

>> Network technology has an important role in the learning process

***Homo Zappiens** are according to Veen and Vrakking a new generation that has grown up using multiple technology devices from early childhood like the TV remote control, the computer mouse, mobile phones, iPod and MP3 players. This has enabled today's children to keep control of information flows, deal with information overload, combine face-to-face and virtual communities, communicate in new ways, and use networks according to their needs. Their relationship with school has changed fundamentally as *Homo Zappiens* consider schools as disconnected institutions, more or less irrelevant to their daily lives as networking with friends, part-time jobs and going out is far more important.

Wim Veen and Ben Vrakking (2006, pp. 10–12).

For learners it means that <u>understanding one's own unique brain functions</u> and learning styles will lead to more confidence, greater achievement and <u>long-lasting learning success</u>. With brain-compatible methods students can learn faster and better, and the improvement can be up to 200 per cent or more. If this sounds incredible, read on.

understanding one's unique brain functions leads to long-lasting learning success

5. School learning in the new millennium

Nearly ten years ago two brain researchers-cum-educators already stated 'the most comprehensive learning includes an <u>absence of threat</u>, careful orchestration of <u>multidimensional teaching</u> strategies, <u>real-life experiences</u>, and an understanding of barriers to learning.' (3)

absence of threat multidimensional teaching real-life experiences

They also presented the following revelations of <u>brain research</u> relevant to teaching and learning:

brain research findings

- Learning involves all systems of the body.
- We process many functions simultaneously.
- The need to make sense of our experiences is innate.
- We learn what we experience and what we are told.
- Emotions cannot be separated from thinking and are crucial to memory.
- We absorb both peripheral and focused information.
- We learn better when we are challenged but unthreatened.
- All senses and basic emotions are integrated differently – we are unique.

Based on these insights which are now slowly <u>becoming common knowledge</u>, what are the <u>implications for learning styles</u> and applied brain research for educators so that school learning will never be the same?

common knowledge implications for learning styles

Among all the possible scenarios I consider the following as the most important ones because they beautifully describe a new set of paradigms for education in this new millennium.

THE MAGIC CLASSROOM
by Chris Mullane

This room is like no other, there is magic in the air
It seems kind of disorganized, and there's colour everywhere.

There are beanbags, cushions, couches,
some dividers and a screen.
And over on the other side, some tables can be seen.

Over there beside the window, the sun is shining bright.
But near the inside wall we see there is a lot less light.

In the background there is music for those who learn by sound.
And earmuffs are here for those who are the other way around.

On every wall there are pictures, each one a story tells;
there are also touchy, feely things and even pens with smells.

How anyone could use this room, I haven't got a notion.
It seems more like a recipe for some kind of magic potion!

Perhaps this room is magic and will cast a special spell,
so that everyone who enters here will learn so very well.

Be they tactile, auditory, or a visual kinesthetic.
An impulsive or a global or a reflective analytic.

No longer need they feel a sense of great frustration
when concentrating, processing, and retaining information!

*This poem was created during one of my seminars 'The Magic of Music'.
Chris is a corporate trainer and has integrated all the principles of
creative, accelerated learning in his training programmes.*

'Brain-friendly' teachers will:
- advise students how to use their learning style strengths independently to their own advantage in their studies at home, at school or at work;
- give visual, auditory, tactile and kinesthetic options routinely for activities;
- structure lesson plans and activities so that all students feel secure in the environment, are taught in their own styles most of the time but are also stretched in their flexibilities at other times;
- include both holistic/global and analytic brain processing styles for learning and self-expression;
- embed the teaching of new material in all the senses, emotions and concrete experiences;
- help students to understand their own learning styles and to recognize that all styles are normal, valid and equally valuable;
- teach appreciation for the complexity, the potential and the uniqueness of every human being.

brain-friendly teachers advise students

give V-A-T-K options

structure lesson plans

stretching their flexibilities

include holistic and analytic learning styles

embed material in senses, emotions, experiences understand own learning styles

appreciation for complexity potential and uniqueness

One can easily imagine what teaching in our classrooms would look and feel like if every educator had the knowledge about the brain and its role in the learning process, if every teacher had learned how to implement these approaches, and would truly respect every student as the unique human being he or she is. And how great it would be if that knowledge could be passed on to parents who then could support their children in learning in a very different way.

knowledge about brain

respect every student

knowledge passed on to parents – support their children differently

The exciting fact is that there are already thousands of teachers (and parents) worldwide who have begun to implement methods and techniques based on latest brain research, and I am pleased to say that through my work I am able to play a small part in the process of making a difference and changing traditional teaching methods for good.

making a difference

ARANUI HIGH SCHOOL

PO Box 15-019
Christchurch 6
New Zealand

Principal G J Plummer
Phone (64 3) 388-7083
Fax (64 3) 388-7913

27 August 1996

Barbara Prashnig
Creating Learning
PO Box 5422 Wellesley St
AUCKLAND

Dear Barbara

I have had some wonderful feedback from your course on Friday. 99% of the staff were bubbly and enthusiastic when they returned to school.

I am very impressed that you were able to work so effectively with such a diverse group. I had felt some trepidation about the cost and disruption of having a large group of teachers out for the day but the results certainly justify the effort.

I now have a substantial group of staff members who are aware of the basic concept involved in learning styles and know that that will begin to impact on our classroom programmes.

Once again, thank you for a very effective day's in-service training.

Yours sincerely

GRAEME PLUMMER
Principal

6. Pioneers at work – from New Zealand to Sweden, to the UK

The many schools in NZ, Australia, Sweden, Finland and lately the UK which have taken up the challenge and introduced learning styles to everyday teaching have done it mainly for two reasons:

1. Their leaders are true pioneers, visionaries and risk-takers; they know what they want for their school, have long-term plans with defined goals and are daring enough to take a calculated risk.

   pioneers, visionaries risk-takers

   daring

2. Their staff and everyone else involved (parents, board members and the wider community) have a particular interest in helping their children to become better learners and equip them with skills that will serve them a lifetime. They are committed and dedicated to making their school a better place for learning, to eliminate underachievement, and are prepared to invest time and money into improving their services to the young ones in our communities.

   staff, parents, board members, community

   committed and dedicated

   invest time and money

And the results speak for themselves. When I visit schools in Sweden, where the learning styles concept has been used for the past ten years, the results are very similar to the changes I am observing in New Zealand schools: discipline has improved (teachers say that there is a much more caring atmosphere since the introduction of learning styles); academic performance has improved (particularly of those students who struggled with learning and were underachieving); the atmosphere in the staffroom has changed (there is much more co-operation, more exchange of ideas and better communication among colleagues); and the school's standing in the community has changed because parents begin to understand that the school is now really working hard to help their children succeed in learning and therefore parents become more interested in their children's schooling.

changes in NZ schools: improved discipline

improved academic performance

among staff more co-operation better communication

parents more interested in their children's schooling

Similar developments can be observed in Singapore, Denmark and the UK where the introduction of LS has improved discipline, learning motivation and most importantly, academic performance. In many cases a knowledge of LS has prevented students from dropping out of school because they are allowed to learn in their own way that best suits them.

improved discipline academic performance prevented dropping out

The illiterate of the year 2000

will not be the individual who

cannot read or write,

but the one who cannot learn,

unlearn and relearn.

Alvin Toffler

What's happening in

students' brains

may redefine teaching.

R. Nummela-Caine

7. The Power of Diversity in a remarkable Austrian school

Hofrat Dr Günter Schmid, principal of the so-called 'Wiedner Gymnasium' reports about a recent, positive development with learning styles at his school which is one of 86 grammar schools in the urban area of Vienna. With a population of approximately 750 pupils and some 70-odd staff it is average in size by Austrian standards and was an entirely unspectacular representative of its species in every other respect as well – until 1998. Could it have been a hint of destiny that the big caesura in the history of a moderately successful school in Vienna coincided with the first publication of this revolutionary book in New Zealand? It would be only too tempting to assume, but I am afraid these two pedagogical earthquakes hit the antipodes independently of one another.

development with learning styles

What happened at this side of the globe was that an experimental stream for highly gifted learners was introduced as an additional special branch in this school and named after the great Austrian philosopher Karl Popper. Ideologically, this was a most daring step at the time, and not surprisingly, it split the team of teachers into two parties: while the "pioneers" literally galloped ahead to develop an entirely novel pedagogical philosophy, the "conservative" group took on a defensive attitude, vilifying what to them was "pedagogical high-treason", and desperately clinging to cherished old habits. The obvious success and popularity of the "revolution" added to the sense of jealousy and envy that precluded any fruitful development since any attempt at innovation, however undisputed in its general applicability, was automatically associated with "those freaks of gifted education" and, as a consequence, rejected without further consideration.

experimental stream

most daring step

pioneers

conservative

popularity of the "revolution"
jealousy and envy

It was at this point – when I was beginning to give up any hope of ever reconciling the two hostile camps within my staff and, as a consequence, to dedicate all my attention to just one half of my school – that I read Barbara's book. Gordon Dryden, in his preface to the first edition, states that "he loves this book", as "it delivers a vital message of hope that is desperately needed by millions of students and parents around the world". In my case, I adored it *from the headmaster's*

reconciling hostile camps

A People Place

If this is not a place
where tears are understood   where do I cry?
If this is not a place
where my spirits can take wing   where do I   y?
If this is not a place
where my questions can be asked   where do I seek?
If this is not a place
where my feelings can be heard   where do I speak?
If this is not a place
where you ll accept me as I am   where can I go to be?
If this is not a place
where I can try to learn and grow   where can I be just me?

William J. Crocker

point of view, as it supplied me with the key to <u>saving</u> <u>my school</u> from literally <u>drifting apart</u> – for the benefit of students, parents *and teachers* alike. The reading of "The Power of Diversity" was probably the most enlightening experience in my life in that it confirmed all my views I had developed in the course of eight years of developing new strategies for gifted education, while at the same time supplying conclusive empirical evidence for considerations we had, to some extent, arrived at only instinctively. Thus, what had been looked upon by some as just a slightly <u>unorthodox</u> partisan view of a <u>handful of freaks</u> was suddenly presented as well-documented <u>irrefutable</u> <u>facts</u>. All it takes to understand and accept them is a <u>double shift of focus</u>: first from learner output (i.e. student results) to teacher input (i.e. methodology) and then again from teacher input to learner intake (i.e. learning styles). If "learner-centredness", "individualization" or "<u>personalization</u>" are to be more than meaningless slogans in modern teacher training, we cannot go on ignoring the existence of <u>individual learning styles</u> in our classrooms. (And this has nothing to do with "gifted education" but obviously applies to any learning situation.)

If <u>students</u> are to be seen not as passive consumers of *knowledge* offered to them by teachers (at which they are bound to be eclipsed by any printed encyclopaedia or DVD) but as <u>active "makers" of their own</u> <u>education</u>, schools should aim at equipping every one of their students with the necessary problem solving skills and competences they will need in future. To achieve this we don't need the most learned experts, nor necessarily the most efficient methodologists, but the ones who are best at empathizing with individual learning styles.

This in itself was not an entirely new discovery to me. But the tool – the <u>LSA assessment instrument</u> – that enables *every* teacher to put themselves into such an ideal situation to deal with their learners at an individualized level struck me as a <u>true revelation</u>.

My hope, when I read Barbara's book, was that well-documented, empirically proven facts when presented by an <u>external authority</u> who had no obvious connection with gifted education would stand a fair chance of being accepted. So I booked a full-range LS

saving my school
drifting apart

unorthodox
handful of freaks
irrefutable facts
double shift of focus

personalization

individual learning styles

students

active "makers" of their
own education

LSA assessment
instrument

true revelation

external authority

Teachers Having Fun
Making Learning Style Tools

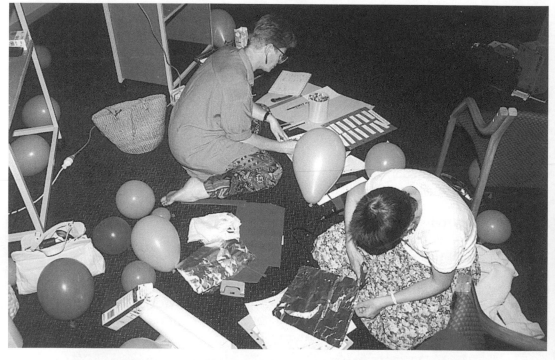

course consisting of four afternoons in a regular working week in May and offered it to teachers on a voluntary basis.

I did point out that the biggest benefit was to be expected for the "suffering": frustrated teachers of "hopeless" classes that had been more or less given up, underachieving or misbehaving students who had given themselves up, and desperate parents who had given their children up. I was pleased to see that many – though not all – of the teachers who were in obvious need of support enrolled for the course, in spite of the heavy time load it put on them. Needless to say that quite a few members of the team of the gifted branch as well saw the point at once and jumped at the opportunity. Altogether the course was attended by 25 teachers, myself and one parent representative.

biggest benefit
for frustrated teachers

underachieving
desperate parents

It was fascinating for me to watch how within one hour Barbara had won round even the most inveterate sceptics. One could literally sense the feeling of new hope, a new sense of motivation taking hold of the entire audience. For some the experience was what it had been to me on reading the book: a confirmation of vaguely held beliefs; to others it brought a reassuring sense of having their individual problems taken seriously.

won round
sceptics
feeling of new hope

reassuring

This was also exactly how students and parents experienced the LSA when they were first exposed to it. The parents association of the gifted branch have meanwhile decided to make a bulk purchase of LSA's for the future generations of newcomers, and the parents of the regular classes have volunteered to take over the whole administration of further testings.

To sum up, the familiarization with LSA has made, and is making, all the difference. After almost a decade of moderately successful attempts to bring pedagogical standards up to date, at the cost of sometimes gruelling internal struggles and conflicts, a whole school now suddenly finds itself on its way into the twenty-first century and is leading the way for others to follow (a neighbouring school has addressed Barbara directly in the wake of our pioneering experience). I had considered it my life's work to achieve this; Barbara did the job for me in the course of four afternoons. Thank you Barbara!'

LSA
making, all the difference

You can make a difference ...

In Maine they tell of an old man walking along the beach
with his grandson, who picked up each starfish they passed
and threw it back into the sea.
'If I left them up here,' the boy said,
'they would dry up and die. I'm saving their lives.'

'But,' protested the old man, 'the beach goes on for miles,
and there are millions of starfish.
What you are doing won't make any difference.'

The boy looked at the starfish in his hand,
gently threw it into the ocean, and answered:
'It makes a difference to this one.'

Past US President George Bush

Since this truly <u>remarkable event</u> of being allowed to work with teachers in such a <u>prestigious school</u> and giving them profound new insights into learning and teaching, various other education institutions in my old home country of Austria are now interested in receiving the same training. I am delighted about this development and it feels like in Sweden and Finland over ten years ago when I brought this concept to these countries. For whatever reason, there is now a true <u>pioneering spirit</u> and students are very happy.

**remarkable event
prestigious school**

pioneering spirit

8. Students, parents and teachers say it in style

When I first heard about the <u>positive effects of learning styles</u> on teachers, parents and students in the USA, I naturally was very sceptical. I thought these American teachers were exaggerating when they reported enthusiastically about higher academic achievements, <u>better attendance</u>, much <u>improved discipline</u> and decreased behaviour problems. Although I was convinced that the knowledge and use of learning styles is one of the most potent remedies to improve teaching and learning in our schools, I had yet to see <u>results in New Zealand</u> and in other countries where I had trained teachers to incorporate learning styles in their daily work.

**positive effects of
learning styles**

**better attendance
improved discipline**

results in New Zealand

And results we got! It turned out that <u>learning styles</u> is not only a wonderful '<u>quick fix</u>' <u>for under-achievers</u> and those students who have difficulties in some areas, but also, more importantly, it is a <u>long-term remedy</u> for those who have <u>serious learning problems</u>, who are in special needs groups or had already been written off as hopeless cases. It is heartwarming and often very emotional when teachers tell stories about <u>incredible progress</u> in their students, and parents rave about the <u>positive changes in their children</u>, their <u>new attitudes towards school and learning</u> and the impact this has had on family life.

**learning styles: 'quick fix'
for underachievers**

**long-term remedy for
serious learning problems**

**incredible progress,
positive changes
in children, new attitudes
towards school and
learning**

Therefore I'd like to share with you, the reader, some of the comments I have received over the past few years which are representative of the positive reactions of thousands of people, young

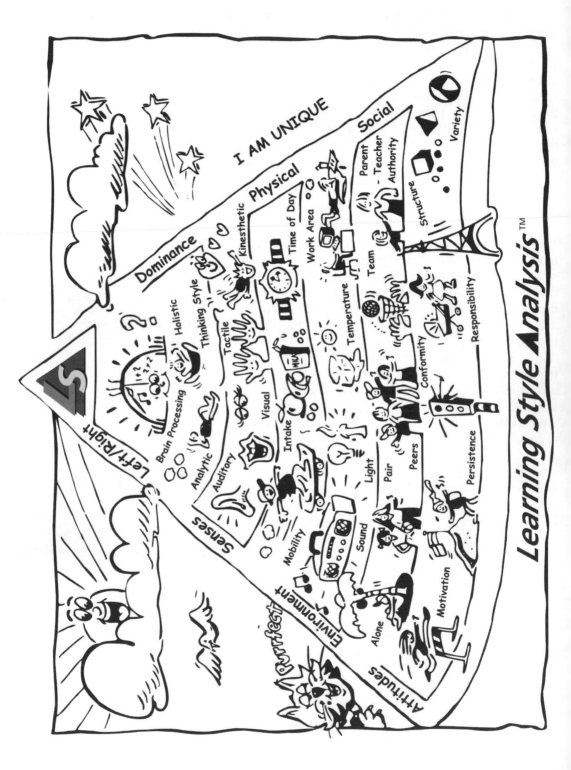

and old, of different races, countries and social groupings triggered by learning styles approaches.

First, let the parents speak:

'It became apparent by the time our son was in Standard 2 that he was not settling into the "normal" education system. Despite bright prospects in the beginning, he was becoming increasingly adept at avoiding most aspects of schoolwork. In the middle of his Standard 3 year he was diagnosed as having ADD (Attention Deficit Disorder) and prescribed low doses of Ritalin which greatly improved his work output. However, he still did not "slot in" and was frustrated in class and spent a lot of time on his own.

'Knowing Ms May's different approach to learning we were keen for him to be placed in her Standard 4 class and the year was brilliant for him. Through her whole-brain teaching style he has regained his self-confidence, made new friends, learned that it is OK to be different and, most importantly, found in Ms May a learning style that really suits him. Finding out that O learns kinesthetically and tactile-visually instead of auditorily has been a major breakthrough and we will constantly search for future teachers that embrace these four senses. The teacher's classroom techniques for our son, such as not insisting he sits at his desk while working, music in the form of accelerated learning tapes to help him relax and focus, and short bursts of Brain Gym® every hour, have all enhanced his ability to learn.

'Although these methods may not be essential for every child to succeed, we feel that all the children in this class have benefited from them. Most importantly for us is that O, who was fast being lost into that percentage of students the education system does not cater for, is now heading in a much more positive direction.'

Sadly, Sheryl May, the teacher at Frankton Primary in Hamilton, New Zealand, who in March 1997 received an Award for Excellence in Education for successfully implementing a 'Holistic Learning

Students enjoying their Learning Style Tools

Courtesy of Pilleval Skolan, Trelleborg, Sweden

Courtesy of J. Anderson-Johns, Intl School Manila, Philippines

Programme', has passed away but Principal
Judy Dixon is very supportive and the whole staff
went through the 'Diploma in Holistic Education';
the school has now become a leader in <u>whole-brain</u>   **whole-brain learning**
<u>learning</u> in the area.

And here's what <u>students</u> say: **students**

'I have found that working with Ms May this year
has <u>improved all my learning skills</u>. It's neat to   **improved learning skills**
know that I can learn freely in a style that I am
comfortable with. For example, I have discovered
that I am a <u>very visual</u> person so I learn well by   **very visual**
seeing things. Therefore, I usually don't learn as
well as I could in the normal classroom structure
where the teacher talks and the students have to
listen. Also, we have not only learned the normal
school subjects like reading and maths but have had
different studies to <u>learn how our brains</u> actually   **learn how brains work**
<u>work</u> and what relaxation does for our learning.
We even cut a brain up – very, very visual! Over
the weeks I have found my <u>teacher</u> is not only my   **teacher**
teacher but also <u>my friend</u>.'   **my friend**

'My <u>learning</u> in 1996 has been <u>very positive</u>. It   **learning very positive**
has made me realize learning is for ever and I feel
pretty <u>confident</u> about myself. I know I can and   **confident**
will be successful. I feel I am important and it is
OK to feel like this.'

Reflecting after five years at Frankton:
'The school is a <u>treasure for learning</u> – one of the   **treasure for learning**
best – and it's a <u>quality learning place</u>. Although   **quality learning place**
it achieves good book work, that's not the only
thing it teaches. It also teaches things on the inside
(which counts). It teaches you to set your goals
and go through with them, also known as walking
your talk.'

9. An action plan for implementing learning styles

It's all right to read about schools which are already
on the way to implementing learning styles and
changing their school around but the question remains
'How can we do it so that it's not too painful?' Well,

Dare to Dream...

1. Write up elements of a successful education system.

2. Draw a mind map – brainstorm a successful education system.

3. Create a song/rap about the education system you'd like to see in the future.

here is a process which has been followed by many schools successfully because it has been trialled, allows the accommodation of individual needs and integrates very well any school's own change programme. Once the decision to go ahead is made, you can use the following action plan which is also part of our in-service programme 'School of the Future Based on Learning Styles'.

accommodation of individual needs

action plan

Ten steps to implement learning styles on a school-wide basis

1. Teacher training (Day 1) *Learning Styles and Classroom Management* including teachers' own personal LSA-Ad profiles

2. Student assessments with LSA questionnaires, production of computer-generated student profiles by the school itself

3. Teacher training (Day 2) *Learning Styles and Student Centred Teaching* focusing on Teaching Styles (TSA-Ed) for teachers and interpretation of student profiles with trained facilitator and production of learning style tools

4. Observation period carried out by teachers trained in learning styles

5. Sharing results with students and parents: interpretation of LSA profiles, homework and study strategies for students; parent evening

6. Classroom redesign: based on students' preferences and with students' input; school-wide co-operation is necessary to achieve the desired outcomes

7. Creating and using learning style tools, produced initially by teachers, later by students and/or parents/resource people

8. Adaptation of classroom teaching to suit analytic and holistic students – lesson preparation to accommodate L/R brain processing plus strategies for multi-sensory teaching to accommodate auditory, visual, tactile and kinesthetic needs

9. Evaluation phase: monitor students' progress and evaluate impact of programme on teachers, students, parents and the community at large

10. Continuation: incorporate new students, train new teachers and continue to build the 'School of the Future Based on Learning Styles' (see Chapter 13).

If you have any questions about this action plan, or how we at Creative Learning can help your school, visit our website **www.clc.co.nz**

Creative Learning

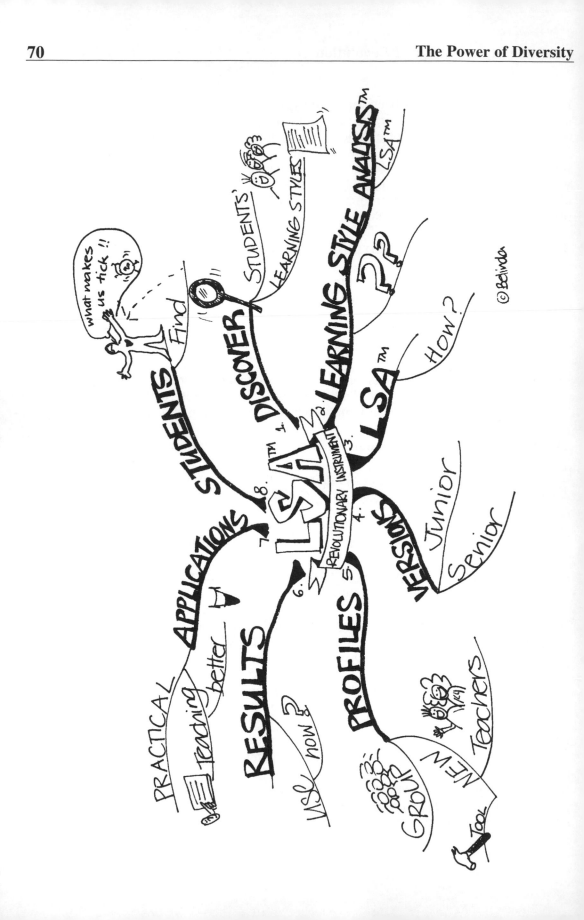

1. Discover your students' best way to learn

For the successful teachers of the future it is vitally important to know what goes on in their students' heads, how they think, what makes them succeed or fail, and how they need to be treated to allow them to grow and develop their full learning potential.

successful teachers

Knowledge about learning styles helps teachers to create a multisensory learning environment which caters as much as possible for each student's individual needs. By utilizing the 'diversity concept' and accepting different styles, teachers will become more effective in their teaching strategies, and students will become more confident learners, being more satisfied with their own learning progress.

individual needs

How someone effectively solves problems, learns and remembers is the key to lifelong success. Even though everyone has the power to learn, few of us really use this power to the full. Why? Because everyone has his or her own style of learning, working and concentrating on something really difficult, yet very few people do it in a way that's best for them. Too often have we been conditioned to use a single style, an approach that is right for some, but not for all of us.

solve problems
learn and remember

own style

conditioned

Research on learning styles explains why certain children in the same family perform well at school whereas their siblings do not. It demonstrates the differences in style among members of the same class, culture, community, religion, or socio-economic group, but it also reveals the differences and similarities between groups. It shows style differences between teachers and their students, how boys' styles differ from girls', and reveals the reasons why some children learn to read easily and others obviously struggle.

differences in style

similarities

Although teachers claim to know their students quite well, research has also shown that they cannot correctly identify all the characteristics of their students' learning styles. Some aspects are just not observable and therefore we need assessment tools.

cannot correctly identify

students' learning styles

Working Style Analysis™

© Dunn & Prashnig

WSA-Corporate

Personal Profile

for

Dorothy Sample

Entered: Tuesday, 6 April 2004

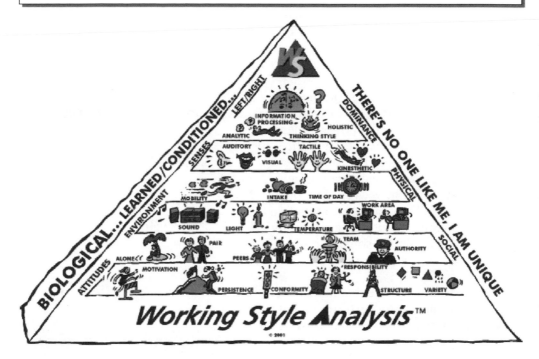

How to make the best use of your WSA results:

 The WSA Pyramid above shows all elements of someone's working style. Mark your most important preferences, non-preferences and/or your flexibilities if you wish.

 Pay particular attention to your Preferences and Non-preferences on Page 2 in your Profile Summary. Apply them when you concentrate on something new and/or difficult.

/3 Find out how flexible you are from the Graphs 1 & 2. Your flexibility is an additional strength in your style, particularly useful in adverse work situations.

 Please note: the WSA is not a test, therefore it cannot be "passed" or "failed". There are no "right" or "wrong" results, only style differences between human beings.

We are continuously improving our assessment instruments but the results remain stored and can be downloaded with all upgrades, currently in eight different languages from www.clc.co.nz

2. What is the Learning Style Analysis (LSA)?

After experimenting with creative, accelerated
learning techniques, using brain-based teaching
methods in my teacher-training programmes for
many years, the development of the revolutionary
'diversity concept' for learning, training and   **'diversity concept'**
working was the next step in an exciting journey.
The first instrument, created together with
Dr Ken Dunn of Queen's College in New York,
was the Working Style Analysis. I have used it
not only to build up my own business and to make
my own staff more effective by utilizing their skills
and drawing out their potential, but I have also   **drawing out potential**
helped thousands of teachers as well as people in
business in New Zealand and overseas to achieve
personal and professional success by understanding
themselves and others.

What is the Working Style Analysis (WSA)?   **WSA**

It is a new assessment instrument, completed in
1996 and derived from the original Dunn & Dunn
learning style model which was created during the
early seventies in the USA. Expanded and improved,
the WSA allows users to find out what their preferred
working and learning conditions are. Research has
proven that every individual prefers to learn, work   **learn, work**
and concentrate in a different way, and information   **in different ways**
intake is greatly enhanced when people can think,
work or concentrate in their favoured conditions.   **favoured conditions**
Factors that determine someone's success are not
only influenced by his or her intelligence or
unique personality, but also by the physical space   **unique personality**
where someone works and concentrates, by the
interaction with people, the time of day, their
physical needs and their frame of mind. (1)

The widespread use, cross-cultural appeal and   **cross-cultural appeal**
successful application of the WSA worldwide
has led to an increased demand for a similar
assessment tool for younger students and its use
in school settings. Again, Dr Ken Dunn and I
collaborated successfully in creating this new
instrument – the Learning Style Analysis.   **Learning Style Analysis**

 **LSA-Senior: Student Version**   Murray Sample 2

Graph 1. Natural / Biological Elements

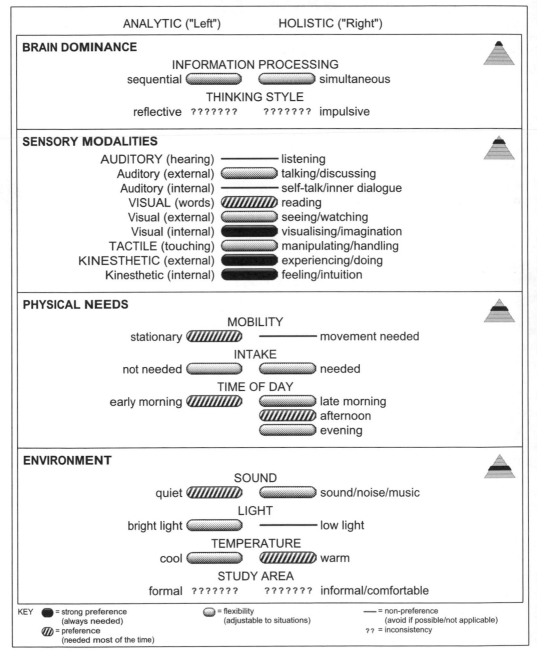

It is the newest learning style assessment tool
available on the market, based on the original
instrument, the Working Style Analysis, and
it comes in two versions: one for primary and
one for secondary school students. For adult
learners, however, the <u>LSA Adult version</u> is
recommended as it also gives insight into style
preferences of grown-up learners.

LSA Adult version

Like adult learners, younger students also prefer
to learn, concentrate and process information in
different ways and every child has a uniquely
different learning style, but, contrary to style
preferences in adults, <u>children's learning style
features</u> change and <u>develop as they grow up</u>.
Therefore it is correct to say that a learning style
profile is a 'snapshot in time' revealing style
elements which remain stable and others which
can change, even daily.

**children's learning styles
develop as they grow up**

The LSA assesses <u>49 individual elements</u> in the
following **six basic areas** which are represented
as layers of a pyramid. The first four of these layers
seem to be <u>biologically or genetically</u> determined
and the last two <u>conditioned or learned</u>:

49 individual elements

**biological or genetic
conditioned or learned**

1. LEFT/RIGHT BRAIN DOMINANCE
   showing **sequential** or **simultaneous**
   brain-processing strategies
   reflective or **impulsive** thinking styles
   and overall **analytic** or **holistic/global**
   learning styles

   left/right brain dominance

2. SENSORY MODALITIES
   including **auditory** (hearing, talking,
   inner dialogue)
   visual (reading, seeing, visualizing)
   tactile (manipulating, touching) and
   kinesthetic (doing, feeling) preferences

   sensory modalities

3. PHYSICAL NEEDS
   identifying needs for **mobility** (preferences
   for moving or being stationary)
   intake/mouth stimulation (eating, nibbling,
   drinking, chewing, smoking) and **time of day**
   preferences (personal biorhythm)

   physical needs

LSA-Senior: Student Version

Graph 2. Conditioned / Learned Elements

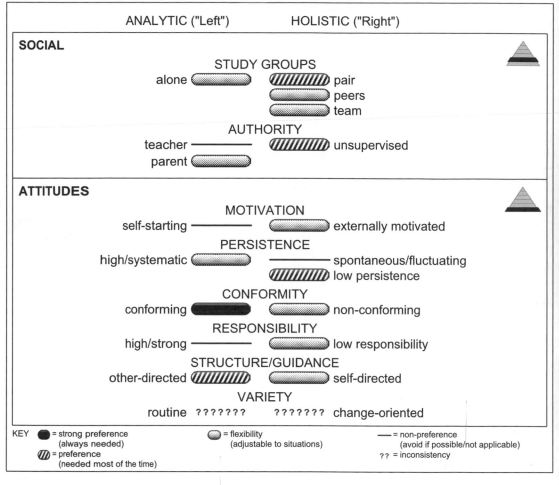

ANALYTIC ("Left")   HOLISTIC ("Right")

SOCIAL

STUDY GROUPS
alone   pair
peers
team

AUTHORITY
teacher ————   unsupervised
parent

ATTITUDES

MOTIVATION
self-starting ————   externally motivated

PERSISTENCE
high/systematic   spontaneous/fluctuating
low persistence

CONFORMITY
conforming   non-conforming

RESPONSIBILITY
high/strong ————   low responsibility

STRUCTURE/GUIDANCE
other-directed   self-directed

VARIETY
routine ??????   ?????? change-oriented

KEY ● = strong preference   ◯ = flexibility   —— = non-preference
        (always needed)   (adjustable to situations)   (avoid if possible/not applicable)
     ▨ = preference   ?? = inconsistency
        (needed most of the time)

DIFFERENCES BETWEEN BIOLOGICAL & LEARNED ELEMENTS:
The results in Graph 1 represent your biological needs when concentrating, reading a study text or learning something new and difficult. Preferences and non-preferences in these areas are usually hard to change and remain mostly stable over a life time. When they are mismatched over a longer period of time they will influence learning motivation, persistence and responsibility in a negative way. For lasting learning success, make sure that your strong preferences are being matched most of the time.
The results in Graph 2 reveal your conditioning, and show with whom you learn best and what your attitudes are when it comes to learning something new and difficult. These elements are not stable in your profile and can change quite rapidly. This usually happens when there are changes going on inside you or in the world around you. To be successful at school it is very important that you develop positive attitudes and always attempt the best you can do because your preferences become your strengths when you use them wisely.

4. ENVIRONMENT   **environment**
revealing preferences for **sound** (needing music/sound or wanting it quiet)
light (needing bright or dim lighting)
temperature (needing a cool or warm learning environment) and
work area (wanting formal or informal/ comfortable setting and furniture)

5. SOCIAL GROUPINGS   **social groupings**
including preferences for working **alone**, in a **pair**, with **peers**, or in a **team**, and
authority (wanting to learn with a **teacher** and/or a **parent** or without them)

6. ATTITUDES   **attitudes**
showing **motivation** (internally or externally motivated for learning)
persistence (high, fluctuating or low)
conformity (conforming or non-conforming/ rebellious)
structure (being self-directed or needing directions, guidance from others)
variety (needing routine/consistency or being change-oriented/needing variety)

The Learning Style Analysis can accurately:

- identify how students learn in class or at home, how they think, concentrate, solve problems and can best master their learning activities;   **identify how students learn**

- assist teachers and parents in creating the most appropriate learning or study environment for every child, either at school or at home;   **assist teachers and parents**

- suggest how to improve study skills and enhance learning motivation;   **improve study skills**

- advise senior students and their parents how to utilize personal preferences for future studies or career planning.   **advise senior students**

     career planning

3. How the LSA works

By responding to a questionnaire which contains a series of statements about themselves, students will receive a computer-generated personal profile and   **questionnaire**

Profile Summary

Murray, your preferences are your strengths when you can use them in difficult learning situations, and your non-preferences become your weaknesses when you have to use them over longer periods of time. This can lead to frustration, concentration problems, low motivation, and learning difficulties. When you are allowed to learn YOUR way, you will enjoy studying more and your academic performance will improve.

Key elements of my learning style when I have to learn something NEW and/or DIFFICULT:

My Preferences: (how I learn best)

BRAIN STYLE: none

SENSES:

 Reading (visual - words)
I remember most of what I read in textbooks or worksheets, so I prefer learning from written or printed information.

 Imagination (visual - internal)
My understanding of new material increases when I visualise what I've seen, heard, read or done.

 Kinesthetic (action, doing/experiencing)
I learn best through physical experiences and love learning situations that require practical involvement. To remember and understand I need to be active with my body.

 Kinesthetic (internal/intuition)
I rely on my intuition or gut feeling during the learning process. For best results, I need to feel good about the things I study.

My Non-Preferences: (what does NOT help my learning)

BRAIN STYLE: none

SENSES:

 Listening (auditory - hearing)
I get bored when I have to listen to lectures, and I don't remember the contents afterwards anyway.

 Self-talk (auditory - internal)
I never talk to myself to understand a new concept or to help me remember a lesson. It doesn't help and I don't need it.

PHYSICAL NEEDS:

 Movement needed (mobility)
I don't want to move around while studying. It distracts me and I prefer to say in one place.

CLASSROOM AND HOME:

 Low light
When the light is not bright enough, I can't study and get tired. Then I feel like falling asleep.

SOCIAL:

 Teacher Authority
I don't like it when teachers tell me what to do. I don't care for their feedback either.

ATTITUDES:

 Self-starting
I don't want to have self-designed objectives or set my own pace for studying. I don't see the point of self-evaluation of my learning progress either.

report, allowing them to <u>identify their individual strengths</u> and personal preferences for learning, studying, reading and general information intake. Through this analysis they will also learn how to recognize and control the elements that can enhance their attempts to solve learning problems. The report helps them concentrate, learn, read and study more efficiently and with greater success and satisfaction. If personal <u>learning preferences are being matched</u> for students in the classroom and at home, these <u>become strengths</u> and will <u>improve their study skills</u>, concentration, consistency and quality of their school and homework as well as their academic performance.

identify strengths

learning preferences matched become strengths improve study skills

Apart from the computer-generated personal profiles the LSA Report gives a detailed explanation of all the <u>individual elements</u> of the LSA model plus advice on how best to utilize personal strengths for learning situations, counteract weaknesses and increase flexibilities.

individual elements

If the <u>recommendations are acted upon</u>, students will find that their overall academic performance, <u>behaviour and concentration improves</u> (to the delight of their teachers and parents). Learning abilities as well as problem-solving skills will be enhanced, <u>school-related stress will be reduced</u> and often learning satisfaction and self-esteem will increase dramatically. This, of course, is reflected in a noticeable <u>improvement in school discipline</u> wherever individual learning styles are the basis for teaching and learning.

if recommendations are acted upon, behaviour and concentration improves

school stress reduced

improvement in discipline

4. LSA Junior, Senior and Adult versions

Both versions have been created to help students gain an insight into their true learning needs and to enable teachers and parents to help them learn in their best possible way.

- The <u>Learning Style Analysis Junior</u> is for students between 10–14 years of age;
- the <u>Learning Style Analysis Senior</u> is for students between 14 and 17/18 years of age.

LSA Junior

LSA Senior

 **LSA-Senior: Student Version**   Murray Sample 2

Graph 3. Learning Style Tendencies

Compare this result with your Left/Right Brain Dominance in Graph 1

ANALYTIC ("Left")	HOLISTIC ("Right")
quiet ▓▓▓	▓▓▓ sound/noise/music
bright light ▓	─── low light
formal study area ???????	??????? informal study area
high persistence ▓	▓▓▓ low persistence
no/low intake ▓	▓ intake needed

Three or more of the following elements: preferring quiet, bright light, formal design/work area, high persistence (to complete tasks without interruptions) and low need for intake tends to suggest an ANALYTICAL (sequential) learning style. On the other hand, preferring sound, soft lighting, informal design, low persistence (completing tasks in bursts while working on multiple tasks simultaneously) and need for intake suggests a GLOBAL/HOLISTIC (simultaneous) learning style (Bruno, 1988; Dunn, Cavanaugh, Eberle, and Zenhausern, 1982).

Recommendations

FOR YOURSELF:
To really improve your study techniques, do this:
- follow the suggestions in your LSA Report,
- share your LSA results with your classmates,
- talk about your learning style with your teachers and the grown-ups in your family,
- see that your learning needs are met whenever possible, in class and at home,
- watch your own success!

FOR YOUR TEACHERS:
Please help your students to understand their profiles, talk about their LSA Report and their personal preferences.
Find out which areas of mismatch between your students' true learning needs and the teaching styles used at your school exist.
This could be the reason for frustration, poor concentration, lack of learning motivation, stress and boredom.
Be aware that style mismatches almost always lead to learning difficulties, low self esteem and underachievement.

FOR THE GROWN-UPS IN YOUR FAMILY:
To help improve Murray's concentration, study skills, learning abilities, motivation and learning attitudes, please follow the suggestions in this LSA Report closely.
Pay particular attention to his preferences and non-preferences when he has to learn something new and/or difficult.
Whenever possible, provide the necessary learning environment at home, accept his unique style, and support Murray's true learning needs.

The <u>reading skills</u> required for the questionnaires have deliberately been kept <u>at a very low level</u> so that administration of this instrument is easy and user-friendly. Although these are reading-based instruments, the reading itself should not be a barrier for students in obtaining useful results.

**reading skills
at very low level**

Sample questions LSA Junior version

'I hardly ever think about eating or drinking when I learn.'
'I get more done when I have a friend to work with.'
'When the classroom is very quiet I can't concentrate.'

Sample questions LSA Senior version

'I remember things better from the early morning classes.'
'When I am interested, no one has to remind me to finish something.'
'It's really difficult for me to sit still for a long time.'

Information about LSA software can be found in Appendix I. For adult students in education institutions the <u>LSA Adult Version is used</u> (formerly WSA Education Version) and for people in the workforce the <u>WSA Corporate</u> is available. They all can be obtained individually or in large numbers from various <u>websites</u>.

LSA Adult Version

WSA Corporate

websites

Our two other revolutionary instruments, the <u>Teaching Style Analysis (TSA-Ed)</u> and the <u>Training Style Analysis (TSA-Corp)</u>, allow teachers and trainers to assess their own styles so that they can compare it with their students' styles. The TSA-Ed instrument will, for the first time, make it possible to reveal <u>mismatches between teachers</u> and their <u>students</u> in a very factual, analytic way. It will help teachers to improve their teaching techniques and adjust to their students' true learning needs.

**TSA-Ed
TSA-Corp**

**mismatches between
teachers and students**

All instruments are freely available on the <u>internet</u>. They can be used individually, in businesses or educational institutions and in-depth training about applications of the diversity concept is available through Creative Learning, NZ, or through one of their international licensed partners or accredited facilitators. (For details see CL website.)

internet

LSA-Junior MINI: Parent Version   William Tester

Did you know?

Please be aware that the non-biological learning preferences (the learned or conditioned elements in Graph 2 of the LSA Profile) will change over time, and often much faster then the biological elements in Graph 1, especially during the early school years.

You may find that, as time goes by, William begins to enjoy learning in different ways, in different study groups or with different people. His attitude towards authority figures may change, and so may his levels of responsibility, persistence, conformity and motivation. But most importantly, you need to know how William's biological style features change as time goes by.

We recommend that you allow William to complete the LSA assessment again in 1 or 2 years' time and thereafter in 3 year gaps until he completes his formal education. Please note that, sometime in the future, William will also graduate from the LSA Junior to the LSA Senior assessment instrument. Please be assured that the Parent and Teacher versions of the Student Report are also available in the LSA Senior version of the tool, so that you will be kept informed about your child's development and learning preferences in high school.

Computer Technology And Your Child

If William has a preference or a strong preference in 4 or more of the below elements of the LSA Pyramid:
*   VISUAL - external/watching
*   VISUAL - words/reading
*   TACTILE
*   KINESTHETIC - internal/feeling
*   TIME OF DAY - evening
*   MOBILITY - stationary
*   STUDY GROUPS - alone,

then he is probably good at working with computers. The internet can be a great source of additional information and further explanations to him. If William battles with a specific subject at school, he will probably benefit from an online tutorial, e-learning or computer-based training, e-books or from commercial educational software. Watch out, however, for excessive computer use, like surfing the Internet when bored or playing too many computer games; and for inappropriate use, like adult sites, adult chat rooms and gambling on line. This is especially true as William enters his teenage years.

Because William will most likely enjoy socialising on the internet, please discuss the topic of internet safety with him. Ruben Rodriquez, director of NCMEC's Exploited Child Unit states that children who are relatively quiet and agreeable are especially targeted in chat rooms. Be especially vigilant if you think your child may not be getting enough recognition or attention.

Is Your Child Truly A Gifted Learner?

These may be the signs that your child is truly a gifted learner:
*   highly integrated in analytic and holistic thinking
*   can learn through all sensory modalities with ease
*   can learn at any time, forgets to eat or do other chores when lost in learning
*   prefers to work alone or with true peers
*   won't accept authority
*   is highly internally motivated - often learns for pure knowledge
*   never gives up - has often extreme persistence
*   dislikes rules - makes his or her own ones
*   doesn't need help in structuring their learning, dislikes guidance.

Please page back and check whether William exhibits some of the above characteristics.

Keep in mind, however, that the above characteristics are just a guideline and not a reflection on intelligence or potential. A gifted learner is someone who learns easily, nothing more and nothing less.

The LSA Adult version has been created for grown-ups who are in any kind of <u>formal education</u>, studying at universities, colleges or through distance education.

formal education

The LSA Report gives suggestions to enhance study skills so that students can <u>monitor their own learning success</u>. To achieve overall improvement in learning and study situations, LSA results should be shared and discussed with teachers, tutors or lecturers where appropriate. By revealing their natural learning needs, the student can then make sure that <u>preferences are met</u> whenever possible, in class and at home.

monitor their own learning success

preferences are met

LSA instruments have been created for the following <u>age groups</u> but if in doubt which version is suitable, the 'younger' version should always be used because the <u>wording</u> of the <u>questionnaire is simpler</u>:

age groups

wording
questionnaire is simpler

LSA Adult: for students at universities and colleges;
LSA Senior: for students 14–18 years of age;
LSA Junior: for students 10–14 years of age;
LSA Junior Mini: for young children (5–9 years of age) and students with low reading abilities

5. The new LSA Mini for very young students

In 2006, we released an exciting new instrument aimed at children aged 5–10 years who find school a challenge. It is based on the premise that every child has his or her unique style of learning, and that if that learning style is satisfied, the child will have more success at school and in other learning situations.

Compared with our other instruments, the advantage of the MINI is the <u>relative brevity</u> of the <u>questionnaire</u> combined with spot on accuracy. The actual report runs for more than ten pages, complete with the analysis, graphs and <u>suggestions</u> how to help the child learn in their preferred style. What's more, the <u>report</u> comes <u>in three versions</u>: one for the student, one for the parent and one for the teacher, so that everybody is aware of the child's natural learning needs.

relative brevity
questionnaire

suggestions
report
in three versions

The new report also helps parents <u>identify giftedness</u> in their children, spot the <u>signs of under achievement</u> and see how <u>safe</u> the child is <u>on the internet</u>.

identify giftedness
signs of under achievement
safe on the internet

Learning Style Analysis™

Senior

prepared for:	Sample Group
7/06/01	Total number in group = 10

Group Percentages I (preferences)

Graph shows the % of people with preferences in the following areas:

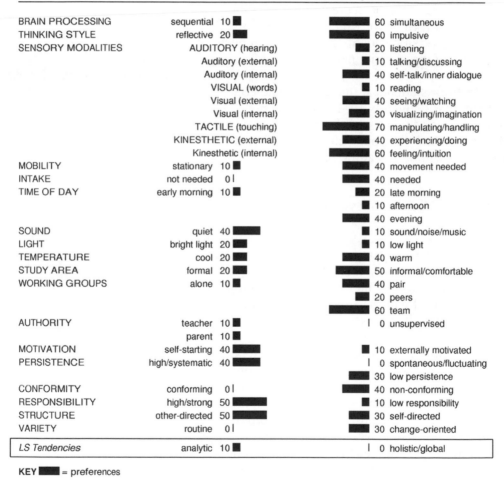

BRAIN PROCESSING	sequential 10	60 simultaneous
THINKING STYLE	reflective 20	60 impulsive
SENSORY MODALITIES	AUDITORY (hearing)	20 listening
	Auditory (external)	10 talking/discussing
	Auditory (internal)	40 self-talk/inner dialogue
	VISUAL (words)	10 reading
	Visual (external)	40 seeing/watching
	Visual (internal)	30 visualizing/imagination
	TACTILE (touching)	70 manipulating/handling
	KINESTHETIC (external)	40 experiencing/doing
	Kinesthetic (internal)	60 feeling/intuition
MOBILITY	stationary 10	40 movement needed
INTAKE	not needed 0	40 needed
TIME OF DAY	early morning 10	20 late morning
		10 afternoon
		40 evening
SOUND	quiet 40	10 sound/noise/music
LIGHT	bright light 20	10 low light
TEMPERATURE	cool 20	40 warm
STUDY AREA	formal 20	50 informal/comfortable
WORKING GROUPS	alone 10	40 pair
		20 peers
		60 team
AUTHORITY	teacher 10	0 unsupervised
	parent 10	
MOTIVATION	self-starting 40	10 externally motivated
PERSISTENCE	high/systematic 40	0 spontaneous/fluctuating
		30 low persistence
CONFORMITY	conforming 0	40 non-conforming
RESPONSIBILITY	high/strong 50	10 low responsibility
STRUCTURE	other-directed 50	30 self-directed
VARIETY	routine 0	30 change-oriented
LS Tendencies	analytic 10	0 holistic/global

KEY ▰ = preferences

6. LSA Group Profiles – a new tool for classroom teachers

The software also generates several different **group profiles** for unlimited numbers of students, allowing teachers to gain a very good overview of individual learning needs among their students. Group profiles are free of charge and very useful for finding out **similarities** and **differences** among individuals or groups, and can help to resolve discipline and communication problems.

Group leaders need to look for **extreme results** above 50 or 60 per cent in preferences and non-preferences, to **subgroup students** with similar needs and apply whatever strategies can be used to accommodate style diversity in learning.

With this knowledge, teachers don't necessarily need to cater to **everyone's individual needs**, because this is impossible in large classes, but any actions they take to **match teaching and learning** styles will benefit the learning process, particularly when teaching something **NEW and/or DIFFICULT**!

Therefore the results from group profiles can be used by teachers (always **together with their students**) to **rearrange the classroom** according to the current group's needs, to discuss how the needs for sound and movement of some (often the majority) do NOT impact on the opposite learning needs of others in class, and to explain why some students will be **allowed to snack** during lessons – only those who according to their LSA really need intake to learn better, and why others will have to wait until the break.

Another important aspect can be discovered and that's **time preferences** of a group with individual exceptions. When a group profile reveals that the majority of the students are **not** 'morning learners' and yet new and/or difficult academic content has to be taught in the morning hours according to the timetable, the teacher can use different methods to match other style needs of this group to **compensate** for one unavoidable mismatch.

Group profiles are not only useful in class for better interaction and more effective instructions, they are also valuable tools for **preparing** teaching programmes and learning materials.

 **LSA - Sen**

prepared for:	Sample Group
7/06/01	Total number in group = 10

Group Percentages II (non-preferences)

Graph shows the % of people with non-preferences in the following areas:

BRAIN PROCESSING	sequential 20 —	0 simultaneous
THINKING STYLE	reflective 40 ——	0 impulsive
SENSORY MODALITIES	AUDITORY (hearing)	— 20 listening
	Auditory (external)	0 talking/discussing
	Auditory (internal)	— 10 self-talk/inner dialogue
	VISUAL (words)	— 30 reading
	Visual (external)	0 seeing/watching
	Visual (internal)	— 10 visualizing/imagination
	TACTILE (touching)	0 manipulating/handling
	KINESTHETIC (external)	— 10 experiencing/doing
	Kinesthetic (internal)	0 feeling/intuition
MOBILITY	stationary 30 ——	0 movement needed
INTAKE	not needed 50 ——	— 10 needed
TIME OF DAY	early morning 20 —	— 30 late morning
		—— 50 afternoon
		— 10 evening
SOUND	quiet 30 ——	— 30 sound/noise/music
LIGHT	bright light 20 —	— 40 low light
TEMPERATURE	cool 20 —	— 20 warm
STUDY AREA	formal 50 ——	0 informal/comfortable
WORKING GROUPS	alone 40 ——	— 10 pair
		— 10 peers
		— 10 team
AUTHORITY	teacher 30 ——	— 30 unsupervised
	parent 30 ——	
MOTIVATION	self-starting 10 —	— 50 externally motivated
PERSISTENCE	high/systematic 50 ——	— 10 spontaneous/fluctuating
		— 40 low persistence
CONFORMITY	conforming 30 ——	0 non-conforming
RESPONSIBILITY	high/strong 30 ——	— 10 low responsibility
STRUCTURE	other-directed 10 —	— 10 self-directed
VARIETY	routine 40 ——	— 10 change-oriented
LS Tendencies	analytic 40 ——	0 holistic/global

KEY —— = non-preferences

Multisensory learning kits can be produced
before the training or class work (see page 154) and
contain the necessary learning tools for all the
different styles during information intake. With the
help of the group profile, teachers can prepare these
tools – particularly in primary schools often with the
assistance of parents or teacher aides – and orchestrate
exercises according to their students' sensory
preferences. Instead of traditional uniform teaching
programmes for everyone in class it is now possible to
have customized, accelerated learning programmes
for individuals within a larger group of students.
This is what can be called real personalization in
education – a combination of teaching to groups of
students with similar preferences AND to individual
learning needs where necessary. (See also Chapter 13.)

multisensory kits

learning tools

**customized, accelerated
learning programmes**

Knowing a group's preferences, non-preferences as
well as flexibilities and then matching students'
learning styles, make any teaching much more
effective and more enjoyable for all participants –
students and teachers alike. Moreover, students
LOVE to see their own group profiles, recognize
themselves in the group, learn more about their
classmates and have a chance of comparing group
preferences with their own ones; not surprisingly, we
have seen that tolerance increases when each other's
style differences are understood, accepted and actually
appreciated. Even bullying stops!

**teaching
effective and more
enjoyable**

**tolerance increases
style differences are
understood**

7. How to use results from the LSA

These instruments help to identify a teacher's
individual own learning style or a student's unique
LS, revealing personal features which are applicable
not only in the classroom but also in the home
environment because personal styles influence
whatever human beings do, and go well beyond the
classroom and the workplace.

**applicable in classroom
and home environment**

They are in fact the basis for our lifestyles, partner
choice as well as the reason for conflict or harmony
between parents and their children, as explained in
Chapters 9 and 10. Interpretation of results always
leads to a much better understanding of our
human diversity.

**basis for lifestyles
reason for conflict or
harmony**

 **LSA - Sen**

Sample Group
Members: 10

prepared for:	Sample Group
7/06/01	Total number in group = 10

Group Percentages III (flexibilities)

Graph shows the % of people with flexibilities in the following areas:

BRAIN PROCESSING	sequential 70	40 simultaneous
THINKING STYLE	reflective 40	40 impulsive
SENSORY MODALITIES	AUDITORY (hearing)	60 listening
	Auditory (external)	90 talking/discussing
	Auditory (internal)	50 self-talk/inner dialogue
	VISUAL (words)	60 reading
	Visual (external)	60 seeing/watching
	Visual (internal)	60 visualizing/imagination
	TACTILE (touching)	30 manipulating/handling
	KINESTHETIC (external)	50 experiencing/doing
	Kinesthetic (internal)	40 feeling/intuition
MOBILITY	stationary 50	50 movement needed
INTAKE	not needed 40	40 needed
TIME OF DAY	early morning 70	50 late morning
		40 afternoon
		50 evening
SOUND	quiet 30	60 sound/noise/music
LIGHT	bright light 50	40 low light
TEMPERATURE	cool 60	40 warm
STUDY AREA	formal 20	40 informal/comfortable
WORKING GROUPS	alone 40	40 pair
		70 peers
		30 team
AUTHORITY	teacher 20	20 unsupervised
	parent 20	
MOTIVATION	self-starting 40	30 externally motivated
PERSISTENCE	high/systematic 10	80 spontaneous/fluctuating
		20 low persistence
CONFORMITY	conforming 50	40 non-conforming
RESPONSIBILITY	high/strong 10	70 low responsibility
STRUCTURE	other-directed 40	60 self-directed
VARIETY	routine 50	50 change-oriented
LS Tendencies	analytic 40	90 holistic/global

KEY ▨ = flexibilities   ■ = preferences   — = non-preferences

Results can be used by students to: **results for students**

- gain important self-knowledge
- understand their strengths and weaknesses
  in learning, remembering and problem solving
- enhance study skills
- prevent misunderstandings between students
  and teachers or parents
- increase learning motivation
- raise self-esteem and confidence
- create a learning environment suited to their
  true style preferences
- be allowed to learn and study 'their way'
- plan their future career.

Although students usually benefit most from
knowing their learning style and how important
this is for school failure or school success, it is
also important for <u>teachers</u> to know their students'   **teachers improve**
learning styles for <u>improving their teaching</u>   **teaching practices**
<u>practices</u>. More information about LSA Profiles
can be found in the LSA <u>Interpretation Manual</u>.   **Interpretation Manual**

Results can be used by teachers to:

- really understand human diversity in their classrooms
- become aware of learning differences between male and female students
- understand biological learning needs in students
- recognize the separate styles of underachievers, slow and 'gifted' learners
- improve communication with students and/or their parents
- help design classrooms better suited to students' individual learning needs
- carry out successful group-work in class
- improve the 'team spirit' of students working together on projects
- enhance student and teacher interaction
- be better capable of matching teaching and learning styles
- deal with at-risk students more successfully
- use time management techniques based on personal styles and biological needs
- reduce stress on a daily basis and in difficult classroom situations
- improve teaching performance and job satisfaction.

Results can be used by parents to:

- understand how different their children are in their learning needs
- support them more successfully in their learning efforts
- learn how to create a learning environment at home suitable to their children's style
- practise more tolerance with unusual style features of their children
- accept that their children have their own unique learning styles
- realize that they are not clones of themselves.

LSA-Junior

Group Results

Teacher Sample

Group member code number	1	2	3	4	5	6	7	8	9	10	11	12	13	14	15	
BRAIN PROCESSING sequential																sequential (analytic)
simultaneous																simultaneous (holistic)
THINKING STYLE reflective																reflective
impulsive																impulsive
SENSES AUDITORY (hearing)																listening
Auditory (external)																talking/discussing
Auditory (internal)																self-talk/inner dialogue
VISUAL (words)																reading
Visual (external)																seeing/watching
Visual (internal)																visualising/imagination
TACTILE (touching)																manipulating/handling
KINESTHETIC (external)																experiencing/doing
Kinesthetic (internal)																feeling/intuition
MOBILITY stationary																stationary
movement needed																movement needed
INTAKE not needed																not needed
needed																needed
TIME OF DAY early morning																early morning
late morning																late morning
afternoon																afternoon
evening																evening
SOUND quiet																quiet
sound/noise/music																sound/noise/music
LIGHT bright light																bright light
low light																low light
TEMPERATURE cool																cool
warm																warm
STUDY AREA formal																formal
informal/comfortable																informal/comfortable
STUDY GROUPS alone																alone
pair																pair
peers																peers
team																team
AUTHORITY teacher																teacher
parent																parent
MOTIVATION self-starting																self-starting
externally motivated																externally motivated
PERSISTENCE high/systematic																high/systematic
spontaneous/fluctuating																spontaneous/fluctuating
low persistence																low persistence
CONFORMITY conforming																conforming
non-conforming																non-conforming
RESPONSIBILITY high/strong																high/strong
low responsibility																low responsibility
STRUCTURE/GUIDANCE other-directed																other-directed
self-directed																self-directed
VARIETY routine																routine
change-oriented																change-oriented

KEY ● strong preference ⦻ preference — non-preference ◯ flexibility ?? inconsistency

8. Practical applications for better teaching

LSA profiles reveal which <u>type of instruction</u>
a student, or group of students, needs to make
information intake or <u>learning truly successful</u> and
fun – through listening, talking, discussing,
reading, watching, thinking, imagining, hands-on
involvement, doing, experiencing or feeling.
For many students, however, the traditional delivery
of learning content through overheads and lecturing
with little interaction is just not the best way to learn.
Through our work with this instrument we have
discovered that New Zealanders, young and old,
are 'hands-on' people who learn best by doing,
not by listening or only watching. For this reason,
over the past few years, and with great success,
we have been introducing various <u>interactive</u>,
self-correcting <u>learning tools</u> to educators –
always tailor-measured to a particular content or
learning programme (see Chapter 6).

type of instruction

learning success

interactive learning tools

Teachers can also find out the kind of <u>environment</u>
their students work best in (for example, light levels
and temperatures they require, how much sound/
noise/music or quiet they need, and what kind of
work area and furniture helps them to concentrate
best). Particularly useful for high school teachers
is knowledge about their students' <u>thinking styles</u>:
whether they are analytical left-brain thinkers who
focus on details and logic, or the more creative,
right-brain thinkers who need the big picture for
better understanding and like to have fun during
the learning process, or those who are flexible
in their thinking and can adjust easily.

environment

thinking styles

Maybe the most valuable information comes from
two areas – <u>attitudes</u> and <u>social groupings</u> –
particularly for teachers of teenage students. LSA
Profiles will clearly show the interconnectedness of
attitudes like motivation (self-starting or externally
motivated), persistence (high and systematic,
spontaneous and fluctuating, or low), conformity
or non-conformity, high or low responsibility,
the need for structure (self- or other directed) and
variety (the preference for routine or changes).
It is usually the <u>combination of these elements</u>,

attitudes/social groupings

combination of elements

In front of the Turkish LSA poster with Ms. Yücel, the principal of the Bahçeşehir primary school in Istanbul

One of the many LS-trained teachers outside this revolutionary new learning space in Istanbul.

Comfortable seating for students at Bahçeşehir University in the 'Holistic Learning Window'

Through Bahçeşehir-Uğur Educational Institutions, our partners in Istanbul, we are now helping to bring students and teachers from a backward, traditional approach to education into the digital age with LS via the internet and the first results can already be seen in practical situations.

the often intangible reasons for students' disruptive
behaviour and their misunderstood or misinterpreted
learning needs, which cause teachers frustration,
anger or despair.

The Learning Style Analysis not only reveals to the
teacher who in his or her class needs to move and
who can sit still easily during the learning process,
but also at which time of day or evening a student
learns best. As an example of <u>mismatch between
teachers' styles and students' styles</u> it is worth
mentioning that we know from research from
around the world that teachers generally work
better in the early morning hours, yet the majority
of students (during primary school years but
particularly in high school) tend to be 'brain dead'
until 11am. This means that they are only beginning
to wake up when they come to school in the morning
and find it very difficult to concentrate, let alone
remember difficult information. A teacher, however,
who is a morning person, expects every student to
be bright and alert, ready to learn at that same time
of day. This is a great fallacy, and <u>time mismatch</u>
is actually one of the most widespread <u>reasons for
underachievement</u> or learning problems.

mismatch between teachers' and students' styles

time mismatch one reason for underachievement

Equally important is information about how
teachers <u>communicate</u> with their students. The way
they interact with each other has considerable
influence on the success or failure of someone's
learning process. Results in the <u>social elements</u>
of the LSA reveal how students work together
and learn best: alone, in a pair, in peer groups
or with a team, and it will become obvious how
they respond to <u>authority</u> – whether they need
supervision or not and how they accept a teacher
or parent watching over their learning.

communicate

social elements

authority

9. Finding out what makes students tick

It is certainly pertinent to ask whether teachers and
parents know which styles their students, their sons
or daughters have, and how to <u>accommodate these
style needs</u> on a daily basis.With the LSA we have
– maybe for the first time – an assessment tool
that goes far beyond psychological, cognitive and

accommodating style needs

There is nothing more unequal than the equal treatment of unequals.

Dr K. Dunn

THOSE WHO SUGGEST
THAT CHILDREN SHOULD ADAPT
TO THEIR TEACHER'S STYLE
DISREGARD THE BIOLOGICAL
NATURE OF STYLE.

DR R. DUNN

intellectual abilities of a student during the learning
process. It gives profound and detailed insight into
biological needs (like sound, light, temperature,   **biological needs**
work area, mobility, intake, time of day and
sensory modalities) and how human brains seem
to function when it comes to thinking, concentrating,
problem solving, and absorbing and retaining new
and difficult information. Beyond that, LSA Reports
show how conditioning or learned style elements   **conditioning/learned**
(attitudes and social preferences) can influence   **style elements**
the learning process to an extent that the student
can become a success or failure at school.   **school success or failure**

Parents have known it for a long time and even
teachers have realized that traditional and formal
teaching methods do not excite the majority of
students in our school systems any longer, that
students are bored, that underachievement,
negative attitudes and discipline problems are
rapidly increasing and that the number of at-risk
students and burnt-out teachers is on the rise.

There will not be much hope of leading students
successfully in this new millennium, and creating
lifelong learners, unless we are prepared to accept   **lifelong learners**
that human diversity exists in our classrooms but
not only in a cultural, social and ethnic sense.

It is time to realize that self-knowledge and a deep   **self-knowledge**
understanding of learning styles might be the   **learning styles**
only way out of the dilemma virtually every
school system around the world finds itself in
these days. It is no coincidence that requests for
learning style assessment software and the
accompanying learning styles training programmes
have dramatically increased recently not only here
in New Zealand but also overseas.

Maybe learning styles IS the missing link between   **missing link**
traditional mass education with its formal learning
methods and the more humane individualized
learning strategies of the future.

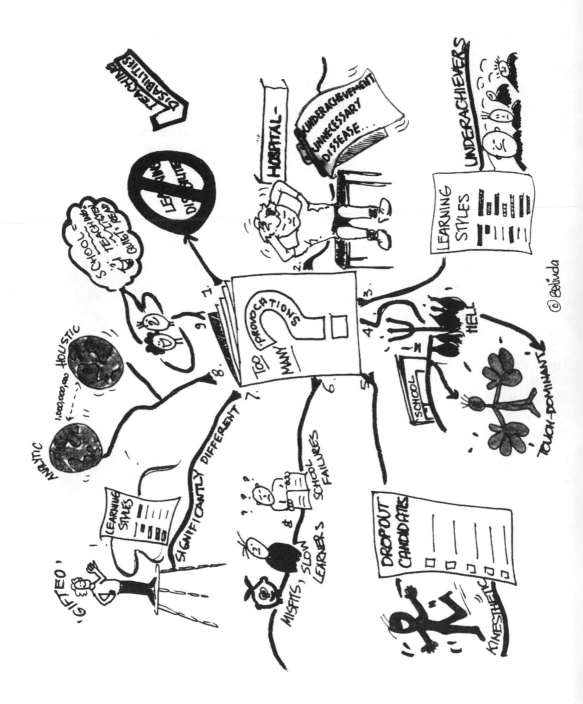

1. There are no learning disabilities – only teaching disabilities

When I first heard this statement – made by one of
the leading researchers in the field of learning styles,
Dr Rita Dunn of St John's University in New
York, at a conference on Accelerated Learning
in Minneapolis in 1992 – I was not only provoked,
I was offended because I had been a teacher
in many different educational institutions (from
primary to secondary schools, to teachers' college
and university) in different countries, and I knew
I had always been highly successful. The results
of my students spoke for themselves, didn't they?
So how dare this woman tell me that *I am the one
really responsible for my students' learning.*

leading researchers

**provoked
offended**

highly successful

Although most of my students always produced
good results, there were also a few who did not
make it, who remained way below their abilities,
who were not really interested in learning or just
dropped out. Still, my colleagues, with whom
I discussed this problem, and I strongly believed
we had done all we could for these students and
it was really their, not our, problem when they
couldn't learn, thank you very much.

**good results
below their abilities
not interested**

not our problem

But the more I thought about Rita Dunn's words
the more I had to question general beliefs about
education and learning. What if she was right?
I began to look into the research and statistics
on learning styles, going back over a quarter of a
century, and I had to admit, the statement which
provoked me and had hurt my professional pride
so much in the beginning became more and more
the truth for me the longer I reflected on it.

**question general beliefs
education and learning**

learning styles

provoked

All these experiences have caused me to rethink
traditional teaching methods and common
learning practices and have set me on a crusade,
literally around the world, to have diversity
accepted in the classroom, different styles
recognized in any workplace or educational setting,
and the need acknowledged to blend them with
creative, accelerated learning techniques.

**rethink traditional
teaching methods**

**diversity accepted,
different styles
recognized,
blended with creative,
accelerated learning**

Whenever I speak to teachers about learning styles

A provocation is awkward in the beginning but gets easier over time.

Edward de Bono

these days, I quote Rita Dunn's statement and
often get <u>similar reactions</u> to the ones I had
when I heard it first: <u>disbelief</u>, <u>confusion</u> or
<u>ridicule</u> on the mild side, <u>anger</u>, <u>cynicism</u> and
often <u>outrage or even hostility</u>, particularly from
educators in high schools and tertiary institutions,
and <u>more from males</u> than from females!

**reactions of
disbelief – confusion
ridicule – anger – cynicism
outrage – hostility**

more from males

Negative reactions are <u>less common from people
in business education</u> – they are amazed to find
such diversity among their trainees and then
are very <u>eager to try anything</u> which will make
their <u>training more effective</u>. Observing these
diverse reactions made me wonder a lot about
<u>teachers and their attitudes</u> towards their students
and learning in general!

**less common from people
in business education**

**eager to try anything
training more effective**

**teachers and their
attitudes**

No matter what educationalists think about this
new approach, research continues to prove it,
teachers who are using learning styles swear by it,
and I know it from individuals and groups I have
introduced to the notion of learning and working
styles. <u>Individualized instruction does work</u> and
I am now convinced that there are no learning
disabilities, only teaching disabilities.

**individualized instruction
works**

If educators continue to <u>disregard human diversity</u>
in their classrooms and are not prepared to teach
to groups with individual styles, too many students
will <u>continue to underachieve</u> and many more will
believe they are <u>learning failures</u>.

disregard human diversity

**underachievers
learning failures**

2. Underachievement – the unnecessary disease in our schools

Over the years, studies on learning styles have
revealed that the learning styles of <u>underachievers</u>
and dropouts are <u>significantly different</u> from
those students who remain in school and finish
their education successfully. Another sad aspect
of this widespread 'disease' in our schools is
that underachievement is often the first step
to becoming an at-risk student, and <u>dropping out</u>
of school is the final <u>unhappy solution</u> for many.

**underachievers
significantly different**

**dropping out
unhappy solution**

The significance of these findings lies in the
necessity to understand that <u>learning style</u> is

learning style

If any learner

leaves your instruction

with a decreased desire

towards your subject

or learning in general,

then you are guilty of

EDUCATIONAL MALPRACTICE

Nikos Kazantsakis

a <u>biologically and developmentally imposed</u>
<u>set of characteristics</u> every human being possesses.
This provides an important insight into the ways
students take information in during the learning
process. It is the <u>individual difference</u> in personal
styles that makes the same teaching method
wonderful for some and terrible for others – even
when the children come from the same family.

**biological/developmental
set of characteristics**

individual difference

The annoying insight for all concerned is that these
underachieving students, sometimes called 'reluctant
learners', '<u>could do much better</u>' as we have all
heard over and over again from teachers at parent
evenings, read in school reports and thought for
ourselves if they would just put <u>more effort</u> into
their school or homework. We as parents look at
these children with despair because we know they
are <u>not dumb</u>, they are actually <u>very smart kids</u> and
we know they CAN do good work, they often
ARE motivated and CAN concentrate ... <u>IF</u> ...
they are <u>interested in the learning task</u>.

could do much better

more effort

not dumb but smart kids

**if
interested in learning**

Teachers, on the other hand, cannot comprehend
why these students can be very <u>successful in some</u>
<u>subjects</u> (often sports, craft, drama, woodwork,
home economics, computers or special interest
projects) where they show all the necessary positive
attitudes: high interest and motivation, persistence,
enthusiasm and the will to achieve their goals.
And teachers always are at a loss to explain why
these same students often <u>fail dismally in academic</u>
<u>subjects</u>, don't do their homework and find school
boring and a waste of time. It is quite obvious that,
<u>despite</u> their often <u>high abilities</u>, these students
do not actively participate in the learning process,
are unwilling to put extra effort into their work and
only do what's necessary for 'getting by'. Often
teachers get very angry when they realize these
students often <u>waste their learning potential</u>.

**successful in some
subjects**

fail in academic subjects

despite high abilities

waste learning potential

No one seems to understand what's going on here
but everyone agrees that they could succeed more
if they were better motivated or just knew how.
Read on to find out what makes them tick and how
all the affected parties can be helped by simply
gaining <u>knowledge about the style features</u> which
underachievers share worldwide in our systems.

knowing style features

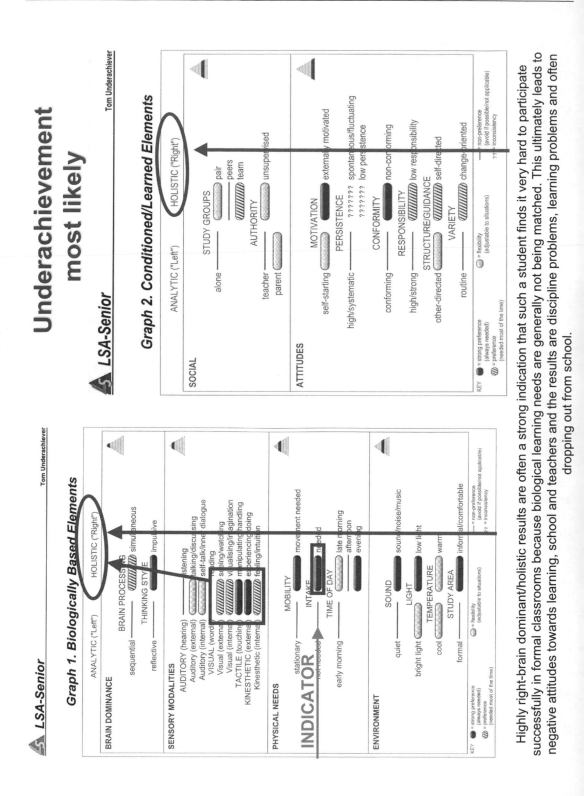

Underachievement most likely

LSA-Senior   Tom Underachiever

Graph 1. Biologically Based Elements

Graph 2. Conditioned/Learned Elements

Highly right-brain dominant/holistic results are often a strong indication that such a student finds it very hard to participate successfully in formal classrooms because biological learning needs are generally not being matched. This ultimately leads to negative attitudes towards learning, school and teachers and the results are discipline problems, learning problems and often dropping out from school.

3. LD: not lazy and disabled but learning-different

According to the Dunn & Dunn learning style model and the research which has been carried out over the years, <u>underachievers</u> and highly at-risk students have <u>eight statistically different style elements</u> compared to students who are successful at school. Such students, however, are <u>not</u>, as the Dunns correctly put it, '<u>learning disabled</u>' (LD) as often diagnosed by their teachers. They are simply, but rather inconveniently for traditional educators, <u>learning different</u> (as 'special needs' teachers well know), have an unusual style combination and generally have strong needs for:

underachievers have 8 different style elements

not 'learning disabled'

learning different

1. <u>Mobility</u> at frequent intervals
2. <u>Variety</u> of learning tools, resources and teaching methods
3. <u>Informal seating arrangement</u> in their learning environment because of their inability to sit on hard chairs for more than 10–15 minutes
4. <u>Low light</u> because their brains seem to get overstimulated, especially by fluorescent light, which often leads to agitated behaviour
5. <u>Tactile/kinesthetic</u> learning tools and resource materials to introduce new and difficult material through their preferred modalities because they are usually not highly visual or auditory
6. <u>Late morning or afternoon</u> for difficult subjects rather than early morning classes
7. <u>Non-authoritative teachers</u> who treat these students collegially and know how to respect their non-conformist thinking
8. <u>Recognition of their high motivation</u> despite their obvious problems which are often caused by inappropriate teaching methods. (1)

mobility
variety

informal seating

low light

tactile/kinesthetic

late morning/afternoon

non-authoritative teacher

recognition of high motivation

When I first heard about these <u>style combinations</u> and how relatively easy it would be to switch these students on to learning, I thought it can't be that simple. My academically trained mind wanted to make me believe that the reasons for under-achievement must be found in much deeper-rooted psychological problems, socio-economic conditions, lack of motivation and parental support, poor study

style combinations

| FRENCH
P. BROADHURST | C+ | A | Sigrun has undoubted ability and can produce very good work. She has yet to overcome her tendency to "wander off" & remaining on-task for the full hour is still a problem at times. She is, however, gaining in confidence, and her exam result was excellent. |
| Social St.
A.L.Fong. | B+ | A | Sigrun has the ability to do even better than what she has produced in this subject. Her assignments, test and her final exam demonstrates total commitment to organisation and research. Polite and very clued up! (Top mark in Soc. St. 73½%) Sometimes a little too talkative. |

| English
D. McGinty | C | B2
54% | The school certificate examination. Sigrun had an awkward slant to the term and did not quite overcome some disorganisation. She is confident orally though she needs to focus clearly on detailing her written work to show her understanding. A competent writer, but she really needs to spend time at home and at school thinking through the ideas she expresses in writing. |
| **SCIENCE** | B | 72 | 21½ | 30 | 75 | Sigrun is slotting down and achieving well, but she must try not to chat in class. JAM |

Form Teacher's Comments: It is evident that while Sigrun is attaining a high level of achievement in some areas, in others she could benefit from a more organised approach to her work. She is always a vivacious, outgoing student who brings to her studies a delightful, original flair.   M.V. McDougall Form Teacher

Dean's Comments: Sigrun should aim to develop sound consistent work habits. She needs to learn her work and revise thoroughly. Some results are most pleasing.   R.J. MacCormick Dean

                        Ruth Jones MA DipEd Headmistress

| **PHYSICAL EDUCATION** | C+ | | | | | Sigrun is energetic, enthusiastic and obviously enjoys all the activities. JL |
| 6 Biology
E. Bowater | C+ | | 4-6 | | | Throughout the year Sigrun's assessment results have been somewhat variable. Some show excellent understanding of biological ideas, but some of the homework-type assignments have a rushed, disorganised air about them. Better attentiveness in class, and better organisation will ensure future success in Biology. |

skills, etc. But then I began to think about **my daughter's**
my own daughter and all the learning problems **learning problems**
she had, particularly during her high school years **during high school years**
in New Zealand schools. I knew she didn't have
psychological problems, we lived in very healthy
socio-economic conditions, she wanted to learn and
there was no lack of parental support. Quite the
contrary, we often overdid it. And on top of that
we also had proof about her high intelligence, **high intelligence**
her many talents and her high learning abilities. **many talents and abilities**

So, 'what was wrong with her?' we began to ask
ourselves as we got more desperate over the years,
hearing from her teachers the familiar 'could do better!'

Despite all our efforts her school reports kept **school reports**
stating the same facts over and over again as you
can see on the opposite page. (I do have her
permission to reveal extracts of her school reports.)
We all dreaded these reports, knowing what would
be in them, feeling the disappointment, discussing **disappointment**
the results, seeing the tears and desperation, hearing **tears and desperation**
the repeated promises and not knowing what to do. **promises**
She was average or below, slowly giving herself up
as a learner in formal education. And here I was,
a caring parent, an educator with all my years of
training and yet I had no clue how to help her, **no clue how to help**
how to make her high school years more successful
(socially she was very successful but learning
was a near disaster) and how to unlock her true **unlock true potential**
learning potential.

If you have experienced a similar situation in your
own family, you will share with me the sorrow and **sorrow and agony**
agony about an underachieving child, the deep
frustration and helplessness and ultimately the **frustration and helplessness**
final resignation that nothing much can be done. **final resignation**

Fortunately enough we did not experience any
other related problems like drug and alcohol abuse
or suicidal tendencies, as often occurs in underachieving students during their teenage years. We
thought we would just have to put up with a strange
phenomenon no one could explain and a 'disease'
for which there was obviously no cure.

And then I found out about learning styles ...

What you bring forth

out of yourself from the inside

will save you.

What you do not bring forth

out of yourself from the inside

will destroy you.

Gospel of Thomas

We had our daughter assessed with the old, original Dunn and Dunn LSA instrument, and for the first time in my life I physically <u>began to understand</u> her <u>true learning style needs</u> when I saw them printed on paper.

understand
true learning style needs

I wish I had known about <u>style differences</u> long ago as it became one of the biggest eye-openers for me and my whole family. All of a sudden it dawned on me how different we all were in our learning needs (as you will see in Chapter 11) and what this child of mine I thought I knew so well needed when it came to learning. At that time she was already in her final year and <u>teachers</u> at her local high school unfortunately were <u>not interested</u> <u>in learning styles</u> because they 'knew what they were doing' and kept telling me that my daughter could 'do much better' (here we go again) if she just studied harder and put more effort into her work. They had made up their minds about underachievers and so had I: from now on I would fight for <u>more</u> <u>understanding</u> of these students' styles and <u>better</u> <u>teaching practices</u> in our schools.

style differences

teachers
not interested
in learning styles

more understanding
better
teaching practices

Regrettably nothing much could be done at her old school (and is still not being done for under-achievers there) but at least my daughter now knew her style, her <u>learning needs</u> and that there was nothing wrong with her. The following year, with <u>appropriate study techniques</u>, she – probably for the first time as an adolescent student – experienced true <u>learning success</u> when she graduated with honours from a self-chosen veterinary nursing course. I had never seen her happier because she had finally done the <u>studying HER way</u>!

learning needs

appropriate study
techniques
learning success

study her way

I had to share this personal experience with you because I see similar problems in many families, not only in New Zealand but also in other countries, causing a lot of <u>unnecessary heartache</u> for all concerned, often ending in tragedy. Therefore I will not give up my quest to have learning styles concepts firmly established in education systems around the world and to help classroom teachers understand human diversity in learning.

unnecessary heartache

To learn without doing

is like making love

without touching.

'Consider:
As a sensory system
the skin is much the most
important organ system of the body.
A human being can spend his life
blind and deaf and completely
lacking the senses of smell and taste,
but he cannot survive at all
without functions performed
by the skin ...
Among all the senses,
TOUCH
stands paramount.'

Montagu (1986)

As long as teaching methods are not individualized and teachers continue to use <u>identical teaching strategies</u> for everyone, knowing they are only effective for some, they <u>will not reach students</u> who need them most, and will keep losing their students in the learning process and, what's even worse, lose them as lifelong learners.

identical teaching strategies
do not reach students

That's why <u>lip service is not enough</u>. Nothing will change as long as teachers say – and I hear it all the time – 'Oh yes, we always tell our students about learning styles' or 'We would love to use learning styles, but we have too many students in our classes', or 'It's a great idea, but we don't have the money to introduce it', etc. All it takes is the doing, and even <u>small beginnings</u> with a <u>pilot group</u> are better than just talking about it. Part of the knowledge about learning styles is the insight into how the <u>human brain</u> seems to process information and how <u>thinking processes</u> work. However, it goes further.

lip service not enough

small beginnings
pilot group

human brain
thinking processes

While step-by-step instruction and rote learning are still favoured methods in traditional education, they are inferior to other learning techniques which <u>activate the right brain</u> and encourage <u>dual-brain thinking</u>. How differently students respond to the same teaching method and why underachieving students clash with so many teachers but get on very well with a few will be explained towards the end of this chapter.

activate right brain
dual-brain thinking

4. School is hell for tactile/touch dominant students

In learning styles, language tactile (tactual) means that sensory information intake happens through <u>touching and manipulating</u> objects. All sensory modalities play an important role in the learning process as described in detail at the beginning of Chapter 6, and people with a tactile preference learn and remember best through <u>hands-on activities</u>. As most young students and many teenagers have strong tactile preferences, it is quite obvious that our traditional school system, with formal instructions mainly based on reading and writing, does not cater for the tactile needs of these students, particularly not

touching and manipulating

hands-on activities

CREATIVE VISUALIZATION

For touch dominant people

Here are three sets of instructions used to show how the imagery technique can be adapted for the touch dominant. All have been thoroughly tested, and even people totally convinced that they 'can't DO that!' find that they can do these with ease. The instructions are brief and the user should feel free to add many more details, from any of the sensory systems; the more details they contain, the more vivid they are.

1. You are walking a tightrope between two trees, about six inches off the ground (so there's no need to be afraid of falling). Feel your feet on the rope as you move along. Each time you set a foot down or lift it up, be aware of the sensation(s) you feel in the foot and the adjustments your body has to make to stay balanced. Go back and forth as many times as you like.

2. You're swimming – having a wonderful time – through a substance that you find pleasing: warm or cool water; blackberry jam; baby powder; sand; your choice. You don't have to worry about breathing or effort, you just swim along through it easily and gracefully. Put your attention firmly on the way the substance you chose for your 'sea' feels on your skin, all over your body, as you swim.

3. You are a broad ribbon of velvet, draped over the back of your favourite chair (or a limb of your favourite tree, or any other support that pleases you). You are absolutely relaxed and absolutely safe and totally comfortable ...

Elgin (1996, page x, preface)

at high school level. Despite the huge amount of information which over the years has been written about learning styles, there is not much literature available about this particular group of learners.

However, I was pleased to have found the recently published book *Try To Feel It My Way: New Help for Touch Dominant People and Those Who Care About Them* by Suzette H. Elgin. The book makes fascinating reading and although I do not agree with everything discussed in it, it is at least one of the few publications describing the problems highly <u>tactile or touch dominant</u> children and adults have. In particular I do not agree with Elgin's unclear distinction between kinesthetic and tactile preferences because, based on my experiences with learning styles, it is very important to <u>distinguish between learners</u> who are highly <u>tactile</u> and those who are highly <u>kinesthetic</u>, preferring whole-body experiences and physical activities during the learning process. It is also not appropriate to call all the 'doing-learners' touch dominant. But that aside, Elgin's book contains a wealth of dialogues, practical hints and exercises to recognize touch dominant children or adults and helps us to communicate better with them.

tactile/touch dominant

distinguish between tactile and kinesthetic learners

The questions now are: Why do these people have problems with communication and why is <u>school so difficult for tactile students</u>? The reason seems to lie in the fact that our Western societies have developed more towards visual (seeing) and auditory (hearing) based information intake and stimulation. We don't know why but, as Elgin says, it may be that in our '<u>Don't touch!</u>' culture more of us *learn* to prefer our eyes and ears. Most likely, it's a combination of the two. (2)

school is difficult for tactile students

'Don't touch!' culture

Not only is our society putting more emphasis on sight and hearing plus rewarding these abilities, but nearly all of our presently used <u>teaching methods</u> rely heavily on <u>visual and auditory</u> skills of teachers and students alike. For young children and primary school pupils it is very much acceptable that they involve their hands a lot, have large amounts of learning materials and they are allowed to 'play' with things during the learning process. But as

teaching methods visual and auditory

Hands-on (tactile activities)

soon as they enter high school, their tactile stimulation during classes is drastically reduced to handwriting (which they don't like anyway) and to computer work (which many of them love); and any other activity with their hands (doodling, fiddling, playing with pens, etc.) is outright forbidden and often punished. Despite all the warnings and reprimands, these highly tactile students – more often boys than girls – will not stop their finger movements, particularly when they are bored or have to listen or concentrate hard.

**in high school
tactile stimulation
is drastically reduced**

forbidden or punished

**when bored,
listen or concentrate hard**

Therefore it is so important for teachers to really understand that manipulating and using their fingers helps tactile students to concentrate, even listen better. The more they are told not to do that, the stronger the need grows and the more they have to suppress it. And that means they concentrate on what NOT to do instead of concentrating on the learning content.

**using fingers
helps to concentrate,
listen better**

But there's more which adds to the misery of touch dominant students – the way they are told to study and the instruction methods teachers use for them. Instead of being allowed to learn with manipulatives (that is, learning tools from a learning style kitset), hands-on activities and movement, they are forced to sit still, listen, read and write. They can do all that but they have to work harder than their visual and auditory classmates because their sensory preferences lie in a different area. That's the reason why such students lose interest, get bored, don't quite understand, fall behind, and finally give up participating because there is nothing in it for them. If you are a highly tactile person and you can't use your hands and fingers or are constantly reprimanded, even a class period of 45 minutes can be hell!

**need manipulatives,
hands-on activities,
movement; when forced
to sit still/listen/read/write**

**students lose interest,
get bored, fall behind,
give up participating**

I wish teachers would understand better what these tactile students really need and learn how to teach them. Being highly tactile AND kinesthetic (which is a very common style combination) was one of the reasons for my daughter's learning problems during high school because these two senses were just not stimulated enough in theoretical subjects and that contributed to her being bored, switching off and falling behind. Had I just known this then!

tactile and kinesthetic

Unusual learning spaces

5. Highly kinesthetic learners: dropout candidates in high schools

It's bad enough for highly tactile students not to be allowed to learn predominantly through their hands, but for the truly kinesthetic students, those who need <u>body involvement</u> and <u>physical experiences</u> to understand the learning content, it's even worse. Sitting in classrooms where there is nothing to do, where moving around is not allowed and where the teacher just talks and talks is not only hell for these students, it actually becomes unbearable. It's no wonder that after a few years of unsuccessfully trying to listen, read and write like most other students, they give up participating and behaving as it is expected of them. They begin to 'play up', they become discipline problems, get together with like-minded (equally kinesthetic) classmates and can create hell for teachers. These <u>boys</u> are usually <u>taller and stronger</u> than their fellow students, and kinesthetic <u>girls</u> are often described as '<u>tomboys</u>', never growing out of their rough and tumble behaviour, never becoming 'ladylike'.

body involvement
physical experiences

**kinesthetic boys are
tall and strong
kinesthetic girls are
'tomboys'**

Due to their very physical style needs which are not matched at all in academic, theoretical subjects, there is not much which interests these students other than <u>practical subjects</u> and <u>sports activities</u> where they are usually <u>very good and successful</u>. They come to the conclusion – often fuelled by their teachers' and parents' beliefs – that they are not the 'learning types', that school is not for them, and over time their learning motivation disappears, school progress diminishes, and being out in the streets or doing sports only becomes much more desirable. First they become <u>underachievers</u>, then <u>discipline problems</u>, then <u>truants</u> and finally school <u>dropouts</u> with a <u>profound dislike</u>, often <u>hate for school</u> and anything which has anything to do with formal learning or education.

**practical subjects and sports
very good and successful**

**underachievers
discipline problems,
truants, then dropouts
dislike/hate school**

In the past these early school leavers could easily go into manual jobs, work hard and, particularly in New Zealand, be compensated for their lack of formal education through their great <u>practical skills</u> and abilities and were able to build a successful life for themselves. But all that has changed now; there

practical skills

Children today are tyrants.

They contradict their parents, gobble their food,

And tyrannize their teachers.

Socrates (born around 470 BC)

If as a student you are

not being taught in

your learning style,

you are being handicapped.

J. Ingham

are hardly any manual jobs left, they are poorly paid and the first to go when companies do 'downsizing' exercises. There is nowhere to go, nothing much to do and no great future prospects for these highly kinesthetic students. Out of this desperation, often paired with social problems, we now see a growing number of young people <u>dropping out of school</u>, with no formal qualification, unemployed and unemployable, taking comfort in alcohol, sex, drugs, gang activities and crime.

dropping out of school

Maybe, if teachers, parents and decision makers in education knew more about learning styles and diversity, and understood and acted upon them, then we might even see fewer teenage pregnancies and suicides in New Zealand, but certainly many more students who <u>want to learn</u> and choose to <u>stay at school</u> instead of giving up.

want to learn
stay at school

6. Misfits, rebels, slow learners and school failures

Now we have investigated underachievement, tactile and kinesthetic learners and their problems in traditional education settings, we can easily understand why so many students become misfits and school failures. <u>Matching learning and teaching styles</u>, better classroom management and creative learning techniques will certainly help all these students to draw out their potential and become more successful at school.

matching learning and teaching styles

There is, however, one group of students who, in addition to their difficult combination of style elements (similar to underachievers yet overall different), do have various <u>other problems</u> like failing health, poor hearing or eyesight, severe social or psychological problems, often slight malfunctions of the brain, or physical handicaps. They are the school failures, the true <u>'special needs'</u> kids, for whom learning styles and creative learning techniques will not be enough to remedy the problems. They are the <u>slow and poor learners</u> and need help from specialists and all the support they can get. But even here a knowledge of style differences can make life much easier for teachers, parents and students concerned.

other problems

'special needs' kids

slow and poor learners

DEALING WITH PROCRASTINATION

For each item below rate yourself from 1 to 5 in the space provided:

1 = Never a problem   **2** = Rarely a problem   **3** = Sometimes
4 = Often a problem   **5** = Very frequently a problem

_____ 1. I delay until the last minute before starting important projects.

_____ 2. I fail to return phone calls promptly.

_____ 3. I pay my bills late.

_____ 4. I say I will do a particular task, but then don't get around to it for a long time.

_____ 5. I show up late for appointments.

_____ 6. I collect materials to use on a project and then delay doing the project.

_____ 7. I avoid situations where I believe I won't be very successful.

_____ 8. I delay answering correspondence.

_____ 9. I feel as though there is just one crisis after another in my life.

_____10. I tell myself that tomorrow I will begin.

Add up your responses and see how you rate. The higher your result the more you are prone to procrastination.

What is the impact of these problems on your daily life, at work or at home?

Can you think of areas in which these affect your colleagues, students or family?

Based on a handout by Educational Research and Advisory Unit, University of Canterbury

Generally so-called 'slow and poor' learners have the following combination of style features:

slow and poor learners

1. Right-brain dominance: need the big picture first, find it hard to think analytically

   right-brain dominance

2. Tactile-kinesthetic preferences: are usually not visual and rarely auditory, but strongly feeling-based

   tactile/kinesthetic

3. Mobility: find it hard to sit still, often fidget

   mobility

4. Late morning or afternoon: have difficulties in early morning classes

   late morning/afternoon

5. Sound: find it harder to concentrate when it's quiet, music enhances their learning

   sound

6. Low light: seem to get overstimulated by fluorescent light, show agitated behaviour

   low light

7. Informal work area: find it difficult to sit on hard chairs for more than 10–15 minutes, need comfortable learning environment

   informal work area

8. Pair/peers/team: don't work well alone, need other students with similar styles to work with

   pair/peers/team

9. Authority: are often afraid of teachers but need them to organize learning tasks

   authority

10. Low motivation: find learning hard, fail frequently, become passive, uninvolved

    low motivation

11. No persistence: give up easily, frequently used phrase: 'I can't'

    no persistence

12. Need structure: cannot do learning tasks without guidance; when left alone, nothing gets done

    need structure

13. Dislike variety: need consistency and routine; change is threatening.

    dislike variety

This complex picture explains why slow and poor learners struggle with school, have very low self-esteem and need all the support they can get from their teachers and care givers who need to know about their style features, their strengths and not only about their obvious weaknesses. Many successful applications of learning styles in the USA have helped these students to become accomplished learners despite their other problems (3) and in New Zealand we are beginning to see similar results.

struggle with school
low self-esteem

Very different from this category of learners are the so-called 'gifted' students who differ dramatically in their style features even from average students as international research findings have shown.

'gifted' students
differ dramatically
from average students

AN INTERESTING COMPARISON:

Students with

LD & ADHD Symptoms	vs.	Holistic Style Features
1. Often fidget or squirm in seats		1. Need mobility; highly kinoesthetic
2. Have difficulty sitting still		2. Strong need for mobility & movement
3. Easily distracted, forgetful, often lose things		3. Short attention span, "scatterbrain", little attention to details
4. Difficulty awaiting turn in group		4. Impulsive thinking; impulsive behaviour
5. Blurt out answers to questions		5. Typical holistic, impulsive, right-brain processing
6. Difficulties following instructions		6. Non-sequential, random brain processing; low auditory preference in information intake
7. Difficulties in attending to learning activities		7. Fluctuating persistence; work in bursts; externally motivated
8. Often shift from one uncompleted task to another		8. Multi-task orientated, non-analytical, need variety, easily bored with just one activity at a time
9. Can't learn or play quietly		9. Need/prefer noise/sound in combination with movement and physical activities
10. Often talk excessively		10. Need social interaction; preference for talking; is peer/group orientated
11. Often don't seem to listen		11. Low auditory preferences; need overview; hands-on instructions; experimental learning
12. Often engage in physically dangerous activities without considering consequences		12. High kinesthetic/tactile preferences, high need for mobility; low responsibility; high non-conformity, resulting in high risk-taking behaviour

7. ADHD (Attention Deficit Hyperactivity Disorder) and LS

The syndrome Attention Deficit Hyperactivity Disorder is being diagnosed in ever-increasing numbers among students in many countries and most teachers find it extremely difficult to deal with their <u>disruptive behaviour</u>. Although there are some students who have <u>neurological disorders</u> causing ADHD and benefit from taking certain <u>medication,</u> many students are sadly <u>misdiagnosed</u>. Their behaviour problems are only partly due to deprived family situations – they are largely based on <u>poorly understood LS needs</u> and style combinations which do not fit traditional norms. The comparison on the opposite page gives a quick overview of LD (Learning Disability) and ADHD symptoms in contrast to holistic LS needs.

disruptive behaviour

neurological disorders
medication
misdiagnosed

poorly understood LS needs

This was the case at Forbury Primary School in NZ where I was in charge of the change project to salvage the school and I could observe over longer periods of time that quite a number of students where given prescription medication against ADHD. They showed many of the symptoms described here, but they certainly did not need Ritalin. Once we had their LSA results, teachers realized that they all had this 'unfortunate' style combination of preferences which looked like ADHD and it was decided to stop giving them the tablets for two weeks and observe what would happen. Of course teachers also <u>matched</u> their <u>learning needs</u> in class and made regular written observations. (See Chapter 13.)

match
learning needs

Several things became obvious quite quickly:
* when these students were allowed to learn according to their <u>natural preferences</u>, their disruptive behaviour stopped;

  natural preferences
* their need for excessive movement was greatly reduced because they could <u>move their bodies</u> during learning tasks;

  move their bodies
* they learned with <u>multisensory</u> activities, that way reducing the need for too much listening and reading;

  multisensory
* most importantly, they were <u>no longer stigmatized</u> and became more flexible and better motivated to participate because they now <u>ENJOYED learning</u>

  no longer stigmatized

  ENJOYED learning

ASSESSMENT of HEMISPHERIC RELATED STRATEGIES (4)

The Mighty Right and the Brain That's Left

i. Read and score each statement from 1 to 10 according to how much it is true for you, (1 being the lowest).
   e.g.   10 = I am 100 per cent like that; that describes me to a T.
        5 = I am like that sometimes/I'm not sure/or it depends.
        1 = No way!
ii. Try to write your first reaction; it is more likely to really describe you than if you think it over for too long.
iii. Write your score for each statement in the column provided.
iv. Be honest with yourself!

	Score
1. I base decisions on objective facts rather than feelings.	
2. I am psychic.	
3. I like using symbols or images in solving problems.	
4. I am artistically or musically creative.	
5. I am logical.	
6. I am good at solving crossword puzzles.	
7. I can read quickly.	
8. My daydreams are vivid.	
9. I can think of synonyms for words easily.	
10. I can remember dreams.	
11. My dreams are vivid.	
12. I am fluent in using words.	
13. I am good at using images in remembering and thinking.	
14. I use a playful approach to problem solving.	
15. I use a serious, all-business approach to problem solving.	
16. I like to keep experiences planned and structured.	
17. I like to read and think while sitting upright.	
18. My thinking consists of words.	
19. My thinking consists of mental imagery.	
20. I like to explain something using a visual presentation.	

SCORING: Left nos: 1, 5, 6, 7, 9, 12, 15, 16, 17, 18   ☐

                Right nos: 2, 3, 4, 8, 10, 11, 13, 14, 19, 20   ☐

Add up the scores for Left and Right. Write them in the boxes above. Subtract the smaller number from the larger, and divide that result by 10: e.g. 74 (left) − 48 (right) = 26; 26/10 = 2.6 (left). The higher score indicates the hemisphere-related strategies you prefer. The larger the number, the greater the preference for that hemisphere. As a rule of thumb, a final score of 0.7 or higher indicates a preference.

8. 'Gifted' students have significantly different learning styles

When talking about '<u>giftedness</u>' we need to clarify what the criteria are, and I have chosen a very good definition by Dr Donald Treffinger, an American specialist in giftedness. He states: 'Giftedness refers to a person's <u>creative accomplishments</u>, over a sustained period of time (that may be years or even decades), in a domain that matters intensely to that person.' (5)

'giftedness'

creative accomplishments

Traditionally, 'gifted' students have been identified by meeting specific criteria, often heavily dependent on rigorous assessments and IQ tests, and then put into <u>so-called programmes for gifted</u> students. With the knowledge about learning styles, many different activities and services should be offered to these students, not just a single, fixed programme, and Treffinger maintains schools should be concerned with the following:

so-called
programmes for gifted

- individualized basic instruction
- appropriate enrichment
- effective acceleration
- independence and self-direction
- personal growth and social development
- career perspectives with a futuristic orientation.

Based on those he urges schools to consider what <u>additional support</u> (people, time, materials) may be needed to expand, extend or enhance the regular programme. (6)

additional support

Various studies on <u>gifted adolescents</u> have revealed that their styles vary significantly from average or even high-achieving students. If you are a teacher, compare the following list of style preferences with the styles your 'gifted' students display, and if you are a parent, this information might give you valuable information on how to support your gifted child because often we don't quite know what to do with these (sometimes 'weird') young people. High IQ and <u>talented students dropping out of school</u> may be highly gifted young people who become unmotivated because conventional schooling does not complement their learning styles.

gifted adolescents

talented students
drop out of school

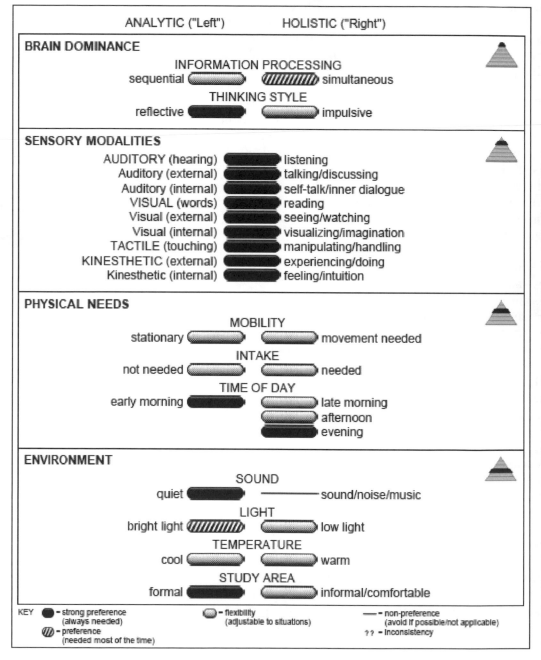

LSA-Senior: Parent Version

Gretchen Gifted

Graph 1. Natural / Biological Elements

ANALYTIC ("Left")   HOLISTIC ("Right")

BRAIN DOMINANCE

INFORMATION PROCESSING
sequential — simultaneous

THINKING STYLE
reflective — impulsive

SENSORY MODALITIES

AUDITORY (hearing) — listening
Auditory (external) — talking/discussing
Auditory (internal) — self-talk/inner dialogue
VISUAL (words) — reading
Visual (external) — seeing/watching
Visual (internal) — visualizing/imagination
TACTILE (touching) — manipulating/handling
KINESTHETIC (external) — experiencing/doing
Kinesthetic (internal) — feeling/intuition

PHYSICAL NEEDS

MOBILITY
stationary — movement needed

INTAKE
not needed — needed

TIME OF DAY
early morning — late morning
afternoon
evening

ENVIRONMENT

SOUND
quiet — sound/noise/music

LIGHT
bright light — low light

TEMPERATURE
cool — warm

STUDY AREA
formal — informal/comfortable

KEY   ● - strong preference   ◐ - flexibility   — - non-preference
      (always needed)   (adjustable to situations)   (avoid if possible/not applicable)
      ▨ - preference   ?? - inconsistency
      (needed most of the time)

The following combination of preferences sets
<u>gifted learners</u> apart from the rest of the student
population yet often causes problems at school
and at home:

gifted learners

1. <u>Left/right-brain integration</u>: can be highly
   analytical or holistic but can also integrate
   extremely well

   left/right-brain integration

2. <u>Multisensory abilities</u>: learn easily through
   several senses but prefer tactile/kinesthetic

   multisensory abilities

3. <u>Early morning or evening preferences</u>: do
   well at these times

   early morning/evening

4. <u>Sound</u>: analytics prefer quiet environments,
   but if strongly right-brained, they like music
   in the background

   sound/quiet

5. <u>Low/bright light</u>: depending on their
   brain dominance

   low/bright light

6. <u>Work area</u>: depending on their brain
   dominance, but show a tendency towards
   formal learning environment

   formal work area

7. <u>Social</u>: prefer to work alone, only accept
   true peers to work with

   alone/true peers

8. <u>Authority</u>: do not accept it, make their
   own rules, don't want to be supervised

   no authority

9. <u>High motivation</u>: internally motivated,
   thirst for knowledge, often learn for the
   learning's sake

   high motivation

10. <u>Extreme persistence</u>: never give up, can be
    stubborn in pursuing learning goals

    extreme persistence

11. <u>Non-conformity</u>: dislike rules, don't mind
    to be told what has to be done but not HOW,
    always want to do it their way, can get
    frustrated and walk out

    non-conformity

12. <u>Responsibility</u>: usually only interested in
    their own projects, can show low
    social responsibility

    responsibility

13. <u>Don't need structure</u>: always know how to
    go about their learning tasks, don't like
    interference from teachers or parents.

    low structure

They often feel <u>isolated</u> or <u>misunderstood</u> and
in contrast to 'average' students they are <u>very
intuitive</u>. They will often <u>go by their feeling</u> in
decision making, when they follow personal
criteria and consider values and relationships.
Again, a sound knowledge of their learning styles
can help to understand and support them better.

isolated/misunderstood
very intuitive
go by feeling

What Analytic Learners Expect From A Teacher

- To focus on tasks and details.
- To provide information in a sequentially organized format.
- To provide outlines and specifics.
- To be tested on details and facts.
- To be left undisturbed and uninterrupted in their thinking process.

What Holistic Learners Expect From A Teacher

- To focus on personal needs and feelings.
- To provide overviews and the big picture.
- To provide guidance and personal interaction.
- To be tested on general concepts and effort.
- To be allowed to socialize during the learning process.

Recognizing What Analytics Say

- Does spelling count?
- Should I use pen or a pencil?
- Will this be on the test?
- Please check my work before I hand it in.
- I need to know what comes first? What second?
- Why can't we do one thing at a time?

Recognizing What Holistics Say

- Why do we have to do this?
- Not now! I'll do it later.
- Is it important? Does it really matter?
- Don't touch the piles on my desk, I'll find it!
- Why do we have to do it now? It will still be here later.
- I can't sit any longer, I need a break.

Based on *A Curriculum Companion, a Visual Staff Training Resource to Teach Global and Analytic Strategies.* Rita Dunn, St John's University, 1993

9. Analytic and holistic students exist worlds apart

When I began to reshape the WSA Model – now in the form of a pyramid – I asked myself if there might be a hierarchy of elements, and by going through the literature on learning styles it became quite obvious: learning styles begin with left- and right-brain dominance, thinking style and brain processing. For that reason these elements had to go at the top of the pyramid because the way a brain processes information influences all the other style elements of a person.

**WSA Model
in pyramid form**

**brain processing influences
style elements**

As we have seen in Chapter 2, the left/right brain metaphor is a very simple one to explain preferences in brain processing styles but there is more to this useful distinction. Hemisphericity – another term for left- or right-brain dominance – manifests itself not only in information intake preferences but also in typical style combinations and resulting behaviour. We therefore need to know what the differences are between left-brain dominant (analytic) students and their right-brain dominant (holistic/global) colleagues. And yet again, research on learning styles and practical experience with the WSA and LSA instruments provide the answers.

**hemisphericity
left/right-brain dominance**

**style combinations
resulting behaviour**

The difference between analytic and holistic styles is like day and night and, one can say, students with these strong preferences are worlds apart. The first divide occurs in the five basic areas where students have the exact opposite needs (in the following list **A** stands for 'Analytics' and **H** stands for 'Holistics'): (7)

analytic/holistic styles

**five basic areas
opposite needs**

1. Sound
    A: prefer quiet while learning
    H: need sound/music/noise
2. Light
    A: need bright light
    H: prefer low light when learning
3. Work area
    A: prefer formal furniture, hard chairs, like to sit upright when learning
    H: prefer informal arrangements, soft chairs, lying or sitting on the floor or on a bed

sound

light

work area

Graph 3. Learning Style Tendencies

Compare this result with your Left/Right Brain Dominance in Graph 1

ANALYTIC ("Left")		HOLISTIC ("Right")
quiet		sound/noise/music
bright light		low light
formal study area		informal study area
high persistence		low persistence
no/low intake		intake needed

Three or more of the following elements: preferring quiet, bright light, formal design/work area, high persistence (to complete tasks without interruptions) and low need for intake tends to suggest an ANALYTICAL (sequential) learning style. On the other hand, preferring sound, soft lighting, informal design, low persistence (completing tasks in bursts while working on multiple tasks simultaneously) and need for intake suggests a GLOBAL/HOLISTIC (simultaneous) learning style (Bruno, 1988; Dunn, Cavanaugh, Eberle, and Zenhausern, 1982).

Graph 3. Learning Style Tendencies

Compare this result with your Left/Right Brain Dominance graph on page 2

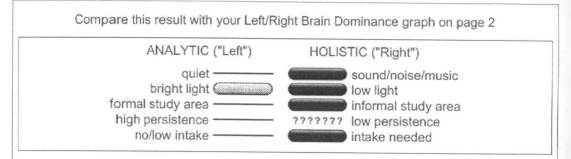

ANALYTIC ("Left")		HOLISTIC ("Right")
quiet		sound/noise/music
bright light		low light
formal study area		informal study area
high persistence	???????	low persistence
no/low intake		intake needed

Graph 3. Learning Style Tendencies

Compare this result with your Left/Right Brain Dominance in Graph 1

ANALYTIC ("Left")		HOLISTIC ("Right")
quiet		sound/noise/music
bright light		low light
formal study area		informal study area
high persistence ???????	???????	low persistence
no/low intake ???????	???????	intake needed

Three or more of the following elements: preferring quiet, bright light, formal design/study area, high persistence (to complete tasks without interruptions) and low need for intake tend to suggest an ANALYTICAL (sequential) learning style. On the other hand, preferring sound, soft lighting, informal design, low persistence (completing tasks in bursts while working on multiple tasks simultaneously) and need for intake suggests a HOLISTIC/ GLOBAL (simultaneous) learning style (Bruno, 1988; Dunn, Cavanaugh, Eberle, and Zenhausern, 1982).

The more **QUESTION MARKS** are visible in a personal profile, the more it is likely that this student:
   a) is under stress,
   b) is currently experiencing confusion or is undergoing change in these areas,
   c) has reading problems, or was confused about the questionnaire (occurs very rarely)
This can lead to behaviour problems, loss of motivation, learning difficulties, underachievement, and ultimately dropping out of formal education. It is important that teachers and parents talk to the student about these areas in their LSA profile and attempt to find out the reasons for these inconsistencies. It is also recommended to redo the profile in 2-3 months' time when the situation has settled down.

4. Persistence
   A: prefer to work on single tasks without interruption until they are finished, have high persistence
   H: like to work simultaneously on several tasks, need frequent breaks, procrastinate, have low persistence

persistence

5. Intake/mouth stimulation
   A: do not eat, drink, chew or nibble when learning, find it distracting, do it when task is completed
   H: work better when snacking, chewing, drinking, becomes part of the learning process

intake/mouth stimulation

Beyond those there are many more features which set these groups of students apart although most people are a complex mix of analytic and holistic features. However, approximately 5–10 per cent of any population are strongly one way or the other and find it hard to flex.

people are a complex mix

General characteristics of ANALYTIC students: they are obedient, controlled, quiet, verbally oriented, reflective, logical, detail oriented, sit upright, respect authority, work well alone, need structure, read a lot and participate in discussions, are conforming, self-motivated and highly responsible, bright and alert in the morning – in short, they are the'ideal students'.

analytic students

'ideal students'

Do you know such students and how do you react to them when they say, 'Will this be on the test?' or 'Does spelling count?' and 'Please check my work before I hand it in.' Depending on your own style preferences and your flexibility, you will either be on the 'same wavelength' and accept such comments or find them baffling and senseless.

There is, however, an ever-growing group of students who have style features most teachers find hard to handle and would certainly describe as distracting from real learning, even destructive.

growing student group
style features

distracting from learning

General characteristics of HOLISTIC students: they are likely to 'play up', are extroverted, noisy, impulsive risk takers, scatterbrained, hate details, slouch in their chairs, chat and socialize a lot, can't

holistic students

General
style differences between

Analytics

don't like to talk
pack days before trip
plan/prepare
compulsive/accurate
obsessively organized
on task/on time
perfectionists
blame others
competitive
outlines/lists/graphs
decision making
don't trust, need proof
worrying/stressed
step-by-step, details
love/need detailed instructions
follow recipes when cooking
wardrobe – things straightened out
single-minded on tasks
logical/reflective
serious/earnest
specialists

Holistics

communicative, motormouths
last-minute packing
dislike planning/carefree
flexible/laid back
sloppy/disorganized
distracted/usually late
not 100 per cent, 'good as gold'
could always be improved
often cruising
mind mapping/summaries/overviews
undecided/oscillating
socialize/many friends
easy-going, less stressed
overview, big picture
prefer general directions
creative cooks/alter recipes
wardrobe – untidy, mess
multiplicity in doing things
intuitive/spontaneous
fun loving/forgetful
generalists

Exercise: check which features you combine in your personal style, compare with your partner.

sit still, often rough and tumble, good at sports, are
night owls and usually 'brain-dead' in the morning,
show low responsibility and learning motivation,
just getting by, are <u>hands-on kids</u> with a very
<u>practical sense</u>, strong non-conformists and tend
to stay away from teachers.

hands-on kids
practical sense

Such students are definitely <u>not the favourites</u> in
our classes and often they are labelled LD (learning
disabled), ADD (attention deficit disorder), discipline
problems, underachievers, at-risk students, school
failures, truants or dropout candidates.

not the favourites

It is amazing that a simple difference in L/R brain
dominance and preference for <u>analytic</u> or <u>holistic</u>
<u>styles</u> should be the reason for such vastly different
behaviours and <u>achievements at school</u>. And that's
exactly what it is: different brain styles lead to
different learning styles which in turn lead to
different school performance. Like it or not, these
partly <u>biologically influenced style combinations</u>
determine success or failure for students because
our education <u>systems</u> still <u>reward analytic styles</u>,
not true potential and learning abilities. Students
who don't fit 'the norm' have very little chance
of success in our present system, and unless
teachers and decision makers <u>accept diversity</u> in
the classroom and fully <u>introduce learning style</u>
<u>programmes</u>, conditions will get worse.

analytic/holistic styles

school achievements

biologically influenced
style combinations
systems reward analytic
styles

accept diversity
introduce learning styles

We have just explored the profound differences
between analytic and holistic students and I hope
this has given you, as a concerned teacher or parent,
a new insight into human diversity. Now we have
to investigate where teachers fit into this scenario.

10. And teachers live in a world of their own!

Given the <u>historic development</u> of the <u>teaching</u>
<u>profession</u> and the problems education is facing
worldwide, we have to ask ourselves a
few questions:

historic development
of teaching profession

Who were the people in the past who formally
educated the young generations? Wasn't it always
the 'learned' men, the clergy and academia? Didn't
they determine the teaching methods? Wasn't it

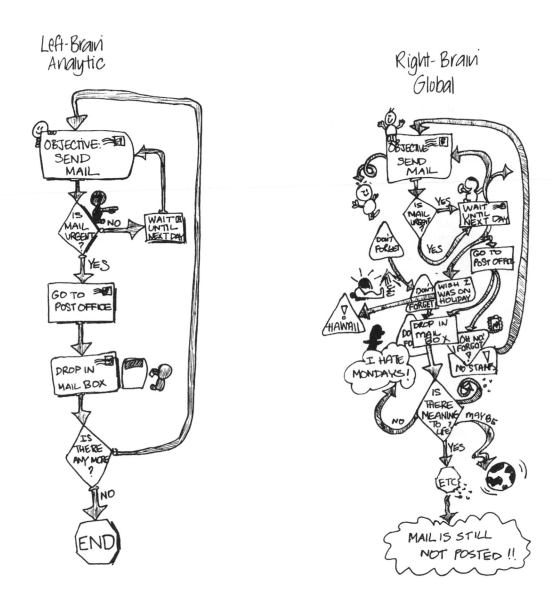

mainly 'chalk and talk'? And what kind of brain
processing styles did these men have? Right,
it was the <u>analytical, logic, left-brain, scientific</u>
approach which still dominates formal education
to this day, despite a world which would need more
people using their 'whole brain' and utilizing their
creative right-brain skills better.

**analytical, logic,
left-brain, scientific**

Whoever went into the <u>teaching profession</u>, liked it
and stayed on (often died on the job), had no real
problems accepting the <u>existing standards</u>, procedures and expectations – and they were all, and
still are, guided by logic, left-brain, analytic styles.
All those who had the same style features fitted in
nicely, were comfortable and passed on their way
of thinking and being through teaching methods
based on <u>analytic preferences</u>. For centuries in
education there was always a near <u>perfect match</u>
between a mainly elitist student population and their
analytic teachers. They quickly and eagerly grew into
the <u>formal ways of learning</u> practised in schools.
Many of the strongly held views about the 'right'
teaching and learning methods date back to these
times, have not yet been eradicated and are still
flourishing, particularly in university education
but also in senior high school settings.

teaching profession

existing standards

**analytic preferences
in the past perfect match**

formal ways of learning

Education had always attracted more <u>left-brain
oriented professionals</u> who fitted the system nicely
and perfected their formal, analytic teaching styles.
It was a simple and quite <u>successful formula</u>:
analytic teachers (lecturers) taught *analytic
subjects* (like the sciences) to *analytic students*
(who had learned to think analytically in high
school) through *analytic methods* (by lecturing
and reading/writing assignments).

left-brain professionals

**successful formula:
analytic teachers
analytic subjects
analytic students
analytic methods**

But then <u>mass education</u> came along and with it
large numbers of students who did not fit the
picture of the 'traditional' student, who struggled
with traditional teaching methods but spared no
effort to make it through formal education. Initially
it was not so bad because those who were <u>not</u>
<u>'academically minded'</u> left school early, found
<u>manual jobs</u> and only those with matching (analytic)
styles stayed on and completed their studies. So
<u>analytic teachers</u> were still at ease and successful

mass education

**not academically minded
found manual jobs**

analytic teachers

Different authors have used different terms to describe the two basic differences in brain processing styles.

ANALYTICAL	HOLISTIC
left hemisphere	right hemisphere (R. Sperry)
reflective/analytic	impulsive/global (Dunn and Dunn)
sequential	simultaneous (Dunn and Prashnig)
introvert	extrovert (R. Ornstein)
high gainers	low gainers (R. Ornstein)
deliberator	liberated (R. Ornstein)
single track	multi-track (A. Gore)
masculine	feminine (J. Nicholson)
logical left-brain	intuitive right-brain (H. Alder)
box and triangle	circle and squiggle (S. Dellinger)
High S and C	High D and I (DISC profiles)
academic parts	creative activities (G. Dryden)

with the remaining students. Since the early 1960s, however, more students stayed longer in formal education and that was the time when all the problems started. All of a sudden, there were vast numbers of students in formal education who would and could not learn the way they were being taught, for whom analytic teaching methods did not make sense and who would have needed very different approaches and learning techniques. But teachers were not and still are not trained for a vastly different and hugely diverse student population with very different expectations, aspirations and ambitions compared to one generation ago. The mismatch between teaching and learning styles is particularly obvious in high schools, vocational institutions and universities. The situation is much better in primary schools where student-centred teaching methods have been practised for many years and learning style techniques are being accepted more readily.

students stay longer in formal education

different learning techniques

mismatch between teaching and learning styles, high schools and universities situation better in primary schools

Traditional, analytic teaching methods are still OK for a small number of students, but the majority would need more integrated, flexible, brain-friendly approaches. Unfortunately most teachers cannot deliver because they have never been trained in these new methods. Many are oblivious, uncertain, reluctant, often cynical about learning styles and creative, accelerated learning, particularly in higher education. Despite student complaints about bad and inadequate teaching practices, most teachers remain stuck in delivery methods they have learned at teacher training colleges many years ago (from very analytical lecturers) and are not even willing to contemplate more user-friendly methods.

teachers have never been trained in new methods

This attitude really alienates traditional teachers from an ever-growing student body demanding modern teaching practices, appropriate for the fast-changing world we live in. Although this is a broad generalization as there are plenty of good and progressive teachers (often frustrated with the system), it seems that many teachers have built a world of their own, which is their comfort zone and which they are not prepared to leave. As I am an optimist, I know that these conditions will change, albeit slowly, and therefore I will continue to work tirelessly for bringing about changes.

students demand modern teaching practices

bringing about changes

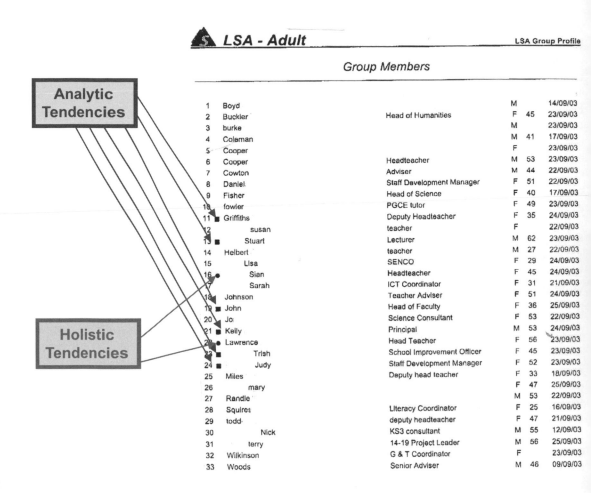

This page from the group profile shows at one glance which members of this group have overall analytic or holistic style tendencies and who is flexible. The people who do not have a symbol in front of their name can flex between logical and feeling-based approaches to learning and problem solving easily. As this is generally the majority in classes, the teacher can then concentrate specifically on the few students who need different strategies while the majority with preferences and flexibilities can be taught together.

11. 'Double-tracking' – a teaching strategy to reach all students

As already described in Chapter 2, Part 3, human beings seem to have three possibilities for <u>information processing</u>: analytic, holistic, or flexing between these two modes which is also called integrated.

information processing

For educators it is therefore very important to recognize and accept these often strong <u>natural</u> (biologically based) <u>style differences</u>, to accommodate and utilize them in their everyday classroom work. When teaching new and/or difficult content, it is advisable to subgroup students with these respective preferences into an <u>analytic</u> and a <u>holistic group</u> according to their LSA results, and assign flexible students to one group or the other.

natural
style differences

analytic holistic group

So far so good, but now teachers have to apply a new way of teaching both groups and that is only possible through 'double-tracking' which means in LS terms <u>switching</u> consciously and continuously <u>from analytic</u> teaching style <u>to holistic</u> strategies and back again in regular intervals during each lesson. This way no students are left behind or need to suffer from teaching methods which go on and on with explanations that do not make sense to them and only switch them off.

switching from analytic
to holistic

In other words: analytic, step-by-step teaching is <u>confusing</u> for <u>holistic students</u> who need the big picture and tend to learn well when they can be emotionally and physically involved in a fear-free learning environment. But holistic, unstructured, self-directed lessons can be very <u>unsettling</u> for <u>analytic students</u> who need routine, order and guidance in a predictable, more traditional learning environment.

confusing holistic students

unsettling analytic
students

For more information, examples, tips and guidelines for teaching analytic and holistic students simultaneously, see my book *Learning Styles in Action,* (Chapter 8, pages 74–9), published in 2006.

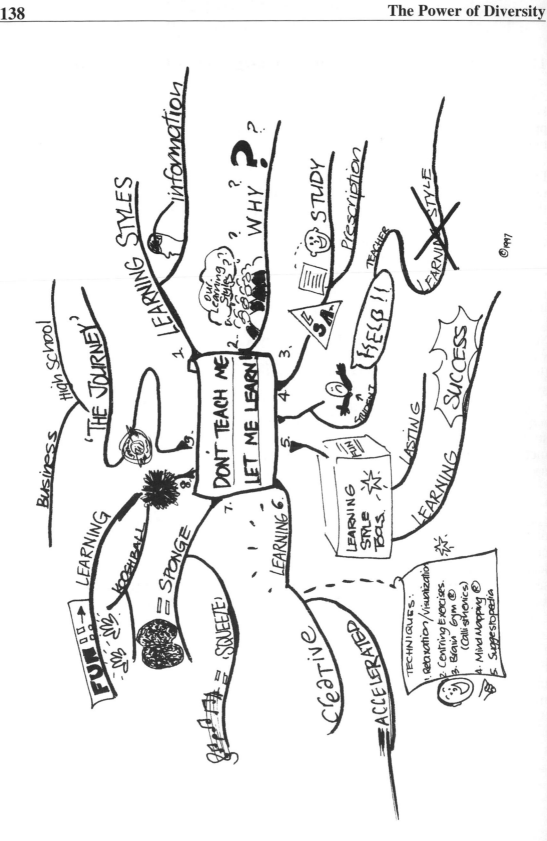

1. Learning Styles (LS) and information intake

As we have already seen, information intake is
strongly dependent on the way people go about it,
and that has far-reaching consequences for their
success in learning and training. By instructing
students through their personal learning style
strengths an immediate <u>behavioural change</u>   **behavioural change**
is noticeable and the <u>failure rate</u> in schools can   **failure rate**
effectively be brought down to <u>zero</u>. The effects,   **zero**
particularly on underachieving students, are instant
because insight into their own learning abilities
leads to ongoing <u>performance improvement</u> in class   **performance improvement**
when they begin to <u>understand their own style</u>.   **understand own style**

The research for underpinning these claims
goes back over 20 years in the USA
and is rapidly growing worldwide. (1)

Among all the elements which make up a person's   **senses**
overall style, four of our six <u>senses</u> (<u>seeing</u>,   **seeing, hearing**
<u>hearing</u>, <u>touching</u> and <u>feeling</u>) are the ones which   **touching, feeling**
most influence <u>information intake</u>, memory and   **information intake**
learning. Translated into more technical terms they
can be described as visual, auditory, tactile and
kinesthetic <u>sensory modalities</u> or <u>perceptual</u>   **sensory modalities**
<u>preferences</u> (see page 140).   **perceptual preferences**

Centres for processing sensory information
are spread all over the brain and <u>develop at their</u>   **develop at own pace**
<u>own pace</u> in each human being. Children first
begin learning and remembering difficult things
by experiencing them <u>kinesthetically</u> (**K**), which   **kinesthetic (K)**
means they need to involve their whole body
for information intake and acquiring basic skills.
The second modality to develop is <u>tactile</u> (**T**);   **tactile (T)**
that's why young children have to touch
everything that interests them – they are learning
through manipulation and interaction with
objects and people. Around age eight, some
children begin to develop strong <u>visual</u> (**V**)   **visual (V)**
preferences which allow them to take information
in more through observing and watching what's
going on around them. Seeing becomes a very
important learning tool. Around eleven years
of age many begin to become more <u>auditory</u> (**A**),   **auditory (A)**

SENSORY MODALITIES
and submodalities

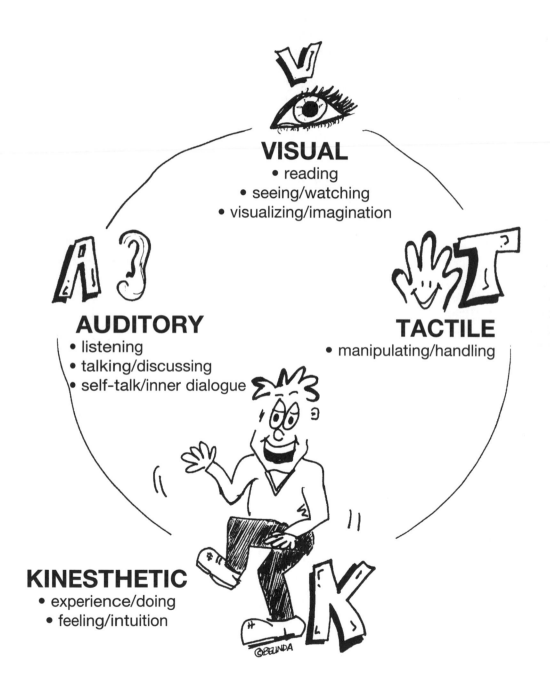

VISUAL
- reading
- seeing/watching
- visualizing/imagination

AUDITORY
- listening
- talking/discussing
- self-talk/inner dialogue

TACTILE
- manipulating/handling

KINESTHETIC
- experience/doing
- feeling/intuition

which means they can now learn well mainly by listening and can easily remember complex information they hear. (2)

However, the majority of school-aged children remain kinesthetic/tactile throughout their primary school years; far fewer students than teachers ever imagined are highly auditory or strongly visual. We found the same results among New Zealand adults (from executives, managers and workers, to polytechnic, university or business school students) by applying our new Working Style Analysis instrument.

most school children
kinesthetic/tactile
few students
highly auditory or
strongly visual

Yet, traditional university and adult education and formal training are still strongly based on auditory/ visual information intake. Hands-on, so-called 'doing learning', or experiential training, is still seen as an add-on to 'serious' or academic learning. Educators seem to be unaware that learning by listening is the least preferred and hardest way for most students to remember complex or difficult information. Auditory learners can remember approximately 75 per cent of what they hear, but less than 30 per cent of the school-aged population in the USA is auditory (3) and the same figure is true for adult learners in New Zealand.

adult education
auditory/visual
information intake

listening
least preferred
auditory learners

less than 30 per cent of
school children

Therefore, when students and adults do not do the things they have been told or can't remember what they were told, it is usually because they find it very difficult to absorb and remember spoken instructions and explanations, particularly if they are given in a series of directives. As we will see in Chapter 10 there also seem to be sex differences which might account for different preferences, styles and behaviour in males and females as well as for misunderstandings and miscommunication between the sexes.

can't remember

spoken instructions
explanations

sex differences

misunderstandings

When it comes to visual preferences, only 40 per cent of the school-aged population in the USA is visual – able to remember approximately two-fifths of what they have read or seen. Figures from New Zealand show an even lower number of visual learners (30 per cent), particularly among adults, but the situation is more complex than that.

visual preferences
40 per cent of
school children in the USA

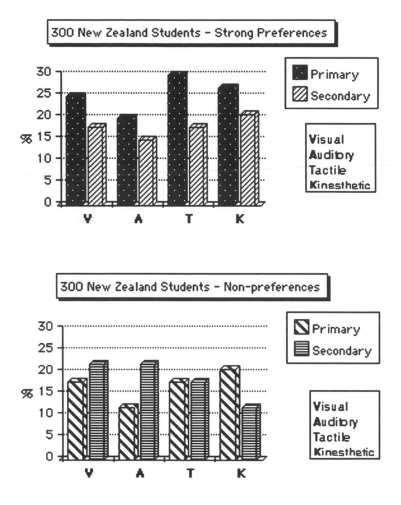

Note that most students display <u>multiple</u> preferences,
and many students are flexible with no preferences,
therefore these figures can exceed 100 per cent when added up.

Visual analytics (people with left-brain, sequential and reflective thinking style) seem to remember words and numbers better; their counterparts, visual holistics (people with right-brain, creative, random thinking style), tend to remember pictures, illustrations, graphs and symbols much better.

visual analytics

words and numbers
visual holistics
pictures, illustrations,
graphs and symbols

If children and grown-ups don't remember a great deal of what they hear and see, how do they remember? They remember what they touch, feel, handle and/or manipulate. These are the tactile (**T**) learners who make up the largest group of children in New Zealand. However, we also found that information intake through their hands is the preferred style of over 30 per cent of adult learners.

touch, feel,
handle, manipulate
tactile learners – T

over 30 per cent of adults

Another large group are kinesthetic (**K**) learners – those who need to experience what they learn. The majority of young children, and many students and grown-ups, learn most effectively and remember best when they do something – play, take a trip, build, cook, create, experience, visit, meet and interact with others. They are able to learn most easily and remember best through whole-body activities (K-external) and an international study has revealed that even gifted and highly talented adolescents are strongly tactile and kinesthetic. That's why we have introduced the use of Koosh balls as a highly effective learning tool, as we will see later.

kinesthetic learners – K
experience

do something

whole-body activities
K-external

Koosh balls
learning tool

By using our Working Style Analysis we discovered that there are also many adult learners who need to feel good about what they are doing (K-internal); it has to make sense to them, otherwise they find it very hard to remember. Unless it feels good they are not even interested or willing to begin a learning experience, and it is nearly impossible to motivate them to do more than the absolute minimum.

feel good
K-internal, make sense
hard to remember
not interested

So far we have considered information intake through the different modalities but for successful learning, working and problem solving we also need to consider how humans process, store and retrieve or access pieces of information.

information intake

process, store,
retrieve/access information

Learning Style Classrooms

Courtesy of St Georges Preparatory School, Wanganui, NZ

Courtesy of Rosegarden Skolan, Västeras, Sweden

It seems that the information intake process does not always equal the <u>information output</u> process. This means that people might well prefer to take in information through their visual sense, which triggers feelings, which in turn help to process, connect and store this bit of information; but when it comes to retrieving it, they might then use a physical movement or touch, combined with a feeling to remember.

information output

As every brain works best through <u>multisensory input</u> (which means involving more than two modalities), imagine a situation where people can take information in through listening only – like in a long telephone conversation. What would they do to remember the content? Depending on their sensory style they might move around, doodle or fiddle to enhance their listening if they are not auditory learners and then, for processing, they might transform what they hear into internal pictures or feelings. Later, when they need to recall the telephone conversation, they might look at something – maybe their doodles – or move or touch something and remember what they heard. Observe how these processes work for you and how you can enhance them.

multisensory input

The more you are <u>aware of your intake and processing styles</u>, the more you will be able to <u>utilize your brain skills</u>, which in the sensory areas seem to be <u>genetically predetermined,</u> particularly in the visual system of the brain. With these experience-independent processes sensory signals are selected and categorized. (4)

aware of your intake and processing styles
utilize your brain skills
genetically predetermined

Knowledge about the range of information intake preferences, the importance of modalities, and how strong they are in each individual, not only helps parents to understand their children's true learning needs better but also permanently changes teachers' and trainers' beliefs about how human beings are supposed to learn. It can give them vital information for <u>preparing</u> teaching <u>programmes</u> and <u>training materials</u> and how to conduct their work with students, accommodating all their modalities. <u>Multisensory learning and training kitsets</u>, as pictured on page 154, are an

preparing programmes and training materials

multisensory learning and training kitsets

The 4 Rs of Learning

1. RESILIENCE:
being ready, willing and able to lock on to learning
students need to absorb information, manage distractions, become aware and persevere when it s dif cult

2. RESOURCEFULNESS:
being ready, willing and able to learn in different ways
students need the skills to question, reason, imagine, link information and make use of resources

3. REFLECTIVENESS:
being ready, willing and able to think more about learning
students need to plan, revise, learn from experience and understand their own learning

4. RECIPROCITY:
being ready, willing and able to learn alone and with others
students need the skill to be self-reliant and depend on others, to collaborate, imitate, show empathy and listen to others

Based on 'Learning-power mind' in *Building Learning Power* by Guy Claxton, 2002, pp. 15–43

This is an excellent, practical book about how to help students become better learners, to build their learning power in the classroom and beyond, and how teachers can teach to this new learning power.

ideal combination of learning tools suitable for any age group and for all possible combinations of modalities in students. More on these kitsets – how to produce and use them – is described later in this chapter or can be found in the Dunn and Dunn books on learning styles (see Bibliography and Further Reading).

combinations of modalities

2. Why students need to know their learning style

Imagine you are walking through heavy fog, not sure where to go, with no equipment to show you the way and no one to ask. That's how students must feel, I imagine, if they have no clue about their own learning style, being lost in the fog of learning where everything becomes a blur because they don't know what goes on in their brain during the learning process. They don't know consciously which strategies they are using, so they can't repeat them next time, even if they have been successful before. Learning actually becomes a trial-and-error process, costing a lot of energy. The result is frustration, stress and disappointment, mixed with occasional elation when things go well. What a roller coaster! Under these conditions even successes don't mean much because the price was too high.

no clue about their own learning style

learning a trial-and-error process frustration and stress disappointment, elation

As you might guess, knowing their personal learning style, actually receiving/touching their LSA Profile and seeing their learning style strengths black on white, can be a huge turn-around, especially for students with low self-esteem due to previous learning failures. In my work with teachers and students I have seen the relief, the astonishment and the pride in their faces when they realize that there is nothing wrong with them, that they don't need to feel awkward because they know they are different. I have heard children say, 'Now I will prove to my teacher that I CAN learn, that I am not dumb.'

seeing learning style strengths improve low self-esteem

relief, astonishment, pride

My request therefore is, every two years have your students' learning styles assessed, discuss their profiles and allow them to learn 'their way'.

every two years learning styles assessed

 *LSA-Junior: Student Version*

PERSONAL REPORT STUDY GUIDELINES

The following Report explains your results shown in Graphs 1 & 2. If you act on the suggestions and guidelines, you will improve your concentration and study skills. But most importantly, you will find that you like learning better and have greater school success!

BRAIN DOMINANCE
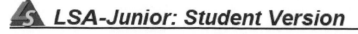

INFORMATION PROCESSING - sequential: (preference)
- You like thinking things through in the right order.
- You often use your logical 'left-brain' abilities.
- You like study projects and assignments that move in a logical order.
- You probably learn best from reading and analysing information.
- You probably dislike jokes and silly stories in class.
- You like teachers who are stay with the subject when they teach.
- You probably like to do one thing at a time and finish what you start.
- You mainly want to learn in well-organized places where you can follow rules.

THINKING STYLE - Think first: (preference)
- You are a more reflective thinker (think first, do later).
- You do best when you have time to think deeply.
- Teachers may think your responses are slow.
- When you come up with an answer, or solution, it is usually well thought out.
- Try to avoid learning situations where you have to make quick decisions.
- Having to think too quickly could cause you stress and your learning may suffer.
- Little change, time to adjust and a steady pace suits your thinking style best.

SENSORY MODALITIES

LISTENING (auditory - hearing): (non-preference)
- You find it difficult to listen for long periods of time.
- You may have problems remembering what was said.
- Even during short teacher talks you often "tune out".
- You have to concentrate hard to follow what the teacher says.
- Try to use your other senses (visual, tactile, kinesthetic and feeling) as well.
- Learn new and difficult information by using the strongest of your senses first.
- Reinforce the learning by using your other senses.
- Use reading, writing, using fingers and/or moving your body while listening.

TALKING (auditory - external): (non-preference)
- You are not a talker!
- You do not like to talk or be with people when you learn new things.
- Having to talk can make you uncomfortable or distract you.
- You often just like to be quiet, read or think about it.
- You do better when you do your learning tasks quietly.
- Your memory improves when you cut out as much talk as possible.
- As being silent in class is not always possible, you need to become a bit more flexible.
- Sometimes you could try doing your schoolwork by talking to others.

3. The LSA Report: a personalized study prescription

When students have responded to one of the LSA questionnaires, their data has been entered into the computer, and their LSA Profile and Report (see pages 74–82) has been printed, a unique document will be available, describing <u>style preferences</u>, <u>dislikes and flexibilities</u>, containing also detailed recommendations for how this student can learn best. Teachers, parents and students themselves will get more than just a description of someone's learning style but a true study prescription, which will, if acted upon, certainly <u>improve academic performance</u> and make life easier for those with so-called learning difficulties.

style preferences, dislikes and flexibilities

improve academic performance

Every <u>single element</u> of the Learning Style Pyramid (see page 18) is <u>described</u> in a separate paragraph in the LSA Report. Following are a few examples of a student's printout (note that the text passages in the Junior Version – see opposite page – is targeted at younger students):

every single element described

LSA Senior Report samples printout:

NEED FOR INTAKE MOUTH STIMULATION: (from LSA Senior)
You usually use some kind of intake – eating, nibbling, drinking, chewing – when concentrating or learning something new and difficult, but also when you are bored, frustrated or impatient. You find it hard to go for long periods without something to eat or drink and you might chew your pens, pencils or fingernails instead. You should give yourself frequent opportunities to eat nutritious foods or have drinks of water and healthy snacks during thinking processes, reading or studying. Just watch out how much you eat or drink because, particularly under stress, you might not be aware of the amounts you take in! (Attention: If you are already smoking, or have tried smoking, you might be in danger of getting addicted to this potentially lethal habit due to your preference for intake!)

AUTHORITY:
You definitely prefer to learn unsupervised or without an authority figure present. You will often do the opposite of whatever a teacher/coach/team leader or parent suggests. However, you can learn with people in authority, but only if they have a collegial approach. It is most important for your study success that you are not under constant control, that you trust the people who are in charge, and that they understand your strong need to study without being controlled all the time. However, you need to prove to your superiors that you have self-discipline in learning, and can produce better results without supervision. If you are about to leave or finish school, you need to take that into account for your future career planning.

Multisensory learning techniques

Tactile discussion which allows to trace the dynamics of this exercise.

PERSISTENCE:

Most of the time following through with your school or homework is up and down, and whether you complete what you start always depends on your interest in the learning task or study assignment. As soon as you lose interest or get bored with your learning you tend to abandon it and do something else. Often the overall situation is much more important for you than the learning task itself. But when you are really excited about a job, your persistence can increase dramatically and you then become very systematic in your approach.

TACTILE (touching):

You are a hands-on learner! When you study, read or concentrate you really like to involve your hands. You probably play with pens, tap your fingers, fiddle and/or doodle a lot – especially when you have to listen for a long time. This increases when you are impatient, bored, frustrated or stressed out in class. To enhance your listening skills and for better memory, always involve your hands. Use Koosh balls for hand stimulation, mind maps for note taking, hands-on learning and models or real objects when you learn something new and difficult. Learning tools you can manipulate are particularly good for you. Involving your hands and fingers when you read helps you to understand and remember better. Your teachers and parents need to know that you learn much better when you use your hands.

MOBILITY:

You find it very difficult to sit still for long periods of time. Having to sit still and listen to the teacher can be deadly for you. Your concentration improves and your brain works better when you can move your body. You change your body posture frequently, often tapping your feet and fidgeting. You really like to move around while studying, concentrating, listening, even reading. When you are bored, frustrated, or under stress, you can become very restless, often agitated – even more so when you have to listen for long periods of time. That's why teachers will often say you are 'hyperactive'. To improve your concentration, make sure that you are allowed to stand up and stretch regularly, walk around, take a break, and then return to your learning task. Moving while you are learning something new and difficult helps you concentrate. Physical learning activities and games are good for your understanding of something new. It is very important that your teachers and parents understand your strong need for mobility. Despite your preference for mobility, be aware that not everyone likes to move around as much as you do! There are people who don't want to be disturbed when they learn, they need peace and quiet. Be considerate.

From these examples you can see that even if you are not familiar with learning styles and diversity, these <u>detailed reports</u> will certainly give you a good understanding about the <u>learning needs</u> of a young person and will help you help them. But of course I do recommend that you learn more about this fascinating concept, particularly when you are a principal, teacher or parent of <u>teenagers</u>.

detailed reports
learning needs

teenagers

RULES FOR TEACHERS

NEW ZEALAND GOVERNMENT 1915

1. You will not marry during the term of your contract.

2. You are not to keep company with men.

3. You must be home between the hours of 8 p.m. and 6 a.m. unless attending a school function

4 You may not loiter downtown in ice cream parlours.

5. You may not travel beyond the city limits without the permission of the Chairman of the Board

6. You may not ride in a carriage or automobile with any man unless he is your Father or your Brother.

7. You may not smoke cigarettes.

8. You may not dress in bright colours.

9. You may, under no circumstances, dye your hair.

10. You must wear at least two petticoats, and your dresses must not be any shorter than 2 inches above the ankles.

11. To keep the school room clean you must:

   * sweep the floor at least once daily.
   * scrub the floor with hot soapy water at least once a week.
   * clean the blackboard at least once a day.
   * start the fire at 7 a.m. so that the room will be warm by 8a.m.

These rules were obviously meant for female teachers only.
Thankfully, life has changed somewhat for teachers!

4. Help, my teacher doesn't understand my learning style!

We have heard this exclamation from students whose parents had arranged for them to get their learning style assessed and who began to understand what enhances their learning and what puts them off. Armed with that knowledge, increased awareness and self-esteem they go back to school and find their teachers are not interested or don't want to know! It's a sad state of affairs, often found in high schools where teachers are too burdened by the curriculum, too stressed out to consider yet another fad (?) and just want to get on with their regular programme. Unfortunately they do not, or do not *want* to consider how a knowledge of learning styles might actually help them to reduce stress, manage their classroom better and equip them with instructional methods useful to all types of learners.

enhances learning

teachers not interested

often in high schools

**learning styles knowledge
reduce stress**

Similar reports come from parents who went to see their children's teachers, presented them with their daughter's or son's LSA profile and wanted them to take their learning style needs into account but teachers brushed their requests aside, discarding them as unimportant or inappropriate. Sometimes they got defensive, saying it is all nonsense. When such a situation prevails, it is most unfortunate, not only for communication between parents and school but also for the progress of the student, because existing learning problems will not go away and strategies prescribed by the school often do not work for the simple reason that they do not take into account style differences. However, if teachers refuse to be part of a learning styles concept there are only two choices parents have: either transfer the child to another school where learning styles are accommodated, or provide all the support they can give at home, create the learning environment their child needs and teach them study skills based on their learning style they can use in class.

parents

learning style needs

unimportant/inappropriate

learning problems

**two choices: transfer child
to other school
provide support**

teach them study skills

In any case, a knowledge of learning styles should always be the basis for student–teacher interaction, for understanding and supporting students in their learning needs and in helping them become more flexible too.

**learning styles
basis for student–teacher
interaction**

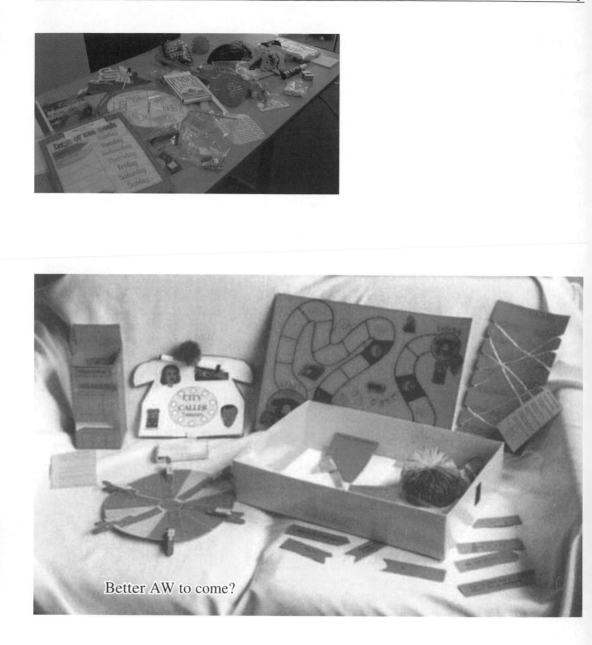

Two different MIPs (Multisensory Instructional Packages) for tactile-visual learners

5. LS tools for lasting learning success

One of the main aspects of student-centred teaching and individualized instruction based on learning styles is to create resources and learning materials which are reusable and can be utilized by ALL students at different times and for very different purposes. For some they will be learning enhancers but for others these tools will be the main activity to learn new and difficult concepts.

**individualized instruction
reusable resources and
learning materials**

Who are the students who benefit most from the use of learning style tools? You may have already guessed – it's the hands-on, highly tactile learners who also have visual and kinesthetic preferences who learn best with manipulatives, have a short attention span, low learning motivation and persistence, are more holistic in their brain processing style and who need variety and multisensory stimulation.

who benefits most?

**hands-on, highly tactile
learners, V/K preferences
manipulatives**

**need variety and
multisensory stimulation**

As you can see on pages 66 and 112, such tools are being used by students in various countries and have helped them to understand difficult information much better than just by reading or only talking about it.

All these tools are self-correcting and easy to make; the most popular ones are:

**most popular, self-
correcting learning tools**

- Task cards/puzzles
- Learning circles
- Wrap-arounds
- Flip chutes/flip boxes
- Electro boards
- Pic-a-holes
- Board and floor games.

Initially, making those tools takes a lot of time but once techniques are known, older students can make their own tools, and in many schools a resource person or teacher aide is helping to create these resources. From our experience with working with schools we also know that parents are often willing to contribute time and materials, particularly in primary schools.

**students
make their own tools
resource person or
teacher aide
parents contribute
time and materials**

INGREDIENTS
OF
CREATIVE, ACCELERATED LEARNING

LEARNING/WORKING STYLES
SELF-KNOWLEDGE
HOW THE BRAIN WORKS
(LEFT/RIGHT BRAIN, ALPHA STATE)
RELAXATION AND VISUALIZATION
CENTRING EXERCISES
BRAIN GYM® (EDUCATIONAL KINESIOLOGY)
WATER
PROPER BRAIN FOOD
BREATHING
MEMORY TECHNIQUES
MIND MAPPING
USE OF MUSIC
KOOSH BALLS
MENTAL STATE OF LEARNER
PHYSICAL STATE OF LEARNER
POSTURE
LEARNING ENVIRONMENT
INDIVIDUALIZED INSTRUCTION
SUGGESTOPEDIA
VISION AND PURPOSE OF LEARNING
GOAL SETTING
ENJOYMENT, FUN AND MOTIVATION
LEARNER'S SELF-IMAGE
ART AND CREATIVITY
MOVEMENT AND DANCE
ACCELERATION OF INFORMATION INTAKE

When put together in a box containing a set of tools about the same learning content you have a 'MIP' (Multisensory Instructional Package) or Learning Style Kitset, as pictured on page 154, which is especially appropriate for learners who require structure. The step-by-step procedures provide clear, sequenced directions that are repeated in a variety of ways until success is achieved.

put together

Learning Style Kitset

structure

If you are interested in creating these tools please consult one of the excellent Dunn and Dunn books on learning styles (see Bibliography and Further Reading) or come to one of our practical workshops on learning styles where you will actually make these tools and then take them away with you (for training dates see www.networkpress.co.uk for Europe or www.creativelearningcentre.com for New Zealand).

make these tools

6. Techniques to achieve creative, accelerated learning

From what has been explained in this chapter so far, it is obvious that more knowledge about styles, diversity and brain functioning will definitely enhance any learning process. However, to make information intake even more successful there are further techniques which, combined with the above, will result in creative, accelerated learning. The following can only be a short introduction to these learning techniques and is meant to be just an 'appetizer' for an extensive 'smorgasbord' of truly revolutionary educational methods available these days. Practitioners who are interested to learn more about this subject will find a comprehensive selection of books in the Bibliography and Further Reading.

further techniques

introduction
'appetizer'
'smorgasbord'

According to the Bulgarian psychiatrist and educator Dr Georgi Lozanov (often referred to as the 'father' of accelerated learning), human learning is the most basic and natural function – easier than breathing or walking. By birthright, learning is an easy, joyful process. Unfortunately, the prevailing, Western educational world view denies that human beings are capable of unlimited learning. Lozanov proved that learning is accelerated by 'desuggesting' limiting beliefs in the learner,

learning – natural function

easy, joyful process

desuggesting and limiting beliefs

CENTERING EXERCISE

Find a comfortable position,
uncross your arms and legs ...
take in a deep breath – hold it – and exhale ...
And with another deep breath
tense your whole body
from your toes to your head ...
... and let go ...
Take another deep breath ...
... and exhale.
Now let your breathing establish a
comfortable rhythm ...

As you are sitting here ...
getting more and more relaxed ...
think back how you came here this morning (evening) ...
Think back how the day began for you.
How did you get up? ...
Where were you? What did you do?
Were you relaxed or in a hurry?...
Did you have breakfast? ...
Who was with you ... or were you on your own?
How did you get here?
Did you drive or walk?
Were you alone or with someone else?
What were your thoughts
when you came up to this building? ...
And when you entered this room ...
how did you feel? ...
what did you say?

... And as you are getting more and more relaxed,
think of all the **problems**
you are carrying around with you right now ...
you **don't need them for today** ...

constantly affirming at <u>conscious and/or subconscious levels</u> that they can learn quickly, easily and pleasantly. An ever-growing body of research results reveals that the <u>link between brain theory</u> and <u>learning practices</u> is crucial for improving mental powers and learning ability.

conscious and/or subconscious levels

link between brain theory and learning practices

The term 'Accelerated Learning', which I prefer to broaden into 'Creative, Accelerated Learning', is now widely used for learning techniques based on understanding <u>how the brain works</u>. They can be applied in any field where <u>information intake</u> is crucial: general education, language learning, vocational and business training, parenting, sports performance, military instructions, self-improvement and management training. The list on page 156 contains <u>methods and techniques</u> which, <u>combined in the right way</u> for every individual learner, can bring astonishing results and drastically <u>improve their learning</u>.

how the brain works information intake

methods and techniques rightly combined

improve learning

Many of these components are of course used on a daily basis in many situations outside learning settings, and the more we apply and combine them the more we are successful in handling problems and <u>mastering difficulties</u>. For the purpose of taking in the information contained in this book, the following <u>techniques will be very useful</u> and you are invited to try them out when going through the individual chapters.

master difficulties

useful techniques

Relaxation/visualization
Before we can even think of getting into any learning or concentration process you need to <u>prepare your body and your mind</u> accordingly.

relaxation/visualization

prepare body and mind

With any gadget we use we readily accept that it has to be prepared for its use (it has to be set up, plugged in or switched on). To reach and maintain an <u>optimal learning state</u> and to deal with stress or anxiety successfully, relaxation and visualization are essential starting points. Lozanov calls this mental state '<u>pseudo activity</u>' where the person experiences relaxed concentration, like in a classical concert – <u>physically relaxed</u> but <u>mentally alert</u>. Although most people can relax in

optimal learning state

'pseudo activity'

physically relaxed mentally alert

CENTERING EXERCISE CONTINUED

Imagine, there is a really nice **bag**
standing right in front of you ...
What does it look like?
Do you recognize it, is it old, is it new? ...
Now **open the bag** and notice
that it is **empty** ...
I want you to put all your **worries** and **sorrows**,
all your problems into this bag ...
one by one ...
Whatever bothers you, put it in!

To show me that you are really filling up
your bag, give me a nod with your head ... good.
Have you found another worry? Put it in ...
Is your bag already full?...
When you have put in your last problem or worry
close your bag ... and lift it up ...
Is it heavy, is it light? ...
Now **carry your bag out of this room** ...
round the corner ...
down the stairs (hallway) ...
... and put all your bags in one place ...
Pile them up, stack them ...

Take a last look at your bag ...
see all the other bags, they are safe there.
If you wish, you can pick up your bag later,
when you go home ...
but you can also **leave it there**,
it's safe, no one will carry your problems away ...

Now **turn around** and **come back into this room**,
feeling light, excited, and ready to learn ...

So, wriggle your fingers and toes,
open your eyes wide, look around,
feel relaxed and **alert** – stretch, and **smile**!

non-stressful situations, they find it impossible
to get into a peaceful state of mind when they are
frustrated, under pressure or stressed out,
especially in learning or work situations. Without
a relaxed body and a relaxed mind it is impossible
to access higher brain functions or draw on
the powers of the right brain, thus limiting
memory input and storage.

**access higher functions
right-brain powers**

The use of music and/or a combination of
relaxation and visualization techniques is the
quickest way to change brainwave patterns
naturally from Beta to Alpha state (see page 174),
to slow down breathing and heartbeat rate, and
to achieve the best state for learning – relaxed
alertness. It is impossible to calm the mind
without relaxing the body.

change brainwaves

**slow down breathing and
heartbeat rate
relaxed alertness**

For this simple reason relaxation exercises should
always start with a physical relaxation, including
breathing, then have a mental relaxation part and
finish with a positive, creative visualization.
Such exercises should be done regularly
before you start a learning session and need to be
learned and practised like any other skill.

**physical relaxation
mental relaxation
creative visualization**

before a learning session

The centring exercise on pages 158 and 160 is
an example of combined relaxation/visualization
which I have been using with great success in
my seminars over many years. I invite you to
follow the given instructions carefully, practise
the exercise a few times and discover whether
it has the desired effect of relaxing you. If you
don't like this particular exercise, try others –
there are many tapes on the market but be careful
that you choose exercises which also contain
positive learning affirmations. Used always
in combination with relaxation and visualization,
they are powerful tools to accelerate your learning
and guarantee success. You must have the patience
and persistence to find out what's best for you.

centring exercise

desired relaxing effect

positive affirmations

accelerate your learning

what's best for you

Centring exercises

When learners have trained themselves into being
more relaxed before they begin learning activities
and have been using the suggested exercises on a
regular basis (either in a group or by themselves),

centring exercises

more relaxed

NZ School Children Preparing for Learning in Koosh Circles

there is one more way of <u>focusing one's attention</u> <u>on the learning process</u>. Especially in groups these 'centring' exercises have proven to be extremely effective for learners of all ages. They can also be used to <u>start classes</u> and precede discussions or group projects. The main purpose is to focus students' attention on the task at hand without jumping into the matter right away to help them relax, <u>make them feel welcome</u> and <u>comfortable</u>; to give them time to <u>mentally prepare</u> themselves; to '<u>switch on</u>' <u>their brains</u>.

focusing attention on learning

start classes

welcome and comfortable
mentally prepare
'switch on' brains

Although you can do these exercises quietly by yourself, focusing on what you have to do, it is recommended to do it with <u>groups</u> of children or adults who are about to learn, concentrate or work on something. Ask all the participants to <u>sit in a full circle</u> so that they face each other, either sitting on the floor or on chairs (if the group is large, it will have to be broken up into two or more circles of approximately 10–15 people). Then the group leader starts the process that will <u>become a ritual</u> over time: he or she holds a '<u>speaking token</u>' to signal to everyone that it is their turn to speak. We find that <u>Koosh balls</u> (see page 180) are very inspirational for this exercise, especially for <u>tactile/visual learners</u> who can control their nervousness by holding them. The leader chooses a phrase like 'I feel like saying ...' or 'Today/right now/this morning I ...' and says what's on his or her mind – either related to the learning session or totally unrelated but necessary to share with the group because it's bothering them and would otherwise interfere with the learning process.

groups

sit in full circle

ritual
'speaking token'
Koosh balls

tactile/visual learners

Each student should only say a <u>few sentences</u> unless something really important comes up and has to be cleared. Then the speaking token is passed on until everyone has had their say. If some children <u>do not want to speak</u>, that's OK, <u>don't force them</u>; maybe at the end they will be ready to contribute. You must always <u>respect</u> their reasons for not wanting to participate yet. When everyone has had their turn, the teacher continues with the set programme. If, however, the group is <u>still not ready for learning</u> after the

few sentences

not wanting to speak
don't force them
respect

not ready for learning

Brain Gym ®

is the registered trademark of the Educational Kinesiology Foundation.

CROSS-OVERS

With your right hand touch your left knee, & vice versa.
Do these movements in quick succession to upbeat music. Do the similar crossover behind your body: with your right hand touch your left heel & vice versa.

Grasp shoulder and look over it, pulling shoulder blades towards each other & breathing deeply...

Turn smoothly to look over other shoulder while breathing out with a 'whooo' sound.
Change shoulders.

Cross legs and balance. Glide crossed arms downwards while breathing out and lift to horizontal while breathing in.
This can be done seated.

stretching

centring exercise, it might be necessary then to add on a relaxation/visualization exercise. This usually happens in groups where students are very stressed out and teachers have to work harder to get them relaxed. Don't forget: it always depends on the group leader how well he or she prepares the whole group for learning!

add relaxation/visualization

if stressed out

prepare group for learning

Brain Gym® (Callisthenics)
Paul Dennison, a pioneer in the field of applied brain research, discovered that a certain sequence of arm and leg movements signals the brain to balance the activities of the left and right brain hemispheres, helping to enhance integration and communication between them. The terms he created were Educational Kinesiology, Edu-K and Brain Gym®, which all mean 'draw out through motion'. Dennison combined traditional body movements (callisthenics) with others he invented, and practitioners over the past 15 years have successfully introduced these exercises on a large scale in schools worldwide.

Brain Gym®

**arm and leg movements
left/right brain hemispheres**

Educational Kinesiology

Whenever you need to concentrate better or your energy gets low during studying or concentrating, try any of the cross-over exercises opposite and experience how these simple and fun movements (particularly when exercised with upbeat music) can rebalance your brain functions and actually re-energize you. Practised on a regular basis you might also notice that your coordination will get better and your memory will improve. An important add-on to all Brain Gym® exercises is to drink plenty of water. The reason is that not only physical but also mental activities, like learning and concentrating, use up body fluids and they need to be replaced regularly. This is particularly crucial during periods of high stress when the water intake should be doubled.

low energy

**with upbeat music
rebalance**

**coordination better
memory improve**

**drink plenty of water
mental activities
use up body fluids**

**high stress
double water intake**

The exercises described so far for accelerating learning and enhancing concentration should either be done before or during learning sessions. The following technique is useful for speeding up information intake and enhancing memory at any time during the learning process.

exercises

before or during learning

enhancing memory

HOW TO CREATE A MIND MAP

FOUR STEPS

1. *Topic in the centre*
2. *Add branches*
3. *Write cue words*
4. *Personalize (add colour, symbols, pictures, etc.)*

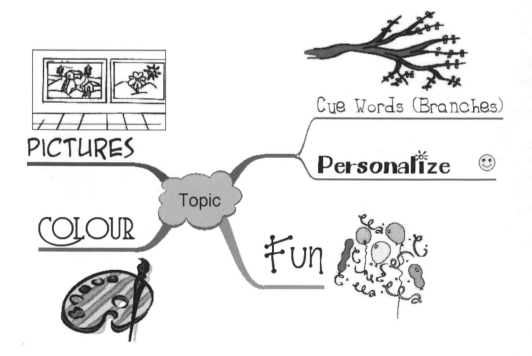

Mind Mapping®

This note-taking technique has become very popular among students over the last few years. Originally created by Michael Gelb, the method has been popularized by Tony Buzan, who called these structures 'mind maps' and registered the name. It was then put into practical applications by Nancy Margulies, Colin Rose and Eric Jensen (see Bibliography and Further Reading).

Mind Mapping®
note-taking technique

Why is it so effective for so many people, young and old? When considering different learning styles, this technique is particularly helpful for holistic thinkers, who need the big overview and who have visual and tactile preferences in their information intake. Analytical thinkers, however, needing a step-by-step approach, and learners who are not highly visual, often experience mind or memory maps as disjointed structures that don't make sense to them. Therefore it is very important for your own learning success to find out your style first so that you can choose the appropriate method for your needs.

effective

holistic: big overview
visual, tactile
analytical: step-by-step
approach

find out your style first
choose appropriate method

If you are a right-brain oriented person, you will find that by using mind maps instead of linear note taking you will improve your memory, save time, get more things done and will be much more creative. The technique can also be used for brainstorming, generating ideas, planning and problem solving. Instead of full sentences, in learning maps we use pictures, symbols, structure, colour and keywords only. For many learners it is much less stressful than traditional note taking and much more fun to do!

right-brain oriented
mind maps
improve memory
save time
more creative
brainstorming/planning
problem solving

less stressful

If you want to try out this technique or improve your already existing mind-mapping skills, follow the instructions on the opposite page and create your own personal mind map similar to the one on page 184 about the different topics of Chapter 7 or any topic of your choice (all chapter summaries are done as mind maps for readers who prefer an overview in a holistic way). Prepare what you need, begin it now and have fun!

try out, improve
mind-mapping skills

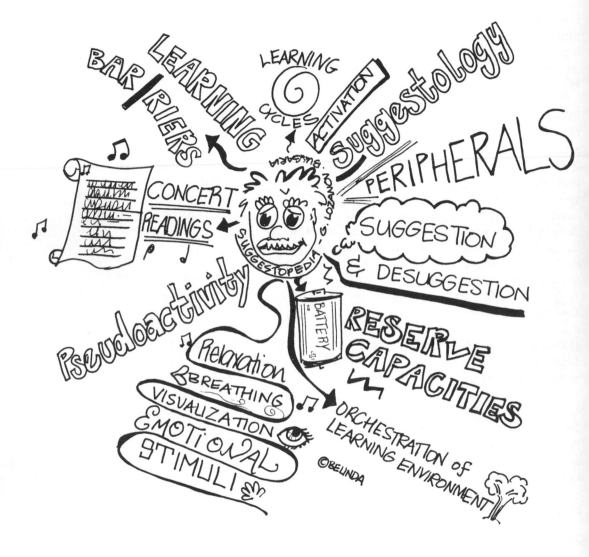

Suggestopedia

For over thirty years, <u>Bulgarian psychiatrist</u> and professor of education <u>Dr Georgi Lozanov</u> has been studying perception and learning. He was the first scientist to systematically research the phenomenon of <u>rapid learning</u>. He called his teaching system '<u>Suggestopedy</u>', based on '<u>Suggestology</u>', the science of suggestion in all its different aspects.

The words he coined refer to the fact that 'suggestion' is used to speed up learning by <u>tapping into human reserve capacities</u>. Suggestopedic teachers <u>organize and orchestrate</u> the <u>learning environment</u> and practise pedagogy based on the use of positive suggestions. (5)

According to Don Schuster, professor at Iowa State University, this revolutionary teaching system clearly <u>accelerates learning</u> by:
a. using advertising-like suggestions to bypass common barriers against rapid learning
b. relaxing students and making learning fun
c. presenting lessons dramatically to help students make vivid imagery
d. reviewing lessons calmly with slow, rhythmic baroque music. (6)

Lozanov's system blends exceptionally well with the individualized learning style approach. After personal training with the 'Great Master', studying suggestopedic methods, and working intensively with our LSA model, particularly with teachers on classroom management and lesson planning based on style diversity I have come to the conclusion that these two <u>holistic models complement</u> each other perfectly because <u>learning styles individualize</u> Lozanov's uniform approach and <u>suggestopedia adds the larger framework</u> to learning styles teaching.

The methods he developed and mainly used for <u>teaching foreign languages</u> the fast way are the historic basis for what is presently known as 'Superlearning', 'Whole-Brain Learning' or 'Creative, Accelerated Learning'.

Suggestopedia
Bulgarian psychiatrist
Dr Georgi Lozanov

rapid learning
Suggestopedy
Suggestology

tap reserve capacities
organize and orchestrate
learning environment

accelerates learning

models complement
styles individualize

Suggestopedia adds
larger framework

foreign language teaching

The Magic of Music

Among the many learning enhancing techniques
of the Lozanov method described explicitly by
two of the top European trainers in Suggestopedia,
Tony Stockwell and Lonny Gold, there is one
aspect I find extremely useful for accelerated
information intake – the suggestopedic text. It is   **suggestopedic text**
based on the ability of the human brain to take in
a certain amount of information at once and store it
in its short-term memory bank. For text layout   **short-term memory bank**
this means 10–12 syllables grouped in
semantically meaningful clusters (for foreign
language texts only 7–9 syllables). Similar to
newspaper columns, this layout allows the reader   **newspaper columns**
to go over text passages quite fast without a lot
of eye movement to the left or right. Skimming   **skimming**
down the text passages with the help of two or
three fingers can bring the reader close to real
speed reading. That is the reason why I have   **speed reading**
chosen the suggestopedic text presentation for
this book.

Peripheral vision, another powerful tool for   **peripheral vision**
fast learning, is also utilized in this type of layout.
Certain keywords, selected from the text and   **keywords**
underlined, are repeated in bold on the right-hand   **repeated in bold**
side of each text column. The effect is that these
keywords, even without reading them fully   **without reading them**
consciously, will be stored in the reader's memory   **fully consciously**
and enhance information intake. This style of text
presentation is my own further development   **further development**
of Lozanov's original suggestopedic text layout
used for foreign language learning as you can see
on the opposite page. (7)

7. The mind is a sponge and music is the squeeze

Music has always played, and still does play,
a central role in the cultures of the world, and
the effects of music on society and on
an individual's emotions, body and mind
have been well documented throughout the ages.

So it is no surprise that, among all the creative,
accelerated learning tools, music is definitely   **music**
the favourite. Once educators have learned how
to use it appropriately and have experienced

MUSIC SELECTION I

Baroque and Pre-classical Music

Slow tempo: 40–60 beats/minute:

A. Albinoni	–	Adagio for Strings in G Minor
J. S. Bach	–	Fantasy for Organ in G Major
	–	Prelude and Fugue in G Major
	–	Brandenburg Concertos
A. Corelli	–	Concerti Grossi, op. 6, No. 2–12
G. F. Händel	–	Water Music, Concerto Grosso op. 3
J. Pachelbel	–	Canon in D
A. Vivaldi	–	Concerto for Viola d'amore
	–	Concertos for Flute and Chamber Orchestra
	–	Four Seasons (Spring, Summer, Autumn, Winter)
LIND tapes, CDs	–	Largo and Adagio

Classical and Romantic Music

Medium tempo: 60–80 beats/minute:

L. V. Beethoven	–	Concerto for Piano and Orchestra No. 5 in B Flat Major op. 73
	–	Concerto for Violin and Orchestra in D Major
J. Brahms	–	Concerto for Violin and Orchestra in D Major, op. 77
F. Chopin	–	Waltzes
J. Haydn	–	Symphony in C Major, No. 101, in G Major, No. 94
	–	Concertos No. 1 and 2 in C Major for Violins and Orchestra
N. Rimsky-Korsakov	–	Symphonic Suite for Thousand and One Nights, op. 35
W. A. Mozart	–	Symphony in G Minor, No. 40
P. I. Tchaikovsky	–	Concerto No. 1 in B Flat Minor for Piano and Orchestra
Rondo Veneziano	–	Mozart, Vivaldi, Venice 2000
LIND tapes, CDs	–	Andante and Allegro, Pianissimo

how it makes the <u>learning process</u> so <u>much more</u> <u>pleasurable</u>, they and their students do not want to be without it. Even if there are students in the group who need absolute quiet and get distracted by background music, there are ways of using music for them as well.

learning process
more pleasurable

Many books about the <u>use of music in learning</u> have been published in recent years, each containing a wealth of information about this topic. The best ones are listed in the Bibliography and Further Reading. It would go way beyond the intentions of this book to try and give a comprehensive account of the use of <u>music as a learning tool</u> but I feel it is necessary to present at least an <u>introductory overview</u>. This, I hope, will make readers interested enough to learn more about the magic of music and investigate more deeply this whole new world of possibilities.

music in learning

music as a learning tool
introductory overview

What is so fascinating about the use of music in learning is that certain styles or <u>types of music</u>, particularly <u>baroque music</u> with its 60 beats per minute, when used as the <u>background</u> to a spoken presentation (known as 'concert reading'), acts as a carrier signal within the brain, activating right-hemisphere functions.

types of music
baroque music
background

In their book, *Accelerated Learning with Music – A Trainer's Manual* (8) – one of the best available on the use of music for learning – Doug and Terry Webb describe <u>music</u> as the '<u>interstate highway</u> <u>to the memory system</u>'. Both Webbs trained with Dr Lozanov and share their vast knowledge about music with their readers, helping them 'achieve success in learning through the <u>strategic use of music</u>'.

music
interstate highway
to the memory system

strategic use of music

As far as the use of music in learning goes, the historic, <u>revolutionary contribution</u> by <u>Bulgarian</u> <u>psychiatrist</u> and educator <u>Dr Georgi Lozanov</u> can no longer be disregarded. His discoveries are the foundation of the educational science known as '<u>Suggestopedia</u>' (explained more fully in this chapter, beginning on page 169).

revolutionary contribution
by Bulgarian psychiatrist
Dr Georgi Lozanov

Suggestopedia

For hundreds of years music has been used to assist in healing the aches and pains of the mind

MUSIC SELECTION II

Uplifting and High-energy Music

Fast tempo: 80–120 beats/minute:

A. Khatchaturian	–	Sabre Dance
M. Ravel	–	Bolero
R. Wagner	–	Ride of the Valkyries
J. Sibelius	–	Alla Marcha (from Karelia Suite)
J. Strauss	–	Radetsky March, Die Fledermaus Overture
J. Fucic	–	Florentine March
W. A. Mozart	–	Overtures Don Giovanni, Magic Flute
L. V. Beethoven	–	Egmont Overture
F. Liszt	–	Hungarian Rhapsodies
J. Rodrigo	–	Concierto Aranjuez
G. Verdi	–	Triumph March from Aïda
G. Rossini	–	William Tell, Overture
G. Holst	–	The Planets
A. Fiedler	–	Anthology of Marches by Boston Pops
O. Liebert	–	Nouveau Flamenco
Rondo Veneziano	–	Venice in Peril, The Best of Rondo Veneziano

Modern upbeat music, movie soundtracks

Brainwave patterns

Beta

When wide awake – the conscious mind: 13–25 cycles per second

Alpha

Ideal learning state of 'relaxed alertness': 8–12 cycles per second

and body. Current research shows us how to improve memory, reduce stress and modify our abilities to heal. One of the latest fascinating findings about the use of music as a learning-enhancing tool has been named the 'Mozart Effect'.

'Mozart Effect'

Researchers at the Centre for Neurobiology of Learning and Memory at the University of California, Irvine, have for several years been conducting experiments that associate musical phenomena with brain functions. Startling results were announced in 1993: after only 10 minutes of listening to the Sonata for Two Pianos in D, K 448 by W. A. Mozart, 36 students were able to perform on an average of 8–9 per cent better on intelligence tests. (9) The scientists are also in no doubt that Mozart should be played to children because they found that pre-schoolers score up to 80 per cent better on tests of spatial and temporal reasoning after a year of daily musical sessions.

association of musical phenomena and brain functions

students perform better on intelligence tests Mozart played to children, score better on tests of spatial and temporal reasoning

The UC Irvine has established the Music and the Brain Information Centre (MBIC) to function as a free source of information on research in music and behaviour. (10)

Don Campbell, one of the great masters in using music for learning enhancement, has now written a book *The Mozart Effect*™ which describes all the different aspects of research findings in this area and to which effect music can be used. It describes the general uses of music to reduce stress, the specialized uses of music to improve memory, awareness and the integration of learning styles, and the experimental uses of music and sound to improve listening disorders, dyslexia, attention deficit disorder and autism. It also explains the therapeutic use of music for mental and physical disorders and injuries.

music for learning enhancement

therapeutic use of music

Don Campbell uses 'The Mozart Effect' as an inclusive term signifying the transformational powers of music in health, education and well-being.

But there is more: over the last 15 years modern music has also been used to help students remember difficult concepts in any subject. By creating songs,

modern music

songs, rhymes, raps

Text for an 'Active Concert' used for a parent group
By Mike Scaddan

Music, man's used for thousands of years,
It's entertaining, soothing and calming of fears.
It can uplift an army who move into battle,
Or surround us in adverts with 'buy us now' prattle.

But this is only a fraction of what *music* can do,
It's importance in *learning* has been discovered too.
Music activates electrical neurotransmissions,
To dendrites enabling more associations.

The more stimulation, the more connections are formed,
To make more associations with knowledge that's stored.
Music then triggers our right-brain *memory*,
And makes learning as simple as A, B and C.

Our brainwaves are made up of *Alpha* and *Beta*,
With *Theta* and *Delta* completing the picture.
Beta is active and used every day,
But for high-level thinking, Alpha's the way.

By relaxing our moods and slowing the waves,
Music stimulates Alpha's creativity phase.
Baroque music's amazing as it matches the rhythms,
Allowing insight and deep thought associations.

So *music* stimulates creativity thoughts,
By altering mood and reducing brain stress.
This *relaxed alertness* is an essential state,
To help us all learn at incredible rates.

© Mike Scaddan, Former Principal, Te Puna School, Tauranga, New Zealand

rhymes, raps and even academic musicals, it is possible for any learner to be more involved in the learning process and retain the content much longer. Putting difficult concepts to music is an invaluable tool for fast information intake and long-term storage for learners of any age.

academic musicals

retain content

**fast information intake
long-term storage**

Considering learning and working styles, the old belief that students learn more and workers perform better in an absolutely quiet environment no longer holds, because research shows that many students (adults as well as children) and people in the workforce think and remember better with music in the background.

quiet environment

**students/people at work
think and remember better
with music in background**

It is also true that a small minority of students (more high school than primary school students and more girls than boys) need absolute quiet while concentrating or taking in new and difficult information. Teachers, educators and parents must respect that need for quiet by setting up classrooms, learning environments and home study areas accordingly. However, even these students can and should be using music for revision and reinforcement of already learned material.

absolute quiet

**music for revision and
reinforcement**

That sounds great, you think, and might want to jump into using music right away – but be warned!

A little knowledge is dangerous and the wrong use of music in a learning environment will achieve the opposite effect. Inappropriate application or wrong timing will certainly create resistance and switch off students' attention.

**wrong use of music
opposite effect**

resistance

The type of music used has to be chosen carefully because sceptical adults and teenagers, particularly those who are used to listening to modern, upbeat music, will resent it. Only with proper information, and careful introduction by a knowledgeable teacher or instructor, will learners accept the type of music which truly enhances and speeds up information intake processes.

**choose music carefully
sceptical adults
and teenagers**

careful introduction

**speed up information
intake processes**

After having experienced various versions of unprofessional use of music in learning and training environments, my advice to educators

Text for an 'Active Concert' used for a parent group continued

Soft *music* as background while learning and thinking,
Or *sound effec*ts to promote wider memory linking.
Music's also helpful with our rhythmic fitness,
But needs to be *calmer* for non-physical business.

BUT before you use music, here is a caution,
The *wrong music* destroys a learning situation.
Music with *lyrics* or heavy rock beat,
Will hamper your learning as you tap your feet.

Plant roots wither on a diet of rock,
It *hinders* the brain if it's played quite a lot.
Rock *doesn't* help learning, an indisputable fact,
But convincing a teenager's not as easy as that.

Instead try *Mozart's* 'Eine Kleine Nachtmusik',
or *Vivaldi's* 'Four Seasons', another good pick.
Pachelbel's 'Canon in D' will also be helpful,
As will others I'll tell you after this recital.

This *Active Concert* that you're taking part in,
Is followed by passive to promote retention.
It's the story of music and an explanation,
And the role it should play in all education.

© Mike Scaddan, Former Principal, Te Puna School, Tauranga, New Zealand

in all educational settings is the following: if you want to be serious about the use of music in your classroom, learn it professionally.

learn use of music professionally

Learn it from the masters in this field, introduce it slowly, and begin to feel the magic of music during the learning process. Finally, enjoy the relaxation music brings, and celebrate the results with your students and trainees.

introduce it slowly

enjoy the relaxation celebrate the results

8. Quiet classrooms – a torture for students who learn better with sound

The strongly held belief that students learn better in an absolutely quiet environment no longer holds true because research has shown that holistic, right-brain dominant students of all ages including adults, think, learn, concentrate and remember better with music, background talking and/or pleasant noise if it's not too loud. Only naturally analytic learners require an absolutely quiet environment and get distracted by music and noises.

holistic right-brain dominant students

analytic learners distracted by music and noises

And here lies the problem: as the majority of those who teach academic, scientific subjects are analytics themselves, they prefer silence when they think and concentrate, therefore expect their students to work in silence too. They constantly remind their students to be quiet and do anything to keep their classes quiet, even at the price of frustration and stress on either side. Such teachers cannot imagine that someone can actually learn better with music in the background because for them it's a serious distraction. They don't know or don't want to accept that for many brains the right sound/music is actually stimulating and helps with concentration and long-term memory. (For more details see Part 7 of this chapter.)

problem analytics

work in silence

keep classes quiet

sound/music stimulating long-term memory

It cannot be said often enough that many students really suffer in quiet classrooms, find silence unbearable, don't want to be there and will do anything to remedy that unpleasant situation for themselves, even to their own detriment: they make noises, click their pens, hum or whistle, drum with their fingers or writing gear, tap their feet, chat a lot but rarely about the lesson content, and often receive punishment. They are the 'noisy' ones,

silence unbearable

they make noises click their pens

punishment noisy

Koosh balls and other tactile
learning tools.

often underachievers, ADHD and other problem students; for them, every lesson where they have to be quiet, every hour of homework they have to spend in silence at their desk is torture. Therefore they will do anything to avoid it or if possible, will switch on music, very loud and often with the wrong beat for better learning – just to escape silence.

To stop their suffering, teachers need to get trained better and know that the use of <u>music works wonders</u> **music works wonders** for the brain and body – and for themselves as well!

9. Want to have a ball in learning? Use a Koosh ball!

To round off the 'smorgasbord' of learning tools, methods and techniques, I'd like to describe one <u>educational tool</u> which has fascinated me ever **educational tool** since I encountered it. It was on the first day of a course on Rapid Learning at Houston University, Texas, some years ago. The teachers there were using brightly coloured <u>rubber pompoms</u>, called **rubber pompoms** <u>Koosh balls</u>, for various exercises. We experienced **Koosh balls** the <u>positive effects</u> they had on our learning as we **positive effects** passed them on to fellow students while giving answers to questions, threw them at different targets during some learning games, or just fiddled with them while we were listening.

Although I was not too sure about the reasons why Koosh balls <u>helped the learning process,</u> **helped learning** I found them so useful that I introduced them to New Zealand educators. They, too, found them very useful in enhancing the learning process of their students and a real Koosh ball craze started which is not over by far. In the meantime it has even spread into corporate training rooms and offices!

It wasn't until I knew more about learning styles and the <u>different needs</u> people have during **different needs** information intake that it finally dawned on me: Koosh balls are the ideal learning enhancement tool for <u>tactile learners</u>! These are the people – young **tactile learners** and old – who always need to <u>fiddle, doodle</u> **fiddle, doodle,** or constantly <u>manipulate something</u>, especially **manipulate something** when they take in new or difficult information, concentrate hard or are experiencing stress. Combined with a <u>high need for intake</u> (when **high need for intake**

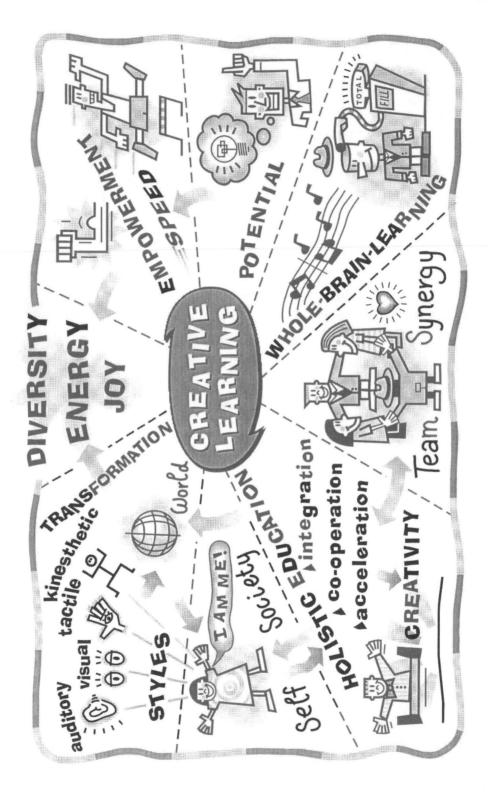

people need to eat, nibble or drink continuously) you have the perfect profile of a smoker as we

perfect profile of a smoker

have seen in many smokers' profiles. However, when these people can fiddle with a Koosh ball *and* have something to nibble or drink most of the time, their craving for a cigarette generally seems to diminish. On many occasions I have observed that they either smoke much less or not at all when they can play with a Koosh ball!

craving for cigarettes diminishes, smoke less when playing with a Koosh ball

We have also seen remarkable improvements in shy children, in nervous adults under stress and in people who usually fiddle a lot. They quickly calm down, their listening skills improve, their attention span is prolonged and they are less fearful speaking in front of groups.

remarkable improvements

calm down

less fearful

But I wanted to know more: who are the people using Koosh balls most during these activities?

who uses Koosh balls?

Results gained from the analysis of our WSA and LSA instruments clearly defined the following groups: primary school children, high school students (in this particular group more boys than girls) and, not surprisingly, far more men than women in the adult group.

primary school children, high school students, more boys than girls, more men than women

That explained why I had seen so many men from all walks of life not letting go of a Koosh ball, once they had begun using it during a training seminar. Then they kept using it back in their own work environment! And the many stories teachers tell me about the success they have with using Koosh balls in class – how these little gadgets have helped boys to participate more in group discussions, to show better discipline and to improve their concentration. Even parents have come to appreciate the magic of these balls for their highly tactile children and know they are not just like any other ball.

Koosh balls in class

better discipline improve concentration

So Koosh balls are not just fancy toys, they stimulate brain activity and learning processes in tactile/visual learners, they relax or activate and are above all a lot of fun to use! If you can't get hold of Koosh balls, allow them to use squish balls, play dough or small soft toys. There are now quite a few other similarly stimulating soft balls available, but nothing beats a Koosh ball I've found.

stimulate brain activity relax or activate a lot of fun

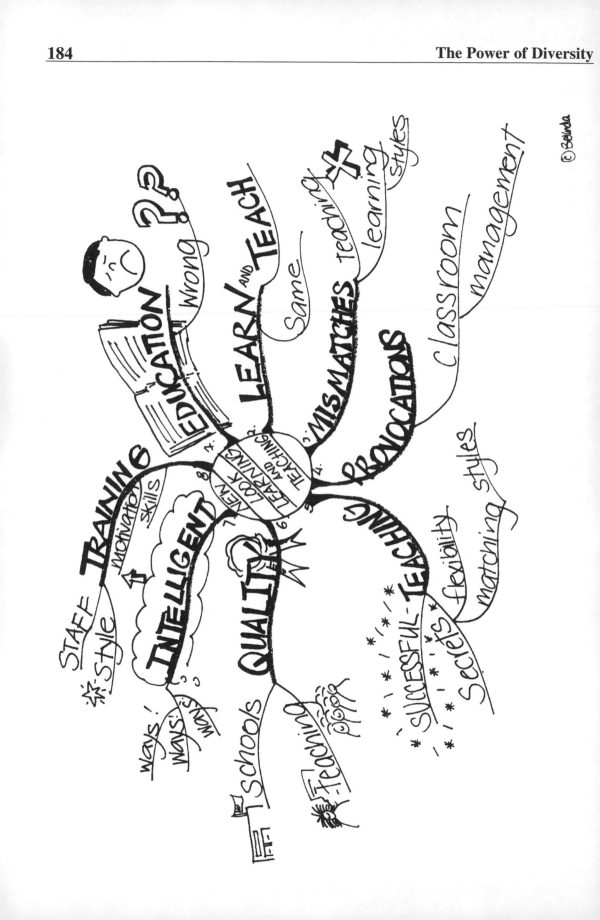

1. What has gone wrong in education?

The term 'educational crisis' is now being used
in literally every country around the world; it's
headlines in daily news and problems of education
are being discussed and debated everywhere.
But the underlying issue is not education, it is
learning. How we have come to regard the role
of learning in our societies, families, the workplace
and in the world at large is the real issue.

educational crisis

learning

the real issue

In the past, value has been placed solely on what
people KNOW, but presently, and even more so
in the future, value will be placed on how people
can LEARN. This in itself represents another
paradigm shift – from *knower to learner*.
The comparison on page 186 makes very clear
how profound the difference is between these two
and how extremely important this new paradigm
of human beings as *learners* is. It values not only
'what we know', it values 'how we know' and
allows us to gain a new attitude towards our own
learning ability which has profound implications
for our mental health from an early age.

**paradigm shift:
from knower to learner**

Let's consider formal education and ask a few
questions: how many thousands of hours do
students sit in classrooms experiencing lectures or
activities which bore them to death, which stifle
their curiosity and their spontaneously emerging
interest? What happens when a child experiences
uncertainty about details of the presentation? How
many hundreds of hours do they spend reading
books? And again, what can students do when they
encounter something they do not understand or
evokes their curiosity? Will they raise their hands
and ask? Only those who are not easily intimidated.
The majority of students, however, learn to ignore
all but their most powerful urges. Slowly but surely
their experiences at school result in a deadening of
their inner sensitivity.

formal education

**lectures, deadly boring
activities**

reading books

**school experiences kill
inner sensitivity**

Unlike the way children learn informally before and
outside school, the entire educational system dis-
courages them from 'tuning' into their own inner
learning processes. They become conditioned to

KNOWER

- Learning is something kids do in school.

- Teachers know and teach and students learn.

- The goal of education is a knower with a particular corpus of knowledge, a particular range of skills and a particular way of behaving.

- Learning is a process used to acquire knowledge, facts, skills and experience.

- Remembering information and patterns in knowledge leads to passing examinations.

- Relevancy is an external association in information and knowledge.

- Uncertainty is a sign of insufficiency and causes discomfort.

- Overall value is WHAT we know.

LEARNER

- Learning is something we all do every instant of our lives.

- Facilitators of learning learn with and, at the same time, about learners.

- The goal of education is a learner who understands how to relate to and learn from knowledge, other human beings and his or her self.

- Knowledge, facts, skills and experience are used to enrich, extend and exercise our capacities for learning.

- Realizing the relationships among meanings forms the basis for 'transference' in learning.

- Relevancy is the process of building meaning into the flow of an individual's attention.

- Self-honesty about uncertainty is a key to developing 'critical thinking'. Uncertainty is illuminative and leads to deeper understandings and insights.

- Main value is HOW we know.

Based on 'Learning Insights' conference handout, 1991

disregard their own meaning, their learning needs, their style and individuality in favour of acquiring machine-like behaviours and uniform outcomes favoured by the system and those who represent it. Consider the following: before children go into formal education, they learn miraculously by developing an inner sensitivity for their learning processes which is their day-to-day experience for years. When they go to school, in the process of being taught various subjects, the message they receive now is: what goes on inside your head is meaningless, pay attention and do as we tell you!

disregard own meaning

uniform outcomes

children learn by developing inner sensitivity

at school

pay attention do as you are told

This whole dilemma has nothing to do with teachers' intentions; this is not the issue. The problem is not WHAT is being taught but HOW it is done. The formal environment and traditional teaching methods continually discourage children from remaining sensitive to their own most essential capacities for learning. It's the overall education experience which turns, almost as a rule, highly energized, curious, eager and alive children into mainly tired, uninterested, uneasy, bored and frustrated students.

education experience turns curious, eager, alive children into bored, frustrated students

This is true for schools in every country I have visited so far, from Finland to Hong Kong, from New Zealand to Sweden, from the USA to Denmark. And what's even more alarming, this unfortunate development can be seen everywhere – despite the school, the teacher, even the socio-economic family status of the student.

It is little wonder that years of negative experiences at school lead to disappointment, learning problems, underachievement, discipline problems, despair, social problems, drug and alcohol abuse, isolation, giving up on oneself and, like currently in New Zealand and other countries, to ever-increasing numbers of teenage suicides, bullying and violence in schools.

negative experiences at school

The following recollection, given to me by Daniela Cassinelli, a teacher from Argentina, says it all:

recollection

'When I started school I had to learn to speak another language. It was not so easy or natural as my mother tongue. I was told not to move, not to touch, not to dance or sing or even play and pretend! Simple grammar, past tense, auxiliary, etc. Sit and write. Use your brain, your logical one. What about knowing intuitively, words coming out just naturally, because we sang them in that unforgettable song or heard them in a funny

If you are in a teaching/coaching role,

or in any sense a facilitator

of learning processes,

always bear in mind

that your own thinking style

probably dominates

your approach to teaching,

perhaps much more strongly

than you realize.

We tend to teach in the same way

we like to learn.

Karl Albrecht

rhyme or had to read them to make those ginger cookies? Why did we have to make this switch from natural, right-brain learning to merely logical left-brain learning? Didn't we all learn to speak a language only naturally and yet successfully? I don't remember mums in the park talking among themselves about having 'learning disabled' children who could not talk. We all could!

Now, at school, not all of us learn the way teachers ask us to. Some of my friends are finding it difficult to sit and copy. I heard my teacher talking about slow learners. My friends heard it too! Now they are worried. They think they are different. But teachers say we are all different and that differences are good. Why can't we learn differently, then? Two of my friends told me that when they are given a test, they feel stressed and that a new feeling of helplessness has started to grow inside themselves and those inner words 'I can't, I won't' are being repeated again and again. How strange, when I was in kindergarten I had this feeling of power, of well-being; the certainty that everything was possible!

Yesterday I heard the teacher telling Mum that my problem was low self-esteem. Mum wonders how I lost it. She remembers me as a clever, inquisitive child, never afraid to try out new things. And then these words: 'disabled learner' and 'low self-esteem'. I see Mum is worried. She doesn't know how to help me and I don't know what to do. I try to remember when it was that I started to feel insecure at school. Maybe the day I was told there were too many mistakes in my paper, or when I saw a number on it and the teacher explained to me it meant 'failed'. Or that day they gave me a long test and they told me to keep my eyes on the paper and to try hard. Yes, I remember my hands were wet and I don't know why. Or maybe the day I wanted to stand and sing; I would have loved to perform the part of the hero in the story I had to read, but there was no time. I was told to read it and to answer the questions in long form. Instead I wanted to stand and act it out.

And then I began to feel bored. I lost interest. I thought: 'This is not fun!' And those low figures in my papers appeared more and more often. I knew I was good at singing, acting, creating, imagining, but there were no figures for those things. I don't know why. We did not do these fun things very often either. I would have loved them too! I was good at them and I felt great about myself when I did them. Sometimes our teacher still talks about respecting differences. I wonder what she means.

2. False beliefs about learning are still alive and well

In the past, <u>traditional teaching methods</u> and educational practices worked well for the mainstream educational systems of Western societies. These days, however, the same systems have to cater for hugely <u>diverse student groups</u> with vastly <u>different expectations</u> and attitudes never encountered before. Despite these profound changes, students and trainees around the world are still being taught by educators and trainers holding on to <u>outmoded beliefs</u> about learning

traditional teaching methods

diverse student groups
different expectations

outmoded beliefs

How Well Do You Listen?

1. Our listening and hearing usually become more acute when we don't have visual cues. In a safe part of your home (where you don't have to worry about tripping or falling), experiment for a half-hour by keeping your eyes closed and simply listening to the world around you. You may also use a blindfold, such as a scarf or towel wrapped around your eyes.

   You will in all likelihood begin to feel sound coming from different appliances. Can you differentiate among them? Is the hum of your refrigerator different from that of the air-conditioner or other appliances? Are you aware of birdsong or other sounds from outside your home?

2. Put this book down and list on a piece of paper the things you hear around you. Do this without concentrating too hard; the point is to be quick and casual.

   Then spend 5 minutes really listening. Close your eyes, exhale, and open the 'lens' of your ear.

   Jot down what you heard in those five minutes. How has the list changed? Do you hear dissonant sounds more clearly? Are you aware of the sound of the refrigerator, air-conditioner, space heater, or other 'background noise' in the room? Can you sense any sounds within your body? Your ears are like periscopes, able to focus on distant or near noise.

Campbell (1997)

and even advocating these <u>archaic methods</u>.
It is therefore no surprise that <u>negative attitudes</u>
towards schooling in general, and traditional learning
in particular, are widespread, especially among people
who had <u>learning difficulties</u> or found it hard to cope
with <u>formal education</u>. Their special ways of learning,
their personal learning styles and preferences were
not recognized and catered for, and that's why they
found learning so unrewarding. Here are the <u>ten false</u>
<u>beliefs about learning</u> which <u>cause high stress and</u>
<u>burn out in teachers</u> and often <u>inability to learn</u>
in students:

archaic methods
negative attitudes

learning difficulties
formal education

ten false beliefs
high stress & burnout
learning disability

Fallacy 1: *Students learn best when <u>seated upright</u> at*
desk or table.

seated upright

Research shows that many human beings perform
better in an <u>informal environment</u>. Making students
sit upright on their chairs does not necessarily make
them more responsive to learning. Studies on high
school students in the USA have shown significant
improvement in maths and English when taught and
tested while the students were seated on cushions,
lounge chairs and rugs, if informal design was their
preference. Our own work with learning styles has
resulted in much happier teachers and students after
<u>rearranging their classroom</u> and establishing informal
work areas for those who need them.

informal environment

rearranging classrooms

Fallacy 2: *Students learn best in <u>well-illuminated</u>*
<u>areas</u> and damage their eyes when they read and
work in low light.

students learn better in
well-illuminated areas

Research shows many students perform significantly
better in <u>low-light environments</u>; bright light makes
them restless, fidgety and hyperactive. Low light
calms them down and helps them relax and think
clearly. The <u>younger children</u> are, the <u>less light</u> they
seem to need! They only need the amount of light for
reading in which they feel comfortable, but their need
for light seems to increase every five years. Teachers
who permit students with low-light needs to work in
low-light corners are always surprised by their
<u>improved behaviour</u>, attention and better grades
within six weeks. Low light is particularly good
for underachievers!

low-light environments

young children
need less light

improved behaviour

Traditional Education

- confines body to limited territory
- confines energy to limited activity
- limits stimulation of senses
- limits social interaction
- limits experiences to the classroom
- subordinates initiative to others
- assumes ignorance

Norm Ericson, IBM

Fallacy 3: *Students learn more and perform better in an absolutely quiet environment.*

Research findings show that many adults think and remember best when <u>studying with music</u>, many primary school children <u>read better with sound</u>, even noise present, and a high number of adolescent students, especially boys and <u>underachievers</u>, learn much better with even <u>loud music</u> or <u>background noise</u>. When students who need sound have to work in quiet environments, they lose concentration very quickly and they will make their own sounds, like finger drumming, pencil clicking, humming, and tapping their feet. Despite countless teacher warnings these distracting noises never stop. The right learning music in the background alleviates this problem. As there are always a few students in each class who need absolute silence while they are learning, <u>each classroom should have quiet sections</u> for those who cannot concentrate with noise, and should also have areas where students can learn with music. Although most <u>teachers prefer quiet</u> learning environments themselves, they need to accept that different brains work differently and that what's good for some is not good for all.

studying with music
read better with sound

underachievers
loud music or
background noise

classrooms should have
quiet sections

teachers prefer quiet

Fallacy 4: *Students learn difficult subjects best in the <u>early morning</u> when they are <u>most alert</u>.*

early morning most alert

This is only true for those we call 'early birds' – but what about the '<u>night owls</u>' and '<u>afternoon learners</u>' of the student population? Research has shown that when students are allowed to learn difficult concepts at their preferred time of the day, their behaviour, motivation and achievements improve. The same goes for test results.

'night owls'
afternoon learners

Fallacy 5: *Students who do not <u>sit still</u> are not ready to learn.*

students need to sit still

Many students <u>need to move when they learn</u>. One American study revealed that half of one school's seventh grade students needed extensive mobility while learning, and when they were allowed to move from one learning area to another while taking new information in, they achieved statistically better than when they had to remain seated in their chairs. Most students who are actively involved are likely to learn more, pay closer attention, and achieve higher test marks than when they just sit and listen.

need movement
when learning

It is <u>not</u> the child who bears

the responsibility for learning,

it is the <u>teacher</u> who bears responsibility

for identifying each child's learning style strengths

and for matching those with

responsive environments and approaches.

Dr Rita Dunn

Fallacy 6: *Eating should not be permitted in classrooms during lessons.*

no eating in class

Many students concentrate better when they can have something to eat, nibble, chew or drink while learning, and many teachers will have observed that a number of students chew on whatever they can get hold of during classes, particularly when they have to listen for a while, when they are bored or nervous. It seems that mouth stimulation helps them concentrate, and as the brain dehydrates during thinking processes, it is essential that students are allowed to have drinks of water whenever needed. Students with a high need for intake should be allowed to have healthy snacks, and with good management techniques there will be no mess in class. Thousands of teachers who have successfully introduced a 'healthy nibbles policy' are proof that it works, and discipline, together with student performance, improves significantly.

concentrate better when eat, nibble, chew, drink

mouth stimulation helps concentrating
drinks of water

healthy snacks

Fallacy 7: *Effective teaching requires clearly stated objectives followed by detailed, step-by-step, sequential explanations until students understand what's being taught.*

detailed step-by-step sequential explanations

While holistic, right-brain dominant learners tend to grasp large concepts first and then deal with the related facts and details, analytic, left-brain dominant learners pay attention to the facts first and use them for building up the whole concept. Only these are the ones who work well with step-by-step teaching. Many, probably most, teachers use analytic styles and a few teach only holistically, using a lot of creativity. Every teacher should (and successful teachers always do) include elements of both styles in their teaching.

holistic R/B learners grasp concepts first; analytic L/B learners need facts first

elements of both styles teaching

Fallacy 8: *Whole-group instruction is the best way to teach.*

Whole-group instruction best way to teach

Some students work well in teams or groups, but many prefer to work in pairs, and others cannot concentrate well with other students around them. Gifted students tend to prefer to work by themselves and some students prefer to work with adults rather than with classmates; others may work well with media rather than with people. The best way to teach is to allow for a variation of social preferences among the students in class.

prefer to work in pairs

gifted students work by themselves

variation of social preferences

A uniform way

of teaching and testing

is patently unsatisfactory

when everyone

is so different.

Howard Gardner

Fallacy 9: *Generally, the <u>older students</u> are, the easier it is for them to <u>adapt to the teacher's style</u>.*

older students adapt easier to teacher's style

While older students require less teacher supervision and <u>less structure</u>, they continue to learn differently from one another, and still have <u>varying learning needs</u>. They do tend to need more independence as they grow older, so giving them <u>options and choices</u> about their own learning is appropriate. This also gives them a chance to develop their responsibility.

less structure
varying learning needs

options and choices

Fallacy 10: *Truancy is related to poor attitudes, home problems, lack of motivation, and other factors which have <u>nothing to do with</u> their preferred <u>learning style</u>.*

nothing to do with students' learning style

Studies of secondary school truants revealed that when their learning style preferences were catered for and <u>their time preferences</u> were <u>matched</u> to their academic schedules, their <u>attendance improved</u> dramatically. Their attendance and learning <u>motivation increased</u> also when they were given a teacher different from the one with whom they had been truant. (1) Although we do not have a study on truancy and <u>learning styles</u> in New Zealand, we know that in some <u>high schools</u> where learning styles have been introduced, the <u>truancy rate</u> has markedly <u>gone down</u> and expulsions are now a thing of the past.

time preferences matched attenance improved

motivation increased

learning styles in high schools truancy rate gone down

Results with learning styles worldwide challenge and disprove these old beliefs, and show that when teachers respond to students' individual learning needs, it takes as little as <u>six weeks</u> to see positive results like <u>increased academic achievement</u> and <u>a decrease in discipline problems</u>. As many practitioners have experienced, even at-risk students begin to learn and feel better about themselves, and teachers no longer despair having them in their class. And even if not every teacher embraces learning styles enthusiastically, the <u>knowledge</u> about <u>diversity in the classroom</u>, a few changes in teaching methods, the insight that the one-style-fits-all approach is outright wrong – all that works wonders in <u>improving classroom management</u>. The unexpected but always <u>positive results</u> delight teachers and students alike.

six weeks to increase academic achievement & decrease discipline problems

knowledge about diversity in the classroom

improving classrooom management
positive results

by Hoana Mitchell, Pukekohe North School, New Zealand

Barbara, dear, when you are near
The whole world explodes
in learning modes.
You've opened our eyes to Learning Styles
Oh! God! We've waited for such a long while
For learning ways to just make kids smile.

We are prisoners of a system set by fools,
Vacationers looking for real learning tools.
In four short days consumers we became
And our restless spirits you surely tamed.
Your profound wisdom has enlightened
our brains
Believe me, girl – we'll never be the same.
As adventurers now in 2003
We'll teach kids in the styles meant to be.

Closed minds protected, you gave us the key
To meet new challenges of education to see.
Out from old comfort zones we must relieve
To help our kids learn so they can conceive
The world and its manifold evolutions
In a way they can feel energy revolutions.

We've analysed and scrutinised
Learning Styles and you know what?
It's all been worthwhile a lot!
LSA and TSA identified our woes,
Mismatching styles we didn't even know.
No wonder even the worms squirmed below.

Left brain, Right brain, what, why, how?
The power of the brain is simply – WOW!

Brain wiring reminds us of things we can do
But also of acts we can never undo.

Symbols, pictures, emotions, sounds,
The brain's capacity knows no bounds.
Music, Mind-Mapping are memory cues
To the magic of Learning Styles we can use.

As for the drum of rap music beat
Watch out you guys for the energy streak!

Hey there, in government you listen here:
Our LSA movement has now appeared.
To reshape your policies is an urgent must
We've had these for too long –
they're gathering dust!

To my people, the Maoris I say:
"We've found the gold."
Learning success for our mokopuna untold.
Too long we've been the educational sheep
Being statistics at the bottom of the heap.

Barbara:
What a fantastic journey this course has been -
The ultimate fulfilment of a long held dream.
In such a short time we've travelled miles
And leave this course with very broad smiles.

We thank God that you
Have been part of our lives.
God bless you, and keep you safe
In your travels worldwide.

This poem was written and given to me after a whole week's training for the 'Diploma in Holistic Education' and expresses beautifully the mood most participants are in after these five days. I am deeply grateful to be allowed to work with these dedicated and pioneering teachers.

3. New classroom management based on style diversity

Traditional teaching methods and educational
practices have made Western school systems strong
and successful over the first half of the twentieth
century, but the same systems now have to service
vastly diverse groups of students like never seen
before. Over the past 20 years virtually every
teacher in every country has been experiencing
problems in class unheard of in the past and most **problems in class unheard**
teachers are ill-equipped to handle situations for **of in the past**
which they have not been trained. This unsatisfactory
status quo, stress and severe burnout among
educators, plus the insight that old teaching practices
just don't work any longer, have led to a search for **search for new & more**
new and more appropriate methods to educate the **appropriate methods**
young. Contemporary wisdom tells us that unless we
succeed in educating every single child AND its
parents, whole societies suffer. School failure and **school failures &**
dropout students put our whole society at risk by **dropout students**
what they do to us, to our children, to our property **put society at risk**
and to our social and welfare systems.

Discipline problems in class, negative attitudes **discipline problems &**
towards school in general, and so-called learning **learning disabilities can be**
disabilities can be eradicated, if teaching methods are **eradicated**
used to reach young people and make them more
responsive. These student-centred methods are based **student-centred methods**
on learning styles, and are particularly useful for **based on learning styles**
students who cannot learn and retain information in
ways traditional education provides.

With the information about learning styles so far
described in the previous chapters and the insights
gained from this new knowledge, we now have to
investigate popular but outdated beliefs about **outdated beliefs about**
learning and teaching which, particularly in high **learning and teaching**
schools, are still the basis for handling students in
class but are far removed from effective and
successful classroom management. If you read the
following statements as a teacher, you might feel
provoked, even offended, and you might think it is **provoked even offended**
impossible to manage classrooms in the suggested
way. I can only tell you that thousands of teachers in
many countries around the world are practising these **practising new**
new management techniques, and on a daily basis **management techniques**
experience greater success with their students and **greater success**
more job satisfaction. If you are a parent reading **more job satisfaction**

What to DO when using
Learning Styles in daily classroom work

Explain to students that the LSA is not a test, that nobody can pass or fail; inform parents that there is no such thing as a correct or better LS profile.

Accept that each learning style classroom must have a comfortable area with dim lighting where students can learn informally on soft furniture or on the floor. This is even possible in high schools!

Avoid switching on the lights in a classroom because YOU need them. Particularly younger students need much less light than adults and get agitated under fluorescent lights.

Involve pupils in creating the best possible learning environment, let them help design a classroom where everyone can learn really well.

Subgroup students according to their sensory preferences and match their other learning needs when teaching new and/or difficult content.

Switch between holistic and analytic approaches, give an overview first, then the necessary details.

Use multisensory teaching strategies, LS tools, learning music in the background and allow snacks and movement for those who need it.

Find out your own Teaching Style (TSA) – it will help you become more flexible and accommodate all students' learning needs much better.

these fallacies, please accept that school <u>teaching IS different</u> from the time you went to school and requires different methods to equip our children with the necessary knowledge, skills and learning attitudes.

teaching is different

4. What NOT to do with learning styles

Never underestimate students' ability to KNOW their LS!
Even young students know deep down how they want to learn, how they can do it best; even if it goes against their teachers' and parents' opinion. Trust their <u>self-knowledge</u> and help them develop their <u>learning potential</u>.

self-knowledge
learning potential

Never give up on underachievers!
These problem students can become very successful learners once their <u>non-traditional learning style</u> combinations are understood, no longer judged as 'weird' but <u>accepted and matched</u> accordingly in school teaching and at home.

non-traditional style

accepted & matched

Never label students according to their sensory modalities!
There are no so-called 'visual' or 'kinesthetic' students because they all have <u>combinations</u> of at least two <u>sensory preferences</u> (some have six and more!). They also have <u>internal modalities</u> like the ability to visualize or feel. Many students possess <u>flexibilities</u> which can become preferences when they are very interested in a subject topic.

combinations
sensory preferences
internal modalities

flexibilities

Never switch on all the lights in a classroom because you need them!
Many students, particularly younger ones need much less light than adults do and get <u>agitated under fluorescent lights</u>. They will not tell their teachers, because they accept their authority but they will get <u>restless</u> and there will be more <u>discipline problems</u>, particularly with underachievers.

fluorescent light
agitates

restless
discipline problems

Never assume all students can learn the same way as you do!
What makes sense for you in learning (like reading, talking) might be very <u>confusing</u> for students who have a different thinking style. If you as a teacher need quiet to concentrate, this does not mean your students can learn well in quiet classrooms too. For many, silence is unbearable and their <u>behaviour</u> will become <u>disruptive</u>.

confusing

behaviour
disruptive

SIX CONDITIONS OF QUALITY SCHOOLS

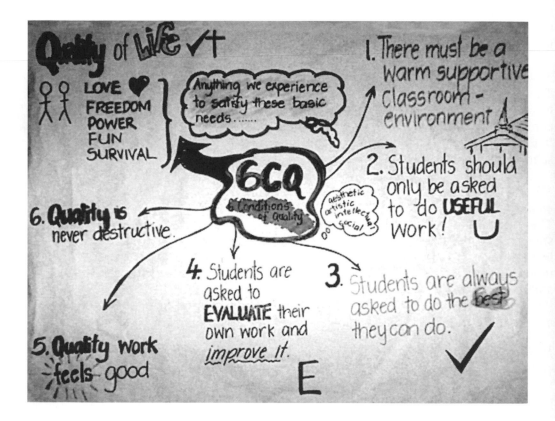

Courtesy of Malfroy School, Rotorua, NZ

5. Quality schools and quality teaching

Some years ago, when the corporate world was
brimming with TQM – Total Quality Management –
which appeared under various names, based on
the work of Dr W. Edwards Deming, <u>quality</u> was
defined as <u>goods or services</u> having characteristics
required by customers and having been <u>produced</u>
<u>without wasted</u> human or non-human <u>resources</u>. (2)
As TQM is both a management method and
a philosophy, it has been widely used in large
organizations, often overemphasizing strategies,
techniques, systems or practices, and at the same
time forgetting people and their individuality.
That might have been the reason why TQM in
education has not taken hold and has been seen
as a much too theoretical system needing to be
strictly followed. However, the desire to create
<u>quality schools</u> is often reflected in a school's
<u>mission statement</u> but its implementation can
get bogged down in too much bureaucracy.

quality ~
goods or services
produced without
wasted resources

quality in schools
mission statement

Through my work with learning styles I also
became involved in the long-term planning of
change processes in schools and the issue of
quality surfaced again. As I did not favour an all
too pragmatic approach, I discovered some very
useful ideas in William Glasser's books on <u>quality</u>
which can be easily <u>combined with learning styles</u>
and <u>creative learning methods</u>. In his first book,
The Quality School, Managing Students Without
Coercion, he describes very clearly that the purpose
of any organization, public or private, is to build
a quality product or perform a quality service, that
the workers in the organization must do quality
work and that the job of the managers is to make
sure that this occurs. <u>In every school</u>, the <u>students</u>
<u>are the workers</u> and right now almost <u>none are</u>
<u>doing quality work in class</u>.

quality combined
with learning styles &
creative learning methods

in schools students are
the workers not doing
quality work in class

Glasser describes it graphically like this: 'Picture the students in a required academic
class at a randomly selected secondary school as a gang of street repair workers. If they
were working as hard as the students are doing in class, half or more would be leaning
on their shovels, smoking or socializing, perfectly content to let the others do the work.
Of those who were working, few would be working hard, and it is likely that none would
be doing high-quality work.' (3)

$$\text{CREATIVE INTELLIGENCE}$$

1. PREPARATION:
gathering information and exploration

2. INCUBATION:
a period of processing in the mind and body

3. THE 'AHA!':
an exciting point of insight

4. VERIFICATION:
insuring the integrity of the insight

5. IMPLEMENTATION:
*putting the information and insights
into a usable framework*

Chris Brewer and Don Campbell (1992)

While <u>students know what quality is</u>, recognize it when they see it and generally believe they are capable of doing quality work in class, all but a few admit that they <u>have never done it</u> and have no plans to do it in future. What's the reason that so many students are <u>not really interested</u> in participating, let alone in <u>producing quality work</u> at school? The most often quoted reason is not that <u>work is too</u> hard, but that it is boring; '<u>boring</u>' meant that they could not relate to the learning task and that it was <u>not satisfying students' needs</u>.

students know what quality is

have never done it

not really interested in producing quality work

work is too boring

not satisfying their needs

And this brings me to the most important message in Glasser's second book, *The Quality School Teacher*:

<u>The six conditions of quality schoolwork</u>:

six conditions of quality

1. *There must be a warm, supportive classroom environment*.
   Without a strong, friendly feeling between students and staff there can be no quality schoolwork and, above all, there must be trust.

warm, supportive classroom environment

2. *Students should be asked to do only useful work*.
   No student should be asked to do anything that does not make sense, like memorizing or rote learning. Whatever they do has to have some use – practical, aesthetic, artistic, intellectual or social.

students do only useful work

3. *Students are always asked to do the best they can*.
   That means students must be given the necessary time to make an effort to produce quality work. They are used to covering ground, not learning, and have hardly ever attempted to do quality work.

do the best they can

4. *Students are asked to evaluate their own work and improve it*.
   Self-evaluation is the most difficult to implement but is essential to achieve constant improvements in students' efforts to produce quality work.

evaluate own work & improve it

5. *Quality work always feels good*.
   It is sad that so few students feel good in their academic classes now. Not only do students feel good as they succeed in doing what they know is quality, but also their teachers and parents feel good observing the process.

quality work feels good

Multiple Intelligences Checklist

Mark those statements that apply to you:

Linguistic Intelligence:
_____ Books are very important to me.
_____ I can hear words in my head before I read, speak or write them down.
_____ I get more out of listening to the radio or a spoken word cassette than I do from television or films.
_____ English, social studies and history were easier for me in school than maths and science.
_____ I have written something recently that I was particularly proud of or that earned me recognition from others.

[____] Total

Logical-mathematical Intelligence:
_____ I can easily compute numbers in my head.
_____ Maths and/or science were among my favourite subjects at school.
_____ I'm interested in new developments in science.
_____ I like finding logical flaws in things people say and do at home and work.
_____ I feel more comfortable when something has been measured, categorized, analysed or quantified in some way.

[____] Total

Spatial Intelligence:
_____ I prefer looking at reading material that is heavily illustrated.
_____ Geometry was easier for me than algebra at school.
_____ I can generally find my way around unfamiliar territory.
_____ I often see clear visual images when I close my eyes.
_____ I like to draw and doodle.

[____] Total

Bodily-kinesthetic Intelligence:
_____ I find it difficult to sit still for long periods of time.
_____ I engage in at least one sport or physical activity on a regular basis.
_____ My best ideas often come to me when I'm out for a long walk or a jog, or when I'm engaged in some type of physical activity.
_____ I often like to spend my free time outdoors.
_____ I would describe myself as well coordinated.

[____] Total

6. *Quality work is never destructive*.   **quality work is**
   It is not quality to achieve good feelings   **never destructive**
   via the addictive use of drugs or to harm people,
   living creatures, property or the environment. (4)

Please consider if all these <u>conditions of quality</u>   **quality conditions**
are already to be found <u>in your school</u> and what   **in your school**
it means on a daily basis for all parties concerned;
or, if only some apply, what the reasons are that
not all six conditions are present yet and what
could be done to <u>improve the situation</u>.   **improve the situation**

6. Many ways of being intelligent: MS vs LS

One of the myths surrounding education is the
notion that human beings have a <u>general capacity</u>,   **general capacity**
called *intelligence*, to deal with all the different   **intelligence**
situations a human being will encounter during
his or her lifetime. For a long time people believed,
and many still do, that this general capacity is
fixed for a particular individual and varies in its
quantity from person to person.

In recent years Harvard professor of education
Howard Gardner has been one of many who
made a major contribution to our understanding
of human intelligence by shattering the 'fixed IQ'
myth. He developed <u>Multiple Intelligence theory</u>   **MI theory**
(MI) based on neurobiological research which
indicates that the human brain is an extremely
complex organ with a much greater capacity for
learning than currently used by human beings.
Originally, Gardner defined at least <u>seven</u>   **seven**
<u>different intelligences</u> which all work together in   **different intelligences**
the brain as an <u>integrated whole</u>, yet each in itself   **integrated whole**
identifiable and capable of enhancement. (5)

More recently, there has been debate about
<u>additional intelligences</u>, and Gardner always   **additional intelligences**
maintained there could be many more faculties
which meet his criteria for intelligence. In 1996 one
more was added, the '<u>naturalist's</u>' intelligence, but   **naturalist**
the main focus is still on the basic seven, of which
all human beings possess varying degrees – in
Gardner's terminology people's '<u>biopsychological</u>   **biopsychological**
<u>potential</u>' which they develop over a lifetime. (6)   **potential**

Multiple Intelligences Checklist continued

Mark those statements that apply to you:

Musical Intelligence:
____   I can tell when a musical note is off-key.
____   I play a musical instrument.
____   I have a pleasant singing voice.
____   I know the tunes to many different songs or musical pieces.
____   I often make tapping sounds or sing little melodies while working, studying
        or learning something new.

| Total

Interpersonal Intelligence:
____   I have at least three close friends.
____   I enjoy the challenge of teaching another person, or groups of people, what I
        know how to do.
____   I like to get involved in social activities connected with my work, church
        or community.
____   I would rather spend my evenings at a lively social gathering than stay at
        home alone.
____   When I have a problem, I'm more likely to seek out another person for help
        than attempt to work it out on my own.

| Total

Intrapersonal Intelligence:
____   I regularly spend time alone meditating, reflecting or thinking about
        important life questions.
____   I have attended counselling sessions or personal growth seminars to learn
        more about myself.
____   I am self-employed or have at least thought seriously about starting my
        own business.
____   I keep a personal diary or journal to record the events in my inner life.
____   I consider myself to be strong-willed or independent-minded.

| Total

Adapted from *Seven Kinds of Smart* by Thomas Armstrong (7)

The original <u>seven intelligences</u> described by Gardner are:

seven intelligences

1. <u>*Linguistic intelligence*</u>: as the ability to read and/ or write well. People who are strong in this area also have highly developed auditory skills, their vocabulary is extensive and spelling is easy.

Linguistic

2. <u>*Logical-mathematical intelligence*</u>: as the ability to reason, calculate and handle logical thinking. People who are strong in this area are highly capable of analysing and classifying information, to theorize and create patterns and hypotheses.

Logical-mathematical

3. <u>*Visual-spatial intelligence*</u>: as the ability to think in pictures and images, see things in relationship with others, to navigate, take great photographs and to perceive the visual world accurately. People who are strong in this area often have the skill to paint or sculpt, even with little or no sight.

Visual-spatial

4. <u>*Musical intelligence*</u>: as the ability to sing, play instruments, compose, appreciate and produce rhythms, pitch and form of musical expression. People who are strong in this area are able to carry a tune, have a good musical ear and are sensitive to sounds in the environment.

Musical

5. <u>*Bodily-kinesthetic intelligence*</u>: as the control of body movements and the capacity to handle objects skilfully, enabling people to express themselves physically, to be active in sports and to 'know' things with their body. Movement and physical activities are very important.

Bodily-kinesthetic

6. <u>*Interpersonal intelligence*</u>: as the ability to work and interact sensitively with other people, to have social responsibility and compassion. People who are strong in this area can listen effectively, negotiate, handle conflicts, cooperate and get along well with diverse groups of people.

Interpersonal

7. <u>*Intrapersonal intelligence*</u>: as the ability to access and understand one's inner feelings, weaknesses, strengths and desires, reflect on experiences, think about thinking (metacognition) and discriminate between inner emotional states. People here often have strong opinions and prefer to be by themselves.

Intrapersonal

MY UNIQUE BLEND OF
H. GARDNER'S MULTIPLE INTELLIGENCES
- SCORING -

Plot your bar graph on the grid below, according to your self-assessment scores, to come up with an intelligence profile that is currently relevant to you.

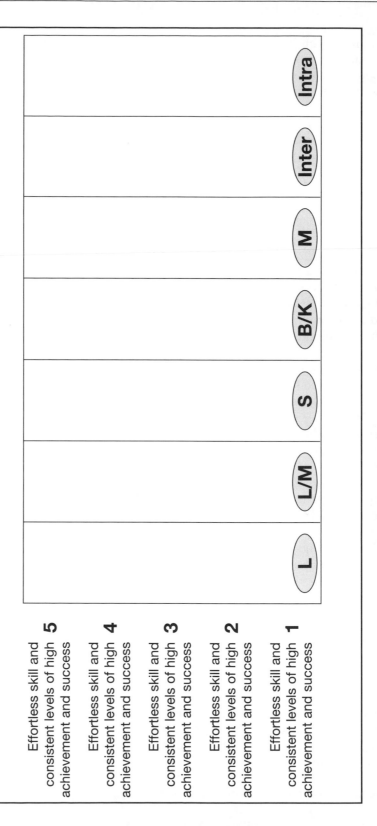

Effortless skill and consistent levels of high achievement and success **5**

Effortless skill and consistent levels of high achievement and success **4**

Effortless skill and consistent levels of high achievement and success **3**

Effortless skill and consistent levels of high achievement and success **2**

Effortless skill and consistent levels of high achievement and success **1**

L   L/M   S   B/K   M   Inter   Intra

L Linguistic   **L/M** Logical-mathematical   **S** Spatial   **B/K** Bodily-kinesthetic   **M** Musical   **Inter** Interpersonal   **Intra** Intrapersonal

MI theory offers a <u>useful framework</u> for curriculum design in schools, and if it is true that there are developmental changes in intelligence through the schooling years, learning experiences must contain opportunities to develop all seven, and Gardner challenges schools to provide experiences for students to develop the different 'ways of knowing'.

useful framework

If you are interested in finding out your personal blend of intelligences, the short <u>questionnaire</u> on pages 206 and 208 will give you a general <u>profile of your multiple intelligences</u> which you can create on page 210.

questionnaire
your profile of MI

Although the MI theory has been enthusiastically welcomed in the USA and tried out by many educators around the world, there has also been confusion, exaggeration and misunderstandings about how to implement this <u>theoretical framework</u>, and I often find that <u>multiple intelligences</u> are being <u>confused with learning styles</u>. I believe that MI made a valuable contribution to make the elusive concept of intelligence more tangible and, utilized carefully by well-trained teachers, it can be a very useful concept to enhance classroom teaching.

theoretical framework
MI confused with
learning styles

Since the publication of Daniel Goleman's book, *Emotional Intelligence: Why It Can Matter More Than IQ*, the debate about academic and life achievements based on intelligence has been expanded by one more dimension – emotionality. According to collated results of brain research contained and interpreted in this best-selling book, <u>EQ (Emotional Quotient) matters more than</u> a person's IQ because, as Goleman argues, our present view of human intelligence is far too narrow, and our emotions play a much greater role in thinking, decision making, even logical reasoning, than is commonly acknowledged. This concept really expands on Howard Gardner's two *personal intelligences* in his MI framework, focusing on the full range of <u>emotional and relationship abilities</u> rather than only on one's mental processes.

EQ (Emotional Quotient)
matters more than IQ

emotional & relationship
abilities

The model of <u>emotional intelligence</u> was first proposed by Salovey and Meyer in 1990 and contains the five following domains:

emotional intelligence

SUCCESSFULLY INTELLIGENT PEOPLE

- motivate themselves and learn to control their impulses

- translate thought into action and know when to persevere

- are initiators and know how to make the most of their abilities

- have a product orientation and are not afraid to risk failure

- don't procrastinate, complete tasks and follow through

- spread themselves neither too thin nor too thick and accept fair blame

- are independent and have the ability to delay gratification

- have the ability to see the forest and the trees

- seek to surmount personal difficulties and reject self-pity

- focus and concentrate to achieve their goals

- have a reasonable level of self-confidence and a belief in their ability
  to accomplish their goals

- balance analytical, creative and practical thinking

Robert J. Sternber

1. *Knowing one's emotions*: self-awareness, recognizing a feeling when it occurs, crucial for self-understanding.

   knowing one's emotions

2. *Managing emotions*: handling feelings so they are appropriate, the capacity to soothe oneself and shake off anxiety, gloom and irritability.

   managing emotions

3. *Motivating oneself*: emotional self-control, delaying gratification and stifling impulsiveness, essential for paying attention, reaching mastery and achieving creativity.

   motivating oneself

4. *Recognizing emotions in others*: empathy and attunement to the subtle social signals indicating what others need or want, one of the fundamental 'people skills'.

   recognizing emotions in others

5. *Handling relationships*: social competence and abilities underlying popularity, leadership and interpersonal effectiveness. (8)

   handling relationships

No one can seriously dispute that these abilities are crucial to live a satisfying, happy life (whatever that might mean to the individual) but, considering the alarming statistics about social ills, particularly in the USA, they seem to be a barometer of dropping levels of emotional competence which does not bode well for the future of society. Goleman states that surveys over the past 20 years are proof that children today, on average, are emotional illiterate as they are doing more poorly in these specific ways: (9)

abilities to live satisfying, happy life

children today emotional illiterate

- **Withdrawal or social problems**: preferring to be alone; being secretive; sulking a lot; lacking energy; feeling unhappy; being overly dependent.

- **Anxious and depressed**: being lonely; having many fears and worries; needing to be perfect; feeling unloved; feeling nervous or sad and depressed.

- **Attention or thinking problems**: unable to pay attention or sit still; daydreaming; acting without thinking; being too nervous to concentrate; unable to get mind off thoughts; doing poorly on schoolwork.

- **Delinquent or aggressive**: hanging around kids who get in trouble; lying and cheating; arguing a lot; being mean to other people; demanding attention; destroying other people's things; disobeying at home and at school; being stubborn and moody; talking too much; teasing a lot; having a hot temper.

When I was young and free and
imagination had no limits,
I dreamed of changing the world.

As I grew older and wiser,
I discovered the world would not change,
So I shortened my sights somewhat and decided
To change only my country.
But it seemed too immovable.

As I grew into my twilight years,
In one last desperate attempt,
I settled for changing my family,
Those closest to me, but alas,
They would have none of it.

And now, as I lie on my deathbed,
I suddenly realize:
If only I had changed myself,
Then by example I might have changed my family.
From their inspiration and encouragement
I would have been able to better my country, and who knows,

I may have changed the world.

Written on the tomb of an Anglican bishop,
Westminster Abbey in AD 1100

If you as a teacher or parent are struggling with any of these issues with your students or children, Goleman's book makes exciting reading, offers valuable insights into the amazing <u>emotional circuits in the brain</u> and gives practical advice on how to deal with these problems from a different angle.

emotional circuits in the brain

Considering the sad statistics about young New Zealanders in the areas of school failure, drug and alcohol abuse, violence, unwanted teen pregnancy, depression and teenage suicide, it seems that this nation, too, has a problem with <u>emotional competence</u>, and maybe even with their moral one as well. Robert Coles, in his very good book, *The Moral Intelligence of Children*, points out that every child is a witness of grown-up morality – or lack thereof (10) and I can highly recommend this book for adding a new and thought-provoking dimension to the intelligence debate.

emotional competence

moral intelligence

In the meantime the search for understanding intelligence has continued and Howard Gardner has now expanded his concept to 8½ intelligences which might not be as clear-cut but certainly worth mentioning:

8. *Naturalist intelligence*: not yet determined where located in the brain, but described as being used in object recognition, one's potential to think about and understand the natural world.

Naturalist

8. *½ Existential intelligence*: not yet fully understood, but seems to be one's potential to think philosophically and to understand life, the universe and things beyond our physical body and world – has elements of the esoteric.

Existential

One thing however, is very certain: MI is NOT learning styles as so often found on internet searches as it deals with information 'output' in the widest sense and LS is responsible for information 'intake' and both concepts complement each other nicely. The Pocket PAL booklet by Mike Fleetham *Multiple Intelligences* (Network Continuum Education; 2007) is an excellent reference book with lots of practical applications in each area and particularly useful for classroom teachers who want to get clearer on this concept.

Teaching Style Analysis – Education

Teaching Style Analysis ™ - Questionnaire Part I

Name:_____ School:_____

Answer the following questions according to the FREQUENCY of their occurrence in your teaching. (Circle one number only for each answer.)

Please rate yourself:
5 – Almost always   2 – Occasionally
4 – Frequently   1 – Hardly ever
3 – Sometimes   0 – It depends/undecided

1.	Do you use background music during your classes?_____	5 4 3 2 1 0
2.	Do you keep your classroom quiet (except during discussions)?_____	5 4 3 2 1 0
3.	Are there computers and other electronic media available in your classroom? _	5 4 3 2 1 0
4.	Do you expect your students to work at their desks?_____	5 4 3 2 1 0
5.	Do you allow students to sit on the floor, cushions or soft furniture in class?___	5 4 3 2 1 0
6.	Is it uncomfortable for you if there is not enough artificial light in your classroom? _____	5 4 3 2 1 0
7.	Do you provide the opportunity for students to work in low-light areas?_____	5 4 3 2 1 0
8.	Are you aware that temperature can influence your students' concentration? __	5 4 3 2 1 0
9.	Do you allow your students to wear warm comfortable clothes in class?_____	5 4 3 2 1 0
10.	Do you instruct your students to work by themselves in your classes? _____	5 4 3 2 1 0
11.	Do you allow your students to work with a friend during classes? _____	5 4 3 2 1 0
12.	Do you provide learning tasks for small groups of students?_____	5 4 3 2 1 0
13.	Are there possibilities for your students to work within team projects in class? _	5 4 3 2 1 0
14.	Are you closely controlling your students' school or classwork? _____	5 4 3 2 1 0
15.	Do you tend to step back and become the facilitator of your students' learning? _____	5 4 3 2 1 0
16.	Are your students required to sit still during the learning process? _____	5 4 3 2 1 0
17.	Do you allow your students to stand up, stretch or move around while they are listening to you or learning something difficult? _____	5 4 3 2 1 0
18.	Do you do energizing exercises (like Brain Gym® or cross-overs) with your students in class to help them concentrate better? _____	5 4 3 2 1 0
19.	Are your students generally allowed to eat, nibble or drink water during class?_	5 4 3 2 1 0
20.	Do you get annoyed when your students chew on pens, pencils and other things while you teach?_____	5 4 3 2 1 0
21.	Do you suggest that students should have their 'most difficult' subjects during morning hours while they are fresh? _____	5 4 3 2 1 0
22.	Are you aware that your students' learning ability is influenced by their bio-rhythm (their best time of day)?_____	5 4 3 2 1 0

1. The way you learn is the way you teach

As we have mainly dealt with learning, information intake, retention and academic achievement of students, it is now time to consider the people who 'deliver' the learning methods – <u>teachers</u> and <u>educators</u>. We have to ask the question whether the personal <u>learning styles</u> of these professionals <u>influence the way they teach</u>, interact with their students, and shape the expectations they have of their students' performance. From my work with thousands of teachers over the past ten years and the data collection from their LSA and TSA results it is quite obvious that virtually <u>everybody teaches through their own learning style</u> because this is the only way they know how and their brain feels comfortable with.

teachers & educators

their learning styles influence their teaching

everybody teaches through own learning style

Whether teachers like it or not, the fact is: the way you learn is the way you teach because what makes sense in your own brain must make sense to everyone else, particularly students, you think. Unfortunately that is not so. Although there are quite a few students whose learning styles match their teachers' learning/teaching styles, there are <u>many more students</u> whose style needs are <u>totally different from their teachers' styles</u> and that's where the trouble begins, as we have already seen in Chapter 5 and will see even more clearly soon.

many students have totally different styles from their teachers

It is also not hard to understand that learning styles equal teaching styles because the strategies which made students successful in their learning during their own studies are of course later being used when these students become teachers. It is very interesting to note that most people who choose teaching as their profession do it for the simple reason that they love learning, have usually been successful learners and love to pass on knowledge to the next generation – in their own way. We all know how these mechanisms can work brilliantly between pupil and teacher (between master and student in the old days) when there is a <u>style match</u> or when the <u>teacher knows</u> about <u>style differences</u> and is capable of being <u>flexible</u> in the teaching methods used. We all have probably fond memories of our <u>favourite teachers</u> which last a lifetime. Whenever such a situation occurs, learning just

style match, or teacher knows style differences or is flexible

favourite teachers

TSA-Ed Model

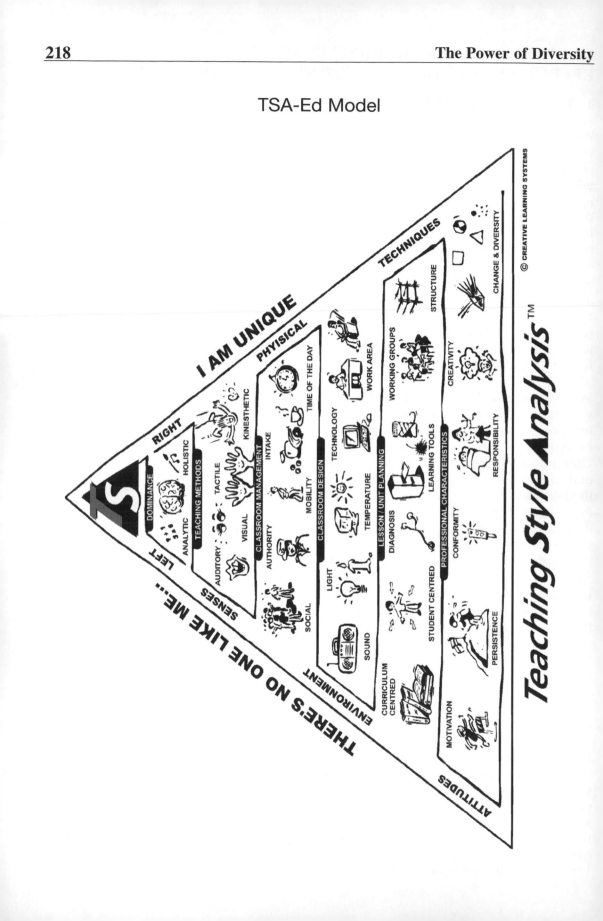

happens naturally; it is joyful, highly satisfactory and always leads to success for both sides.

One might think this is the way learning and teaching in our system should always happen, but we all know how often these processes can be disastrous for everyone concerned, and how much despair, frustration, stress and ill feelings are involved when <u>teaching goes wrong</u> because the main reasons are ....

teaching goes wrong

2. The TSA-Ed – a professional development tool

After we had developed a highly reliable and useful tool to assess students' learning styles, it became clear that we needed an instrument which would reveal how <u>teachers deliver the curriculum</u>, but more importantly, how they come across under pressure, how they <u>interact with their students</u> and what they expect in learning and teaching. Like the LSA, this instrument is also based on a pyramid model, has most of the elements of the LSA and consists of graphs, detailed personal reports and an action plan. (See pages 216–224.)

teachers deliver the curriculum
interact with their students

For each graph there is an in-depth description of the person's general and personal results, and an <u>action plan</u> can be completed for each sector wherever changes are desired. The <u>monitoring system</u> at the end is a valuable help for implementing the selected new strategies on a daily basis through which personal progress can be monitored and <u>techniques adjusted</u>.

action plan

monitoring system

techniques adjusted

It was created as a professional self-development tool for <u>practising educators</u>. Since the launch of the TSA-Ed instrument thousands of teachers have gone through the questionnaire and discussed and compared their style features with colleagues and friends. Many have reported that once they became aware of certain techniques they were often (over)using, they endeavoured to learn about <u>new techniques</u> and began to consciously use different teaching strategies much more <u>based on the learning needs of their students</u>. This has also helped them to become more flexible in their approaches, accepting <u>diversity in the classroom</u> more and reducing stress. More and more educators are becoming aware that instructional methods of the

practising educators

new techniques

based on the learning needs of their students
diversity in the classroom

TSA-Education
Personal Profile

 **TSA - Ed**

Graph 1: Teaching Style

	traditional / analytic	flexible / adaptable	individualistic / holistic
1A. TEACHING METHODS			
auditory: listening	−30 to −10		
auditory: discussing			+30 to +50
auditory (internal): self-talk			+30 to +50
visual: reading			+30 to +50
visual: observing			+30 to +50
visual (internal): imagination			+15 to +30
tactile: hands-on			+20 to +35
kinesthetic (external): physical			+15 to +30
kinesthetic (internal): feeling			+30 to +50
1B. MANAGEMENT STRATEGIES			
social: alone			+15 to +30
social: pairs			+30 to +50
social: peers			+30 to +50
social: teams			+30 to +50
energizing exercises			+30 to +50
authority and control		−5 to +10	
movement and mobility			+30 to +50
intake awareness			+25 to +40
time of day awareness		+10 to +25	
1C. CLASSROOM ENVIRONMENT			
temperature awareness			+35 to +50
light levels	−30 to −10		
work area / design		+5 to +20	
technology			+20 to +35
music / sound		0 to +15	
1D. PLANNING TECHNIQUES			
curriculum-centred	−15 to 0		
student-centred			+30 to +50
diagnosis / assessing styles	−20 to −5		
learning tools		0 to +15	
student grouping: alone		+5 to +20	
student grouping: small groups			+30 to +50
student grouping: whole class	−50 to −30		
set structure		+5 to +20	

Scale: −50, −40, −30, −20, −10, 0, +10, +20, +30, +40, +50

past are no longer appropriate because they make it impossible for many students to develop their full learning potential. During the past 25 years, research has shown how it is possible to teach students of all ages either by <u>matching their individual styles</u> or by teaching them to teach themselves by <u>finding out their preferences</u> and capitalizing on their <u>personal learning style strengths</u>. This simple concept explains why some children perform well in school and others – often from the same family – do not, or fail altogether. Research also explains how boys' and girls' learning styles differ and why some children learn to read early and very well, and others do not.

matching individual styles
finding their preferences
personal strengths

3. Mismatches between teaching and learning styles

Results from schools in New Zealand, Switzerland and Sweden show very clearly a <u>mismatch</u> between <u>teaching methods</u> based on teachers' styles and <u>students' learning needs</u> as the group profiles reveal on the opposite page. The biggest mismatches are generally in the areas of <u>kinesthetic and tactile</u> preferences, as well as the need for <u>mobility</u> which teachers often do not share, particularly with their younger students. Another striking mismatch is the need for <u>sound in students,</u> particularly among male teenagers, and the need for a <u>quiet</u> learning and teaching <u>environment among teachers</u>. The same is true for <u>low light levels</u> which many <u>students</u> prefer, and <u>brightly lit classrooms</u> which <u>teachers</u> prefer. An expected and, through American research, well-documented mismatch is the fact that teachers are much <u>more auditory than their students</u>, which has lead to the age-old complaint by teachers that their students just don't listen! There is of course a widespread difference in attitudes between teachers and their many students, particularly among under achievers. Results show that <u>adolescent students</u> these days are much more <u>non-conforming</u>, show <u>less persistence</u> when it comes to difficult learning tasks, and are of course <u>less responsible</u> than their teachers. However, highly successful students show a much greater match in their learning style features with their teachers, and that's probably one of the reasons why they do so much better at school.

mismatch between
teaching methods
students' learning needs

kinesthetic & tactile
mobility

sound for students,
quiet environment
for teachers
students: low light
teachers: brightly lit

teachers more auditory
than students

adolescent student
more non-conforming
less persistence
less responsible

TSA-Education
Personal Profile

 **TSA - Ed** _____ **Sample five**

Graph 2: Brain Dominance

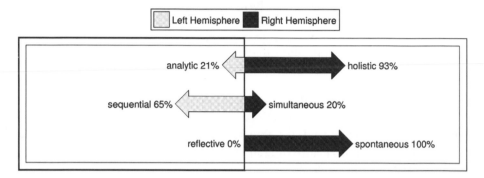

Left Hemisphere   Right Hemisphere

analytic 21%   holistic 93%

sequential 65%   simultaneous 20%

reflective 0%   spontaneous 100%

Graph 3: Professional Characteristics

low   flexible   high

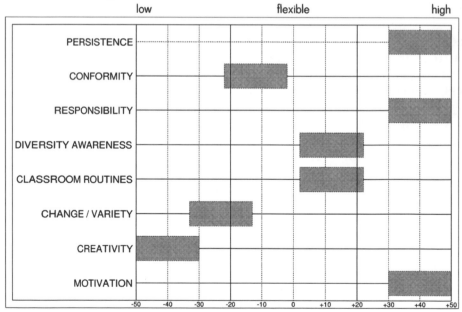

	-50	-40	-30	-20	-10	0	+10	+20	+30	+40	+50
PERSISTENCE											
CONFORMITY											
RESPONSIBILITY											
DIVERSITY AWARENESS											
CLASSROOM ROUTINES											
CHANGE / VARIETY											
CREATIVITY											
MOTIVATION											

Please note: the graph above shows elements that can be influenced or changed. If the score is in the FLEXIBILE area, it means that attitudes can change according to the situation.

In addition to all the above-mentioned mismatches between teaching and learning styles there is one which causes endless frustration, conflict, and often serious trauma, resulting in loss of motivation, low self-esteem and finally the inability to learn with success. It is the profound difference between analytic, left-brain oriented teachers and holistic, right-brain oriented students, and all the related style features described in Chapter 5 and explained in detail from page 127 onwards. For positive attitudes towards school and lifelong learning strategies such a mismatch can prove fatal because we now know beyond the shadow of a doubt that young children, primary school pupils and under-achievers are much more holistic in their thinking than their teachers or their older and/or successful fellow students. Analytic, step-by-step teaching based on logic and consistency is confusing for holistic students who need to know WHY they have to learn things, who need to see the big picture, and for whom feeling good is the most important aspect about learning.

analytic, L/B teachers holistic, R/B students

fatal mismatch

young children, pupils & underachievers ~ holistic

analytic teaching, logic & consistency is confusing for holistic students

feeling good ~ most important in learning

Whenever we get results from assessing teachers' working/learning styles and compare them with their students' learning style needs it saddens me to see how strongly analytic most teachers are in their thinking (and teaching), not only at university level where we have also seen grave mismatches between the styles of lecturers and their students, but particularly in primary schools where these analytic teachers really struggle to teach their highly holistic pupils – pupils who need variety, movement and an informal work area, whereas teachers try to instill routine, have them sit quietly in rows of desks, and cut out individuality as much as possible. A similar scenario can be observed in high schools where teachers have long given up on underachievers. But teachers cannot be blamed solely for this unsatisfactory situation. I believe they all do their best with the knowledge and the means they have and they all have been trained, like me, in a system that requires uniformity, rewards formal teaching methods and expects conformity. They have never really been trained to recognize individual learning needs, to accept individuality and capitalize on diversity in the

most teachers strongly analytic thinkers

highly holistic pupils

underachievers

system ~ uniformity rewards formal teaching expects conformity

TSA-Education

Results and Action Plan from TSA Profile

△ _TSA - Ed_   **Sample five**

1B. MANAGEMENT STRATEGIES

This graph describes your management strategies in the classroom which are often based on your personal experiences during your own schooling. It reveals how you manage the physical and social learning needs of your students.

YOUR PERSONAL SCORE

> Your current management strategies seem to be already very individualistic/holistic and you are acutely aware of your students' individual learning needs in class. Congratulations! Given your high awareness in this area combined with learner-centred management techniques you tend to use in your classroom, it should be easy for you to notice changes in your students' energy levels, alertness, responsibility and learning motivation. You have already developed a variety of approaches and know when to use them and for whom. Please keep up the good work!

A few questions worth considering:
Do you allow your students to work in groups, with a friend, or do they mostly learn alone?
Do you build in energizing exercises when you notice your students are tired?
Are you the ultimate authority in the classroom and do you look over their shoulders, or do you allow your students to learn in their own way?
Can you accept that some of your students can concentrate better while they move around and that not everyone can sit still for lengthy periods of time?
Do you allow them to drink water or nibble on something healthy while you are teaching them?
Are you aware that students have different time preferences for learning new and difficult content and that the morning hours are not the best time for many students to concentrate on new and difficult learning content?

MY SELF-ENHANCEMENT ACTION PLAN 1B:

1. **WHAT** can I do to improve my Classroom Management Strategies? (my **GOAL**)
2. **HOW** will I do this? (my **ACTION**)
3. **WHEN** will I take concrete action to move closer to matching my students' learning needs with my teaching strategies? (my **TIME FRAME**)

IN CLASS:

1. WHAT?_____
    _____

2. HOW?_____
    _____

3. WHEN?_____
    _____

IN PLANNING:

1. WHAT?_____
    _____

2. HOW?_____
    _____

3. WHEN?_____
    _____

classroom. The main thrust of all Western education systems has been, and still is, uniformity in class, information dissemination, and assessing/recording results. <u>Learning outcomes</u>, goals and objectives are still <u>more important than the learning process</u>.

learning outcomes still more important than the learning process

That's why I am working so avidly to spread the word with the help of so many teachers who are already experiencing the magic of learning styles, who now know there is a better way and who are achieving incredible results never thought possible. How do they do it? All it takes is some professional training, some goodwill, a lot of practice and a skilful combination to experience teaching success.

4. How to increase motivation and professional skills

Teachers, principals, administrators and managers in virtually all Western countries are suffering from <u>heavy workloads</u> due to changes in their present educational systems and radical new curriculum developments, causing severe <u>stress and burnout</u>.

heavy workloads

stress & burnout

However, instead of having staff in schools who out of <u>despair and frustration</u> often fit into the categories of Traditionalist ('good ol' days'), Do Nothings (retired on the job), Verbal Abusers, By-the-Book Bureaucrats, Meeting Dominators, Narrow-Minded Nit Pickers, Chronic Complainers, Blind Followers, Sceptics, Sarcastics, and Cynical Inflexibles, institutions could have competent people on their staff who <u>feel at ease</u> with the demands made on them, honestly <u>love the work they do</u>, and who are <u>open to change</u>.

despair & frustration

**feel at ease
love their work
open to change**

A simple four-step plan based on matching styles can bring about enhanced collaboration, increased productivity, <u>better skills</u>, improved performance among teaching and administration staff, greater <u>job satisfaction</u>, more pride and higher motivation for everyone.

better skills

job satisfaction

Many schools in New Zealand have already gone through this programme or are in the process of retraining their staff by following this plan, which

DISC Model

The DISC Model suggests that people generally display one of the four basic behavioural styles

DOMINANCE:
High Ds are interested in the new, the unusual and the adventurous. They love a challenge. They have one goal in mind – that is to make things happen – and happen now. When results are at stake, it brings out the best in them. They are great problem solvers and will work long hours, continually, until a tough problem is solved.

INFLUENCE:
High Is want to be liked and usually like others – sometimes indiscriminately. They have the ability to talk smoothly, readily and at length. They will not be overlooked, or uninvolved. Is are consistently trying to inspire you to their point of view.
They are great motivators and work well with people.

STEADINESS:
High Ss are generally easy-going and relaxed. They like to build a close relationship with a relatively small group of associates. Ss are usually very dependable, predictable and loyal. They operate well as members of a team and coordinate their efforts with others with rhythm and ease.

COMPLIANCE:
High Cs are humble, precise and will do whatever is expected of them to the best of their ability. They strive for a stable and orderly life and tend to follow procedures in both their business and personal life. They are systematic thinkers and workers, precise and attentive to details they perceive as important.

The DISC Model is based on the book *The Emotions of Normal People* by William Moulton Marston (1) and was computerized in the 1980s.
Presently there are 21 versions of various reports available, and DISC Reports can be ordered through *Creative Learning Company* (see Appendix II).

has also relevance for European schools as my
ongoing work shows in these regions.

Step I: Assessment
a. All teachers are assessed for their individual
    <u>learning style</u> with LSA (Adult Version) and   **learning style**
    their teaching style with the TSA-Education
    (<u>Teaching Style</u> Analysis)   **teaching style**
b. All board members are assessed for their
    <u>working style</u> with the WSA   **working style**
c. All administrators are assessed for their personal
    <u>administration style</u> with EFL (Administrator   **administration style**
    Version) Excellence for Learning – DISC. (2)

Step II: Information and Training
a. Discussions about different working, teaching
    and administration styles among all staff –
    learning to understand and <u>appreciate diversity</u>   **appreciate diversity**
b. Explanation of different profiles through
    trained facilitator, and considering practical
    ramifications of different styles for daily work
c. <u>Review</u> of administrators' and board members'   **review**
    styles with <u>management group</u>   **management group**
d. <u>Review of teachers' styles</u> and implications for   **teachers' styles**
    their classroom teaching
e. <u>Assessing students</u> in primary, intermediate   **assessing students**
    and secondary years with the LSA Jun. or Sen.
f. <u>Training teachers</u> in the use of the LSA and TSA   **training teachers**
    instruments and application of their results;   **explaining**
    explanation of students' learning style profiles   **students' LSA profiles**
    on an individual and group basis to students
    and <u>involving parents</u> in this process.   **involving parents**

Step III: Comparison and Planning
a. Comparing teachers' and administrators'
    <u>perceptions of each other</u>   **each others' perception**
b. <u>Comparing</u> main areas of their teaching style   **comparing**
    profiles as well as their learning, management
    and administration <u>styles</u>   **styles**
c. Working out strategies for <u>positive interaction</u>   **positive interaction**
    and <u>team building</u>   **team building**
d. Comparing students' and teachers' profiles
    using individual and group profiles
e. Planning for <u>in-service staff training</u>,   **in-service staff training**
    <u>meetings and projects</u> using strategies which   **meetings & projects**
    are suitable for different styles, which help
    with personal growth, which are motivational
    and enhance cooperation.

STAFF TRAINING IN STYLE

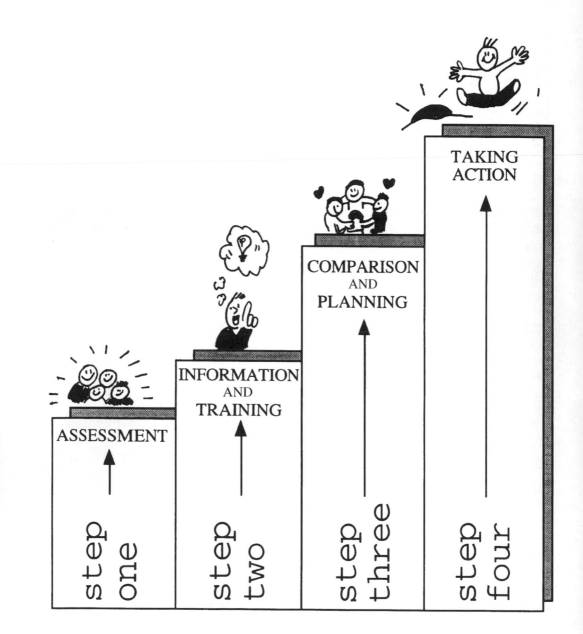

Step IV: Taking Action

a. Implementation of new strategies for staff
interaction, training and teaching methods;
classroom performance based on learning
styles and creative, accelerated learning

implementation

b. Compulsory management training for all
administration and board members, but
optional for teaching staff

management training

c. Monitoring increase in productivity and
performance of staff; carrying out
adjustments if necessary

monitoring

d. Documentation of positive changes among
staff and effects on students, parents and
the wider community. (For full change
programmes see pages 326 and 331).

documentation

When personality types are understood, diversity
in administration and management styles is
cherished rather than levelled out, teaching and
behavioural styles are matched with students'
learning styles in daily classroom situations, and
educators will experience less stress and burnout,
and more pride and job satisfaction. Principals and
administrators will be able to do their high-pressure
jobs with greater effectiveness, and the community
at large will be more satisfied with the services
provided by educational institutions.

**teaching & behavioural
styles matched
with learning styles**

job satisfaction & pride

greater effectiveness

If we accept that no two human beings learn
the same information at the same time the same
way, we also have to accept that, if schools
introduce learning styles and individualized
instruction, all students have a much greater
chance to fully develop their learning potential,
despite social, economic, gender, ethnic, and/or
cultural differences.

**greater chance to
fully develop
learning potential**

These are truly revolutionary thoughts compared
to traditional views that 'learning disabilities and
underachievement are facts of life which can't be
changed' as one high school principal put it
so succinctly. Although these new concepts might
sound as if a revolution was about to happen, I
know from experience that wherever learning styles,
student-centred teaching and creative, accelerated
learning (so-called holistic teaching methods) are
being introduced, it is rather an evolutionary process
because of resistance being encountered on the way.

revolutionary thoughts

evolutionary process

The reason is that human beings seem to <u>respond to change</u> in the way Arthur Schopenhauer described it so well: (3)

respond to change

'All truth goes through three stages:
at first it is ridiculed,
then it is violently opposed,
and finally it is accepted as self-evident.'

Looking at the illustration on the opposite page, reflect on changes your organization has already undergone and how you and other people responded, particularly when the change or 'truth' was unwelcome. Or think about the changes you have gone through in your private life and how you reacted before you were capable of seeing the 'truth' and welcoming the change.

For our own, our children's sake and for the sake of the many adults who are still carrying <u>negative memories of learning</u> through their lives, let's hope that this particular truth – accepting, <u>appreciating</u>, and catering for <u>human diversity</u> in any <u>learning or working process</u> – will be widely accepted sooner rather than later.

negative memories of learning
appreciating
human diversity in learning and working

5. Secrets of successful teaching – flexibility and matching styles

From whatever has been said about better teaching, learning styles, student-centred approaches and individualised instructions, there are two more aspects which will not remain secrets any longer:

1. <u>Matching students' learning styles</u> with the <u>appropriate teaching styles</u> will always lead to successful interaction between teachers and their students, and result in improved learning outcomes.

matching students' styles with teaching styles

2. <u>High flexibility</u> for achieving genuine style matches is maybe more important, and teachers need to be confident in choosing their methods and strategies, and must be prepared to try something else when the usual methods don't work. But this 'something else' should not be trial and error, but based on a sound knowledge of students' learning style needs. But isn't that what teachers are supposed

high flexibility of teachers

TSA - Ed

Group Percentages

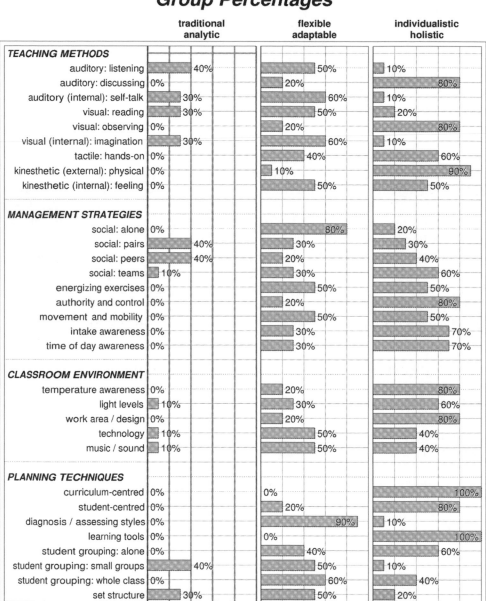

	traditional analytic	flexible adaptable	individualistic holistic
TEACHING METHODS			
auditory: listening	40%	50%	10%
auditory: discussing	0%	20%	80%
auditory (internal): self-talk	30%	60%	10%
visual: reading	30%	50%	20%
visual: observing	0%	20%	80%
visual (internal): imagination	30%	60%	10%
tactile: hands-on	0%	40%	60%
kinesthetic (external): physical	0%	10%	90%
kinesthetic (internal): feeling	0%	50%	50%
MANAGEMENT STRATEGIES			
social: alone	0%	80%	20%
social: pairs	40%	30%	30%
social: peers	40%	20%	40%
social: teams	10%	30%	60%
energizing exercises	0%	50%	50%
authority and control	0%	20%	80%
movement and mobility	0%	50%	50%
intake awareness	0%	30%	70%
time of day awareness	0%	30%	70%
CLASSROOM ENVIRONMENT			
temperature awareness	0%	20%	80%
light levels	10%	30%	60%
work area / design	0%	20%	80%
technology	10%	50%	40%
music / sound	10%	50%	40%
PLANNING TECHNIQUES			
curriculum-centred	0%	0%	100%
student-centred	0%	20%	80%
diagnosis / assessing styles	0%	90%	10%
learning tools	0%	0%	100%
student grouping: alone	0%	40%	60%
student grouping: small groups	40%	50%	10%
student grouping: whole class	0%	60%	40%
set structure	30%	50%	20%

Please note: the above graph shows the percentage of selected group members in all three categories, adding up to 100%.

to do anyway, you might ask. Supposed maybe, but very few teachers are actually flexible enough to <u>change their methods according to their students' learning needs</u> because most teachers have a very limited repertoire of teaching methods – remember, they have all been trained by the same analytical system – and when the few well-known strategies don't work, they are soon at their wits' end, blaming everyone and everything else for their students' failure and finally give up on them.

change methods according to students' learning needs

Another reason for this unfortunate situation is the fact (again based on research findings and our own experiences in data collection) that <u>teachers</u> are among the <u>least flexible people</u> of all professional groups. The majority have <u>very strong preferences</u> based on analytic, <u>left-brain dominance</u>, paired with very <u>strong beliefs</u> about what's right and wrong in learning. They find it very hard to flex and adjust, prefer to stay with what they know, even when this knowledge is outdated, and generally <u>resist change</u>. Often I hear from cynical teachers that there is no need for them to change because their methods have been around for the last 150 years, have worked for many students and if someone has to change it is surely the students who should get their act together! This is a very regrettable state of mind, far more often found among high school and university teachers than among primary school educators. This attitude needs to change because too many <u>students</u> really <u>suffer from</u> such <u>inflexibility</u> and are often lost for good from lifelong learning. For those of you who have already accepted the notion that everyone can learn, you will agree that this is a standpoint that is no longer acceptable.

teachers
least flexible people, have very strong preferences, are left-brain dominant have strong beliefs

resist change

students suffer from teachers' inflexibility

Teachers who are now working with learning styles realize that it is they who have to be the <u>most flexible person in class</u>.

teacher has to be most flexible person in class

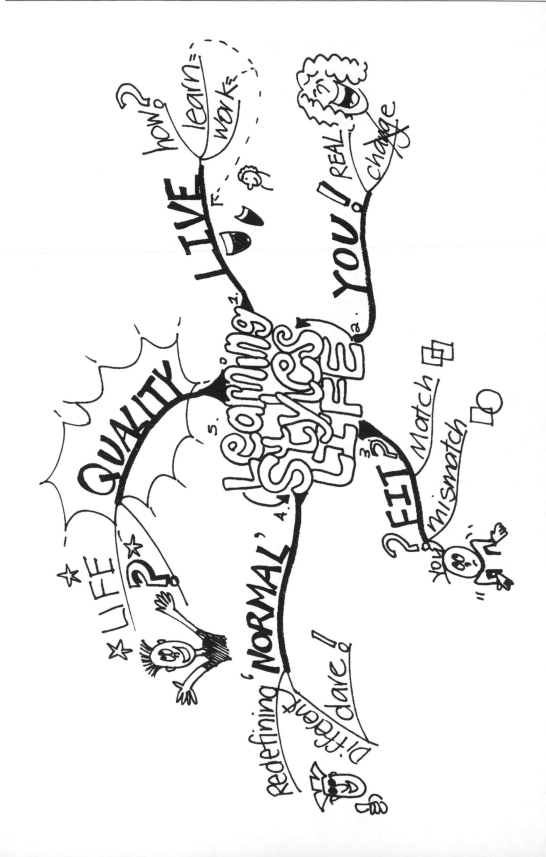

1. How you learn and work is how you live

From our investigation into <u>style differences</u> in the areas of learning, teaching, working, stress management, communication and partner choice, it is already more than obvious that the way we do things doesn't end here – style differences go far beyond that. It is appropriate to say that learning and working styles are not only that – they are really <u>life styles</u>. The main differences are once again the basic ones: <u>analytics, holistics and flexibles</u>. No matter how well you play roles in your work environment, when you go home you either slip into another role and act out another style, or most of the time you revert back to your true style. It is easy to imagine how (when not understood and appreciated) these <u>style differences cause problems</u> on a daily basis, not only in the workplace, but also between partners and among family members.

style differences

life styles
analytics, holistics,
flexibles

style differences
can cause problems

Just consider this:
• Are you a person who needs lots of stimulation which you get by creating dramas at home, by causing disruptions with people at work or by pursuing somewhat dangerous hobbies?

• Or are you the type who doesn't like to socialize very much, enjoys sitting quietly at home reading a good book and gets stressed out at work when no one else does?

Style differences based on <u>left/right-brain processing</u> deeply affect even seemingly unimportant aspects of our daily lives, like:

left/right-brain processing

• <u>cooking</u>: <u>analytics</u> usually need a <u>cookbook</u> and follow recipes very diligently; <u>holistics</u> usually <u>throw together something creative</u>, unable to repeat the same dish twice;

cooking
analytics – use cookbook
holistics
throw something together

• squeezing the <u>toothpaste tube</u>: <u>analytics</u> always squeeze it from the end, <u>roll it up</u>, close the cap; <u>holistics</u> always <u>make a mess</u>, squeeze it from the middle, never roll it up and can't be bothered to put the cap on, which drives true analytics crazy;

toothpaste tube – analytics
roll it up
holistics – make a mess

STYLE DIFFERENCES
of strongly analytical/holistic people

- or consider shopping: analytics make shopping lists, plan every purchase and spend their money – even if they have lots of it – very wisely and never on unnecessary items; holistics, however, do all of that spontaneously; they loathe shopping lists, and when they do write one, they usually leave it at home, and they hardly ever know precisely where their money has gone. And so it goes on. The examples on the opposite page illustrate these situations and show you a more humorous view of style differences.

shopping – analytics make shopping lists

holistics – spontaneous loathe shopping lists

Reflect on your own relationships and you will realize the number of examples is endless. Marriages, the most committed form of relationships, go wrong when husband and wife fail to acknowledge, or resent, each other's complementary differences even after years of living together.

relationships

marriages
go wrong
fail to acknowledge, resent
complementary differences

So, what's the message in all that? You may have already guessed and it can't be said often enough: Know Thyself! It might sound like a paradox, but the better you know yourself, the more chances you have to understand others and the more likely it is that you will get on with them.

2. Some things never change – the real YOU

Increased self-knowledge will give you yet another advantage: you will realize who you really are, what makes you tick, what you can change and what you can't. By understanding your personal style features, your preferences, your flexibilities, your dislikes and even your intelligences more accurately, you will also realize what your core qualities are. These insights are particularly important when you are under stress or encounter adverse situations. Based on the unique way your brain works, you will always fall back into your basic style features under such conditions because your brain will go into survival mode. It has to, because under threat it cannot and will not consider options; all it will do is help you survive, whatever 'survive' might mean to you. And that can sometimes be a nasty surprise when you don't know the basic patterns

self-knowledge

core qualities

basic style features
brain goes
into survival mode

Most people live ...
in a very restricted circle
of their potential being.
They make use
of a very small portion
of their possible consciousness,
and of their soul's resources
in general,
Much like a man who,
out of his whole organism,
should get into a habit of using
only his little finger.

William James

of your behaviour, your thinking, learning or acting – in other words, your real YOU.

Let me illustrate this with the following example:

When things are going well, everything is to your liking, your needs are met and you can do things your way, you will most certainly feel comfortable, probably enjoy yourself and also be able to display flexibility when necessary and appropriate. You cruise along, are satisfied with your accomplishments, probably like yourself for that, you notice that you are in harmony with others, you are nice to them and they are nice to you. And then something happens – something unexpected and unpleasant, upsetting the whole pleasant scenario. Unless you are an incredibly balanced person or know yourself extremely well, you will notice that within a very short period of time – often within moments – your behaviour and your style changes, most often to the negative. In such situations people often display behaviour so very different from their usual one, and do or say things they later regret. These can be times when people hardly recognize their partners or workmates because all of a sudden they are so different from their usual self. Often they don't even recognize themselves, may get very upset and wonder what has got into them. These mechanisms can repeat themselves time and again, and people have no clue how to break their patterns.

Unless you learn what makes you tick and how your personal style features affect you in every situation, you have no chance of controlling your behaviour, let alone preventing your emotions control you. But when you know yourself, your core features, your strengths and weaknesses, your boundaries, your breaking points, you can develop strategies to prevent going over the edge because you know how you would react automatically if you didn't know yourself. Like it or not, some of your style features will never change, particularly your biological ones (see pages 74 and 76) as they are responsible for who you are. You'd better learn to live with them, use them to your advantage and capitalize on your strengths. Remember: you are a special human being with a unique brain and a unique style combination, and although you cannot control what happens to you, it's always in your power to control how you react.

controlling your behaviour or emotions control you

some style features will never change

who you are

capitalize on strengths

3. Match and mismatch – where do you fit?

There are at least three fatal consequences from not knowing your true style, being unaware of all your preferences: it affects your daily life, how you feel about yourself and how you

three consequences

affects daily life, feel about self,

WORK SMARTER, NOT HARDER

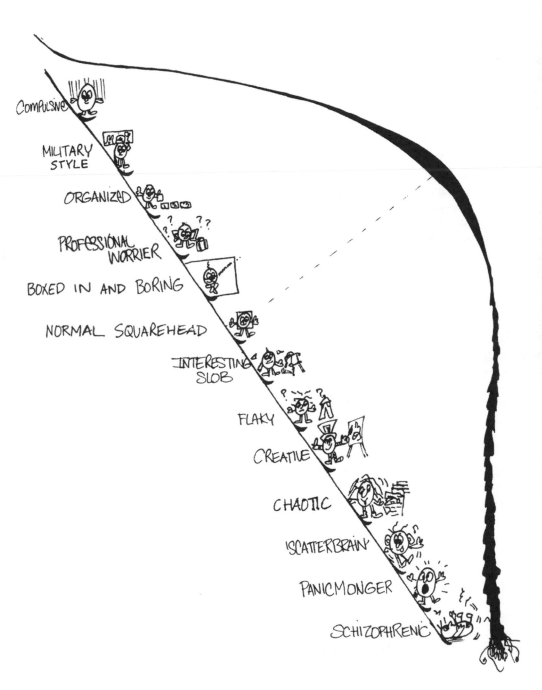

perform at work. It's a vicious circle: the more you suffer from these consequences, the more you are inclined to adopt different styles and play different roles in addition to your social roles.

work performance

By not knowing what your real strengths and preferences are, you will often unconsciously try to fit into other people's requirements and do things *their way* which might not be *your way*. That's very often the reason why so many people in their jobs lose motivation, or despair at tasks they think they can't do.

not knowing strengths and preferences

their way not your way

The following example illustrates this process:

example

You might have experienced that you quite like doing a job or a difficult assignment but the way it has to be done, because 'that's the way we do things here', does not really suit you. You find it hard, so you try harder; you try out different roles, different approaches to get the task done, but despite all your efforts, it actually drives you crazy after a while. You are frustrated and feel stressed out. Then you either throw in the towel (if you can), get more miserable until the thing is finally over, or delegate it to someone else who probably experiences half the stress and might even enjoy doing the job you couldn't come to terms with!

way to be done

does not suit you

frustrated
stressed out

Your final conclusion is: you are not suited for such tasks, you'll never be able to do these things and you should probably change your job! WRONG! You just experienced a typical example of mismatched styles. It's not true that you were not suited to the job but your style was not compatible with the way the job was supposed to be done! It had nothing to do with your capability of carrying out the task; if it had been possible to do it *your way*, it might have been a lot easier and you might have enjoyed the process more.

not suited

change job

mismatched styles
your style
not compatible

capability

easier
more enjoyable process

The majority of people who leave their jobs don't do it because of their inability but out of frustration about the way they have to do it.

frustration

My Best Practices

**To become aware of your learning strategies,
your 'Best Practices', answer the following questions.
Take your time to really think and reflect.**

1. How I like to learn: _____

_____

2. Where I like to learn: _____

_____

3. When I like to learn: _____

_____

4. Why I learn: _____

_____

5. When I don't learn: _____

_____

6. What stops me from learning: _____

_____

When you <u>know your style</u> you can, most of the time, <u>work through your preferences</u> and avoid playing roles or following trial-and-error approaches; no longer do you have to do tasks the 'hard' way, no longer do you have to believe you are just not good at difficult jobs.

know your style
work through preferences

The more often you work with <u>mismatched styles,</u> the more you will come to believe that you are not good at anything, which means you will struggle to be <u>persistent in your work performance</u>. Due to its importance it's worth repeating: it is not your <u>lack of ability</u>, it is mainly a <u>mismatch</u> between your style and the way you are made to do a job (or learn, if you are a student). This is the reason why so many people become <u>successful after they leave</u> environments which didn't suit them any longer; they had outgrown the style of the organization they were in before – family, educational institution, large corporation, government body, etc. Finally they were allowed to do things their way and to their surprise it worked! If they had really <u>known their own style</u> and their true preferences <u>before they set out to do new things</u>, you can imagine how much easier it would have been to be <u>successful</u>.

mismatched styles

persistent in work
performance
no lack of ability
but mismatch

successful
after leaving

know own style
before doing new things

successful

Maybe you can relate to this story:

Just imagine a boy growing up with siblings in a family where strict rules and regulations are the norm. From an early age on it is obvious that this child is a 'misfit'. He struggles through school, leaves without qualifications, does not want to go to university as his parents had hoped and is also not interested in working in the family business. He doesn't get much support for his 'weird' ideas as his interests are totally different from all the other family members' interests; only his grandmother stands by him and helps him to follow his dream. With the help of his father he tries several jobs, but without success, and finally leaves home and his disappointed parents behind. His teachers have told him he'll never make it, never come to anything and his parents have finally given up on him. By travelling the world he gains life experience, saves some money and is finally able to realize his dream. Away from his family he experiences success based on his true talents and he becomes rich and famous. Everyone who knew him as a child can hardly believe his transformation – only his grandmother, who always believed in his special gifts, who always said 'I know it, one day you'll make it,' would not have been surprised if she could have lived to see his success; she always knew.

Do you know of people who have had similar experiences?

Graph 2. Conditioned / Learned Elements

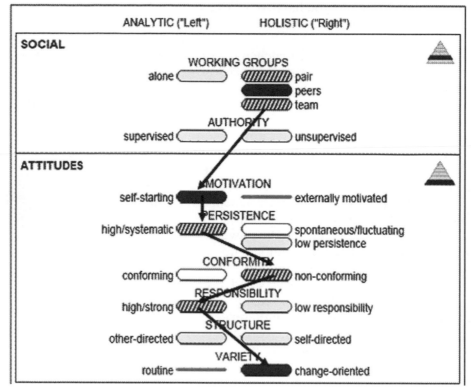

ATTENTION:
Currently you seem to experience an **INTERNAL CONFLICT** based on the following COMBINATIONS OF ATTITUDES:
self-starting/non-conforming/strong responsibility/change-oriented

You might need to re-assess your present work situation, what's required of you in your daily work and whether it fits with your values and beliefs. Read through your Personal Report describing your Attitudes and find out where the reasons for your conflicts lie. A well thought-through Action Plan can help you achieve the desired changes or necessary improvements.

If a zig-zag line can be drawn between preferences and strong preferences in Graph 2, this is a strong indication of an inner conflict of a conflict with the system this person has to work under.

4. 'Learned analytics' and inner conflicts

Over the years I have become more aware of certain style combinations, particularly in Graph 2 of people's **style combinations** WSA profiles. For a long time we were not quite sure what that meant, but during many business seminars, coaching sessions and discussions about the way people fit or don't fit into systems, we discovered the **fit into systems or not** following: the majority of people are more holistic **majority is holistic** and right-brain dominant in their information intake, problem solving and thinking, however, the systems **but systems require** they have to work under require analytic, **analytic approaches** sequential approaches.

This in itself would not matter if human beings could easily switch between these two modes, but only a **switch modes** minority of people can do that easily. So we learn to adjust: instead of following our 'gut' feeling, we use logical strategies, even if they don't make sense, don't feel good and don't lead to success. This conditoning starts early in school where step-by-step **early conditioning** learning is the norm and continues into working life where we are forced to fit into systems and do as we are told to keep our jobs.

A mismatch between the way many of us would like **mismatch** to learn or work and what we HAVE to do over longer periods of time always leads to frustration, under **frustration** performance, stress, and burnout. The first signs are **stress and burnout** uneasiness, yet we disregard that and continue until our inner conflict becomes unbearable or the conflict **inner conflict** with 'the system' escalates and we get results like the one opposite. The more pronounced we can draw a zig-zag line, the stronger this conflict is and often **zig-zag line** leads to resignation, quitting a job or giving up on **strong conflict** studying altogether.

One could say that 'learned' analytics can be very flexible in adjusting their abilities to requirements but once stretched beyond a certain point, they often cannot continue physically because their health is suffering. **health suffers** This is the point where people change jobs, migrate or turn their life upside down. To make this process easier or less traumatic, our LSA and WSA instruments can be used as reliable predictors and have saved many people unnecessary pain in recognizing the early **early warning signs** warning signs of style mismatch. **of style mismatch**

Do you have a zig-zag line in your Graph 2?

'*The qualities that make for a happy and genial life*

are these: a small estate with fruitful vineyards,

a fire to curtail the rigours of winter, a contented

mind, a strong and healthy body, frankness tempered

by tact, congenial associates, happy guests, a table

spread with simple viands, wine not in excess but

enough to drive away care, yet virtuous with all,

sound sleep to make dark hours fly, no longing

for change, just contentment with what you are,

no fear of death, nor yet a desire for it.'

Free quotation of an ancient Roman poet

5. Do you have a quality life?

When we are born we do not know what the basic
components of a quality life are – survival, love, fun,
personal power, freedom – but we all are capable
of knowing what feels good, what feels bad and the
difference between the two. Immediately after birth,
we become aware that it is <u>better to feel good</u> than   **better to feel good**
bad and quickly learn that it feels good to eat
because all <u>survival behaviours feel good</u>. Almost   **survival behaviours**
immediately we also learn that it feels good to be   **feel good**
<u>loved</u> and, later, to love. Based on our ability to   **to be loved**
feel good, we also learn how important it is to <u>have</u>   **have fun, to be free**
<u>fun, to be free</u>, and to have some control over what
happens to us and around us, which is <u>power</u>.   **power**
Glasser maintains that these basic needs are built
into our genetic structure, and from birth we must
devote all our behaviour to attempt to satisfy them. (1)

Quality, therefore, is anything we experience that is
consistently satisfying one or more of these basic
needs. It is important to understand that <u>maintaining</u>   **maintaining**
the <u>quality of our lives</u> is so vital that for many of us   **quality of life**
it can become a matter of life and death. For example,
we are probably the only living creatures who, given
all the means of physical survival, still may choose
to <u>commit suicide</u> when we desperately feel lonely   **commit suicide**
or powerless. People still choose to die because
they believe the <u>quality of their life is so low</u>, and   **quality of life very low**
there is so <u>little chance it will improve</u>, that their   **little chance to improve**
existence is no longer tolerable and <u>death is a more</u>   **death a more**
<u>favourable option</u>. This is particularly tragic when   **favourable option**
young people have reached that conclusion, and
given the world's highest rate in teenage suicide in
New Zealand, there is obviously a dramatic lack of
what they perceive as quality in their lives. To help
prevent more of these sad incidents we need to look
at our own lives first and how we as parents and
educators can <u>create quality for ourselves</u> and at the   **create quality for**
same time for our <u>children</u> and students.   **ourselves and our children**

I invite you to honestly consider your own life and
check it out for the five <u>basic needs</u> constituting   **basic needs of quality life**
a <u>quality life</u>:

Five Basic Needs of a Quality Life

Survival

Love

Personal Power

Freedom

Fun

W Glasser

1. Is your <u>survival</u> guaranteed? Do you live in   **survival**
   physical, emotional, financial comfort?
2. Is there <u>love</u> in your life? Do you love and are   **love**
   you being loved? If not, how does it feel?
3. Do you have <u>personal power</u>? Can you control   **personal power**
   what happens to you and around you? And if
   not, how do you react?
4. Do you have <u>freedom</u> of choice, thought, action?   **freedom**
   Are you free to move, to speak, to be yourself?
5. Do you have <u>fun</u> on a daily basis? Are you able   **fun**
   to experience joy and delight regularly?

Based on Glasser's basic needs of a quality life, let's
consider the daily school life of students who struggle
in class, who experience frustration, boredom, failure
with all the related unpleasantries – do they still have
a <u>quality school life</u>?   **quality school life**

Please follow my train of thoughts from the most
elusive quality to the most basic one and ask yourself:
- Do they have <u>FUN</u> in class (not just during the   **fun**
  breaks)? Are they ENJOYING their lessons and
  teachers and are they DELIGHTED to go to school
  every day?
- Do they have <u>FREEDOM</u> to choose subjects,   **freedom**
  topics? And are they allowed to be themselves, to
  move while learning, to speak with classmates in
  working groups?
- Can they control what happens to them in class?
  Do they still have the <u>PERSONAL POWER</u> they   **personal power**
  had as a baby, as a young, adorable child?
- Do they feel <u>LOVED</u> by their teachers? (What a   **love**
  nonsense! Teachers are not there to love students,
  they are there to teach and test them!). Is there a
  loving feeling among students and teachers in
  their school?
- How do they <u>SURVIVE</u> the daily drag? Are they   **survival**
  physically comfortable during these many hours
  they have to spend in class (on hard chairs etc.)?
  And are they emotionally safe? Is there no bullying
  and is yours a '<u>caring</u>' school or a '<u>scary</u>' school?   **caring or scary school**
- You might be surprised by the obvious answers
  and how on these terms the <u>quality</u> of school life   **quality reduces from**
  <u>reduces</u> dramatically <u>between primary and</u>   **primary to high school**
  <u>secondary school</u>.

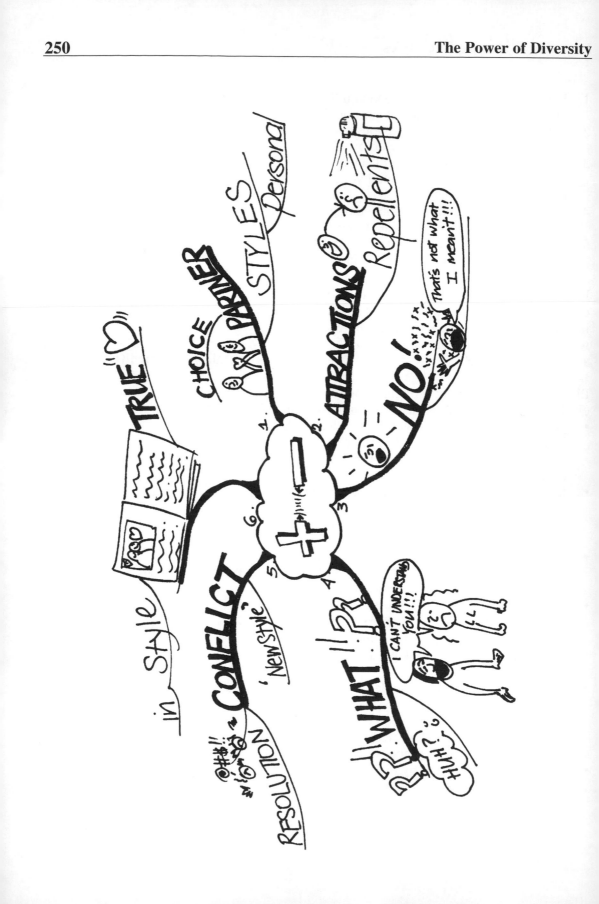

1. Partner choice and personal styles

The old saying 'opposites attract' could not be
more true when it comes to choosing a partner
for a personal relationship. It seems that we are
generally attracted to someone who has all
the style elements we either don't have ourselves
or would like to have. For business or working
relationships, however, a different pattern seems
to be true – we tend to choose people who are
rather similar in their working style. We can relate
to our colleagues and superiors much better
when they think and work like us. Significant
style differences in this area usually lead to
serious conflicts unless the two parties
respect and appreciate each other's diversity.

But for couples, different rules apply. Time and
again I have seen that both partners, though
compatible in many ways, display needs at the
opposite end of the scale in their individual
Working Style Analysis.

Although the following descriptions are very
general and there are many exceptions to these
rules, they are nevertheless widely applicable
to couples and often lead to misunderstandings:
she is an impulsive, holistic thinker, most of
the time following her intuitions and feelings,
he is a reflective analytic, usually going by
his logical mind and rationalizing everything;
he hardly ever feels the cold, she does; one is
a 'night owl', the other an 'early bird'; he needs
mobility and is kinesthetic/tactile, she prefers to
sit quietly and is more auditory/visual; one always
prefers noise and/or music when concentrating,
the other needs absolute quiet; and on it goes.
The combination of opposites is endless.

Let's leave it to psychologists to explain why we
feel attracted to our opposites. I can only advise
you what to do when these style features begin to
cause problems, which in the long run might, and
often do, cause the breakdown of the relationship.
With climbing divorce rates, increasing numbers
of single-parent families, and too many children

choosing a partner

**style elements we
would like to have**

**similar working style
with colleagues
think and work like us**

**serious conflict unless
respect diversity**

couples – different rules

display opposite needs

**impulsive, holistic
intuition and feelings
reflective, analytic
logical and rationalizing**

**night owl – early bird
kinesthetic/tactile
auditory/visual
noise, music
absolute quiet**

attracted to opposites

**can cause problems and
relationship breakdowns**

♀ ♂

DIFFERENCES

♂   ♀

♂	♀
Often detached	Often emotional
Often obsessed with sports	Sports less important
Talk mostly about 'things'	Talk mostly about 'people'
Less talkative in private	Less talkative in public
Take things literally	Look for hidden meanings
Less responsive listener	More responsive listener
Focus more on solutions	Like to discuss problems
Less willing to seek help	Seek help readily
Often seek conflict	Tend to avoid conflict
Fearful of commitment	Eager for commitment
More sadistic	More masochistic
More sex-oriented	More love-oriented
Have fewer close friends	Have many close friends
Less trusting	Often too trusting
Shop out of necessity	Often shop for enjoyment

Based on an original idea from *He & She – 60 Significant Differences*

Between Men & Women by Cris Evatt, 1992

coming from broken or reconstituted families, it is <u>more important than ever to understand our different styles</u>. It is not enough to accept them grudgingly. We need to <u>appreciate our diversity</u> and make it work to our advantage so that attractions don't become repellents. But what can we do?

important to understand different styles appreciate diversity

2. When attractions become repellents

In the <u>beginning of a relationship</u> we are usually fascinated by the way our chosen one behaves and goes about things because it's all <u>new and exciting</u>. We tend to appreciate, often glorify, style features we like and readily overlook the ones we are not too comfortable with. When the relationship continues and the initial firestorm has cooled off a little, you can bet that <u>real style differences</u> are now <u>surfacing slowly</u> but steadily. As you learn more about each other, you discover quite a few aspects which are so different that you get a little <u>concerned about your compatibility</u>. But you are still very much in love and you tell yourself that all these little '<u>bad habits</u>' will eventually <u>disappear</u> over time, that he or she will <u>change for the better</u>.

beginning of relationship

new and exciting

real style differences surface slowly

compatibility questioned

hope bad habits disappear or change for the better

Then something occurs which will remain a <u>mystery</u> for you if you don't know anything about styles: despite your attempts to <u>change</u> or 'fix' <u>your partner</u>, he or she stubbornly <u>remains more or less the same</u> and your <u>disillusionment</u> as well as disappointment <u>grows</u>.

mystery change or fix partner but remains the same disillusionment grows

The <u>diversity which had attracted you</u> to your partner in the first place begins to <u>cause further uneasiness</u>. You are amazed that many of these originally <u>fascinating features</u> have long <u>lost their attraction</u> and begin to bother you because they just <u>don't fit your style</u>. But you still love your mate very much, so you tell yourself again 'if I try harder <u>maybe he or she will change</u> and then we will be <u>totally compatible</u> and <u>really happy</u>'.

diversity attracted you causes uneasiness

fascinating features lost their attraction don't fit your style

will maybe change be totally compatible, really happy

As this unfortunately only happens in love stories,

DIFFERENCES – SIMILARITIES
in general

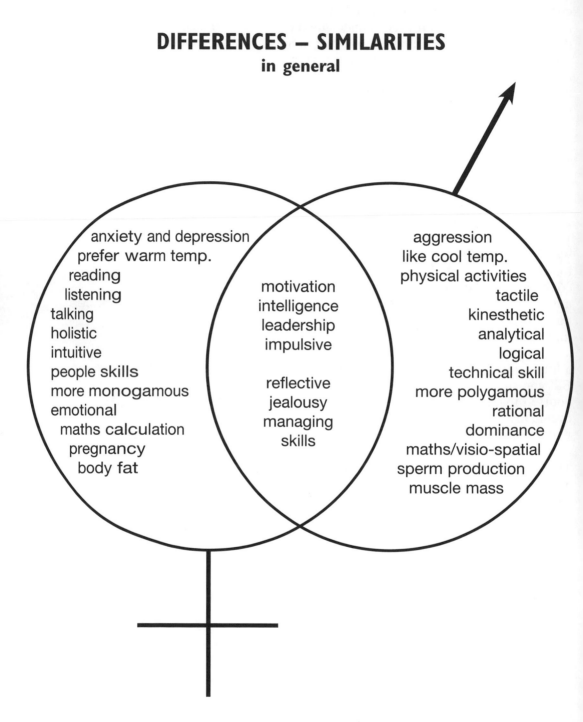

Left circle (♀):
anxiety and depression
prefer warm temp.
reading
listening
talking
holistic
intuitive
people skills
more monogamous
emotional
maths calculation
pregnancy
body fat

Overlap:
motivation
intelligence
leadership
impulsive

reflective
jealousy
managing
skills

Right circle:
aggression
like cool temp.
physical activities
tactile
kinesthetic
analytical
logical
technical skill
more polygamous
rational
dominance
maths/visio-spatial
sperm production
muscle mass

Relationships between men and women can be much more successful when
there is a recognition of inherent biological differences, a respect for one
another's diversity and a valuing of shared qualities. (1)

you are now entering the either sad or dramatic
stage of your relationship where these early
attractions have finally turned into repellents.
And like a disease they are slowly destroying
your love and compassion.

**early attractions
turned into repellents**

Here you have only two choices: either to leave
the relationship (something an ever-increasing
number of people do these days) or to stay, trying
to figure out what's going on, getting counselling
or just hanging in, hoping for the best. People
who leave usually follow the same patterns and
are bound to make the same mistakes in their new
partner choice until they begin to really understand
how diversity works. Those who stay often learn
to put up with less than acceptable situations,
believing it's their destiny to suffer.

two choices:

leave or stay

hoping for the best

make same mistakes

It could have been much easier had you just
known both your own and your partner's style,
respected each other's diversity, cherished your
compatibility, and worked to overcome your
differences so that you could truly complement
each other and grow together.

**much easier
partner's style
respected diversity**

**complement
grow together**

The great danger in not understanding
true style differences between partners is that
one is quick to judge different preferences as
something that should be changed for good, and
to misinterpret different behaviour as something
the other partner does to us on purpose to make
life harder. When we consider that particularly
biological style features of a human being
change very little over a lifetime, cannot be
altered easily by sheer will and seem to manifest
themselves as habits, it is not hard to comprehend
why we always fight a losing battle with
our partners by trying hard to change them,
improve them and fix them.

**not understanding
true style differences
misjudge preferences**

misinterpret behaviour

**biological features
change very little**

**become habits
fight losing battles
trying to change,
improve, fix them**

If you want a clearer picture about yourself in
this particular area, please look at the biological
style elements displayed on page 74, and mark
the ones which are true for you. Do it without
compromising, without considering present
circumstances, or taking into account how you
have to do things right now.

**biological
style elements**

We love each other's physical differences,
but we can only love each other's
differences of character, mind, values
and sensitivity once we actually
understand them.

There are thousands of marriages
beached on the bleak sands of
mutual incomprehension.

'Why on earth does he or she
react so differently from me?'

Moir and Jessel (1989)

Ask your <u>partner</u> to do the same if you wish,   **partner**
then <u>compare the results</u>. You might be surprised   **compare results**
by how many <u>differences</u> you have discovered   **differences**
and pleased to see in which <u>areas</u> you both
are <u>truly compatible</u>.   **truly compatible areas**

We can conclude the <u>mystery about attractions</u>   **mystery about attractions**
<u>becoming repellents</u> in following the thoughts   **becoming repellents**
so accurately expressed by Anne Moir and
David Jessel in their book *BrainSex*: 'It is hard to
understand nature's plan in arranging this <u>inherent</u>   **inherent**
<u>incompatibility</u> between the two sexes of the   **incompatibility**
species. Maybe if we all felt and thought alike
we would soon get bored with each other. But
sex would surely be less of a disaster area if these   **differences**
<u>differences were recognized and understood</u>.   **recognized and understood**
Science is doing what it can, by producing
the evidence that the minds of men and women
are different. The rest is up to us.' (2)

3. Males and females CAN communicate in style

Many books have been published over the past
few years describing <u>communication differences</u>   **communication differences**
between males and females, containing valuable
exercises and giving lots of advice on how to
<u>overcome these difficulties</u>.   **overcome difficulties**

These differences are already obvious in young
children, where <u>girls</u> are more '<u>person-centred</u>'   **girls – person-centred**
and <u>boys</u> are more '<u>thing-centred</u>'; these features   **boys – thing-centred**
carry on in adult communications, where <u>women</u>
<u>talk mostly about people</u>, their problems, reactions   **women talk about people**
and responses. Even when women talk about
careers these days, a great deal of these work-
related conversations are about people. <u>Men talk</u>   **men talk about**
mostly <u>about business, sports and politics</u>, often   **business, sports and**
about cars, gadgets and tools. They can discuss   **politics**
at length how things are made, how they work,
how to fix them and how they affect the world.
Many <u>men get irritated</u> by women's highly   **men get irritated**
personal subject matters, and many <u>women are</u>   **women are bored**
<u>bored</u> by male topics and cannot understand
how someone can get excited about a car engine
or results in sports competitions. (3)

Conflict Resolution
'NewStyle'

*Remember at least three conflicts you had in the past
and try to find answers to the following questions:*

1.   How did these conflicts start?

_____

_____

_____

_____

_____

2.   Who or what fuelled them?

_____

_____

_____

_____

_____

(Continued on page 260)

The answers to these questions and your knowledge about diversity should
give you a clear insight into your patterns and how to avoid them in future.

The book with the same title as the heading of
this sub-chapter by Deborah Tannen explains so
brilliantly that growing up in different parts of a
country, having different ethnic and class back-
grounds, even age and individual personality,
all contribute to <u>different conversational styles</u>
which can cause disappointment, hurt and blame.
Very appropriately for the differences between
male and female talking patterns, she describes
that <u>male–female conversations</u> are always <u>cross-</u>
<u>cultural communication</u>. By culture she means
the combination of habits and patterns acquired
from past experiences because boys and girls
grow up in different worlds, even if they grow
up in the same house, and as adults they 'live'
in different worlds, reinforcing patterns
established in childhood. (4) We also have to
do away with the conventional wisdom and
'common sense' making us believe that the
<u>more time people spend together,</u> <u>the better</u> they
will <u>understand each other</u>. If you don't know
yourself and your partner's style – not only in
conversation but also in learning, working and
living – you will not be able to overcome the
<u>differences</u> which attracted you in the first place.

The <u>failure to communicate</u> is one of the basic
facts of life. Given our new understanding about
<u>style differences</u> women need no longer complain
about men's lack of communication, because
men's brains are structured that way. And yet,
she truly wants him to express himself, *he* wishes
she wouldn't press him. In the book *BrainSex*
a <u>familiar male complaint</u> is described and a
contrasting <u>female viewpoint</u> given: "'She always
says I don't talk to her. I don't understand.
I am sure she knows what I'm thinking but that
isn't good enough for her." ... "Sometimes
he listens, but he hardly ever talks to me. It's hard
to talk to a drunk, and yet it's the only time he
shows me any real feelings." Alcohol breaks down
the barriers between the discrete compartments
of the male brain.' (5) Physiologically speaking,
in the female brain, the centres of reason and
emotion are more closely connected. Therefore

**different
conversational styles**

**male–female conversations
always cross-cultural
communication**

**more time together –
better understanding
of each other**

differences

failure to communicate

style differences

**familiar male complaint
female viewpoint**

Conflict Resolution 'NewStyle'

3.   *How did you feel during the conflict?*

_____

_____

_____

_____

_____

4.   *What did you think about your counterpart(s)?*

_____

_____

_____

_____

_____

5.   *Who or what terminated the conflict?*

_____

_____

_____

_____

_____

The answers to these questions and your knowledge about diversity should give you a clear insight into your patterns and how to avoid them in future.

she is better equipped to analyse, rationalize and
verbalize her emotions. Something many of us
have long known intuitively is now finally being
acknowledged by scientists: the fact that male
and female brains work differently.

verbalize emotions

**male and female brains
work differently**

Taking all the obvious and not so obvious male
and female differences into account, I believe
knowing one's personal style, true preferences
and brain processing functions should be the
starting point for any attempt to try to understand
diversity and deal with differences. It just makes
any human interaction so much more successful
and takes the guessing out of the process.

**knowing one's personal
style**

**makes human interaction
more successful**

Eric Jensen, in his book *The Learning Brain*, has
a whole section called 'Sex and Gender' in which
he sums it up very nicely: 'Males and females truly
live in a different world created by the processing
of very different sensory information.' (6)

**different world processing
of different sensory
information**

4. Conflict resolution 'NewStyle'

Most of the stress in major relationships stems
from the misconception that men and women
are essentially the same. That's the reason
why *he* cannot understand why *she* spends
so much time agonizing over their relationship,
and *she* cannot comprehend why *he* spends
so much time tinkering with the car or working
and/or playing on his computer. Life would
be much easier if we only acknowledged how
different we are from each other.

**misconception
men and women the same**

agonizing over relationship

tinkering with the car

different from each other

Next time you encounter conflict of opinion,
dissatisfaction, impatience or miscommunication
with people at work or with your loved ones,
you can be sure it's due to style differences.
Practise some new approaches and surprise
the people around you with more flexibility
and greater understanding of different needs and
styles. You could respond to different styles either
by matching their style – which means you learn
to do things 'their way' even if it is not 'your way'
(this method will make you more flexible and is
usually a success recipe for creating great rapport

**conflict of opinion
dissatisfaction, impatience**

style differences

**more flexibility
greater understanding**

matching styles

make you more flexible

How MARTIANS (males) cope with stress

- become focused and withdrawn
- feel better by solving problems
- lose temporary awareness of everything else
- do not burden others with their own problems
- retreat, go quiet and find solutions
- do something else to forget problems
- become distant, forgetful, unresponsive
- on solving the problem become attentive again

How VENUSIANS (females) cope with stress

- become overwhelmed and emotionally involved
- feel better by talking about problems
- continue talking about logically unrelated problems, worries, frustrations
- openly talk about their problems and feelings
- share feelings of being overwhelmed
- need loving friends
- become emotionally involved in other people's problems
- by talking and being heard, the stress disappears

MARTIANS NEED TO:

- Listen without offering solutions
- Help solve problems without quick-fix attitude
- Feel trusted and appreciated

VENUSIANS NEED TO:

- Talk about their problems and feelings
- Accept without giving advice or criticism
- Have their feelings validated

Based on an idea from: *Men Are From Mars, Women Are From Venus* by John Gray, 1993

with the people around you) or you could do it
by showing <u>more love or compassion</u> for
the other person whose behaviour is different
from yours and up to now has often upset, even
outraged you, because you didn't understand
their style.

more love, compassion

You'll be pleased to discover how much <u>easier</u>
<u>interaction</u> on any level of a relationship will be
when you practise <u>conflict resolution 'NewStyle'</u>.
The exercises on pages 258 and 260 should help
you to make this change process more effective.
There is now a vast variety of books available
on this topic; the ones which are practical and
have helped me most are listed in the Bibliography
and Further Reading.

easier interaction

**conflict resolution
'NewStyle'**

5. A true love story in style – with a sad ending...

The 23 years of my second marriage are a glowing example of what happens if neither partner truly understands style differences and diversity. Had I known then what I know now about different styles and non-preferences, biological needs and diversity, I would have saved myself and my family a lot of money, disappointment, heartache and despair. I would have realized that our daily frustration and uneasiness came from misunderstanding and misinterpreting different brain processing styles which created adverse behaviour. But, as we have discovered, it is never too late to learn more about ourselves and different styles.

With love, tolerance and understanding we finally began to enjoy each other's diversity but this didn't happen until we both had our WSA and LSA profiles and sat down to compare them, element by element. Although we thought we had known each other, we got a real shock by discovering that I am naturally much more analytic than my husband! For all these years, particularly during highly emotional times, he had obviously found it very hard to be always logical, reflective ('cool, calm and collected') in our discussions because that was the way we generally interacted. I had no clue that he actually wanted to be much more spontaneous and carefree, which I often saw as just silly or irresponsible. As we both did not know ourselves as we could have, and were not used to communicating in matching styles, we got into arguments, verbal fights, bitterness, disappointments, the lot. The result was that we split up and were determined never to get back together again. But then, after a year and a half of separation, we started talking again – business only at first – and in this process we rediscovered our compatibilities, and with more insight into style differences we were also able to overcome mismatched areas of our styles with humour and we had learned to appreciate each other on a very different level. The deep love which had always been there can now blossom again in a very different climate, based on friendship and true understanding of human diversity.

Sadly it was not to last – my husband died after a short, tragic illness in April 2005 and I miss him dearly.

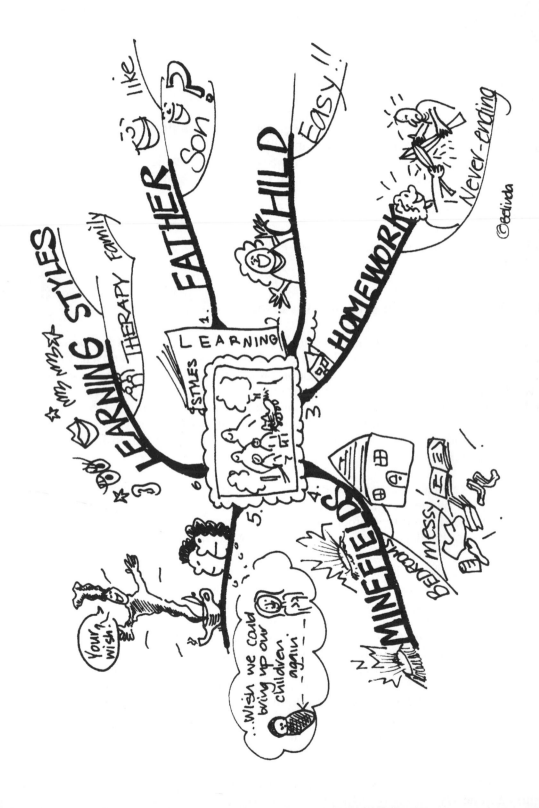

1. Like father – like son?

In previous chapters we have discussed at great length matches and mismatches between teachers and their students, between partners in private relationships, and now it is time to look at style differences between parents and their offspring. As you already know, opposites attract when it comes to partner choice and therefore it is no surprise that married couples usually have style preferences at the other end of the scale; they are usually diametrically opposed to each other, particularly in their biological style features. But how about children?

style differences between parents and their offspring

When we talk about style differences and similarities, please note that we only talk about natural, biological children of a couple; we are not talking about adopted children or children from reconstituted families. Research carried out in the USA only dealt with biological offspring because the question of interest was, how do genetics influence learning styles? For many the answer will be surprising, but when we consider the difficulties we often have with our children, it's not hard to accept that the first child has very different learning styles from its father or mother. Only the second or third child resembles one of the parents or a sibling in their style features.

biological children

how genetics influence LS

first child
different learning styles

So, if you have only one child, don't expect it to be like you although it might have many similarities and compatible areas, particularly in the learned or conditioned areas (like motivation, conformity, responsibility, structure and variety) of your style profiles. However, in the biological elements you will find a style combination usually not matching yours and that can lead to ongoing, often seemingly unresolvable conflicts, particularly during teenage years. But even earlier on, conflicts based on style differences become visible, often between fathers and their sons, based on the differences in analytic and holistic styles. The majority of children are still strongly holistic when they begin school, but most fathers, being strongly analytic, expect their sons to be rational, logical, highly responsible and

biological elements
not matching parents

conflicts

between fathers and sons

most children
strongly holistic
most fathers
strongly analytic

The easy part is learning how to do new things.

The hard part is giving up what we normally do.

A mind once stretched

by a new idea

can never go back

to its original dimension.

Oliver W. Holmes

more formal when it comes to schoolwork. The boy whose brain works very differently despairs because nothing is ever good enough; he knows he can't meet his father's high expectations, and finally either gives up or becomes rebellious. Mothers, who are generally more right-brain dominant, understand the needs of their sons intuitively better but can often do very little to help resolve the conflict between fathers and their sons, and so everyone suffers in their own way.

**mothers
more R/B dominant
understand needs
intuitively**

Later on we will see how styles can be matched and conflicts resolved with the help of understanding learning styles, and family life can be much more harmonious – something we all need these days.

To accommodate the style needs of one child can be difficult enough but to get on in peace with your spouse and with several children can sometimes seem impossible; yet again, a knowledge of one's own and everyone else's styles in the family can be a great help. As we now know there is hardly ever the same style between parents and their first child, but the situation is very different when we consider the second and third child in a family.

**knowledge of everyone's
styles in the family
great help**

2. This is such an easy child!

How often have you heard this exclamation, usually uttered by a parent who already has experienced some disharmony with another (or some other) of their children? Research and our own work with learning and working styles has shown that the second and more often the third child of a couple can resemble one parent very strongly in its style and that's why it gets labelled 'easy'. It is 'easy' because a style match always feels good; you are on the same wavelength and understand each other even without words. Wherever there is a true style match between parent and child there is a mutual understanding which cannot be reached when there is a mismatch present.

**second or third child
can resemble one parent
in its style
style match feels good**

mutual understanding

In practical terms this might mean that both of you want it quiet when you concentrate, or that you love to do physical things together, or that you

I believe that imagination is stronger than knowledge –

That myth is more potent than history.

I believe that dreams are more powerful than facts –

That hope always triumphs over experience –

That laughter is the only cure for grief.

And I believe that love is stronger than death.

Robert Fulghum

share the same interests in reading, talking and
listening, or that you both are early birds or night
owls. In any case, you will have many areas of
compatibility leading to shared interests, which   **shared interests**
leads to more closeness. You want to be together   **more closeness**
because you enjoy each other's company very much.
In some families this can lead to favouritism and
exclusion of the other children, even the spouse,
creating disappointment and a lot of unhappiness.

Whenever you have such a situation in your own
family, make sure you and your partner fully under-
stand styles and diversity, have the whole family   **styles and diversity**
assessed, and begin immediately to discuss style
differences and similarities, because it is crucial
that all family members understand the reasons   **reasons for**
for conflict as well as harmony.   **conflict and harmony**

How to utilize the results of learning and working
style profiles will be discussed at the end of this
chapter, and you will find some useful hints for
clearing the air and improving the family climate.

3. Homework: the never-ending battle in some families

One area in which style mismatches between parents   **style mismatches**
and their children can lead to constant frustration,   **parents and children**
irritation, even fights, is that of homework. All
parents know homework is important and most
children resent it. How come that in the same family
there is no problem with homework for some kids,
they sit down, do what needs to be done, seem to
cope well with even loads of homework and the end
product is always neat and tidy? And then there are
these other children for whom homework is nothing   **homework:**
but a constant struggle: they don't want to do it,   **constant struggle**
always have something more important to do, and
when they finally sit down to get on with their
homework, don't stay with it, find every possible
interruption and usually end up with half-finished,   **interruptions,**
shoddy work. And their work area – you can't even   **half-finished**
look at the mess! There is no wonder, you think,   **work area – a mess**
that they can't produce good work under such
conditions: their school books strewn all over the
place, the radio blaring (if you allowed it), food
everywhere, and in the midst of it your daughter,

Dialogue between Parent and Tactile Child at Homework Time

Child: 'Mum? I need some help – I don't get this!'

Mother: 'That's because you aren't even looking at it! How do you expect to learn anything that way? It's not written on the ceiling, you know! As usual – you're just not trying.'

Child: 'I am trying, but it's too hard! I just don't get it, that's all!'

Mother: 'Look, Sharon, I don't have time for this nonsense. You pay attention to your work, and don't let me see you staring out the window or up at the ceiling. Keep your eyes on your page and try again – and please don't bother me with any more of your ridiculous excuses!'

Adapted from *Try To Feel It My Way: New Help for Tough Dominant People and Those Who Care About Them* by Suzette Haden Elgin, 1996

or more often, your son – <u>slouching</u>, not sitting on the chair, or most of the time <u>lying</u> stretched out <u>on the floor</u> or on the bed. You go out of your way to help them, support them, sometimes even do parts of the homework for them, just to get these daily unpleasantries out of the way. You try your best, <u>you get frustrated</u>, your nerves are at break point, you plead, cajole, <u>even threaten</u>, and when you have succeeded for a few days, the moment comes and you are back to square one – the <u>child doesn't want to do homework</u>. Despite all your efforts, deep down you know there is not much you can do about this hopeless situation and finally <u>you give up</u> educating them HOW to do homework properly and leave them to themselves.

**slouching,
lying
on the floor or bed**

**you get frustrated,
even threaten**

**child doesn't want
to do homework**

you give up

Sounds familiar? I can feel for you because that was the scenario we had in our house all through our daughter's high school years – it was a <u>constant battle</u> and usually <u>all of us were the losers</u>. I could not understand why my daughter sometimes would do her homework in no time, although the quality was not the best, but at least she did it, and at other times she would just forget, leave it half finished or find excuses for not doing it at all – and then she would go to school without it.

**constant battle
all of us were the losers**

I had no clue why she was so <u>resistant to doing homework</u>. I knew she was bright and could produce very good work – if she was interested and wanted to, but I didn't know how to make her WANT to learn. For years I had given her what I thought was <u>good advice</u> on how to do homework, and I know for many of you the following sounds very familiar because we have all heard it from our parents and said it to our children. Whenever it was time for homework (usually right after school or after a short snack after coming home from school) I would say to my daughter: 'Go to your room, switch off the radio, turn on the lights, take out your books, sit at your desk – upright please – and do your homework.' For me this was <u>the only thinkable way of doing homework</u>; that's how we had to do it and that's how everyone does it, because it's <u>the right way</u> to do it, right?

**resistant to doing
homework**

good advice

**the only way
to do homework**

the right way

Wrong! It wasn't until I found out about learning

Sequence of Events

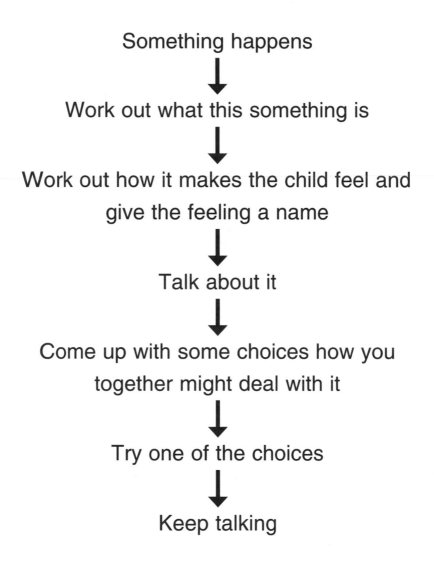

Something happens

↓

Work out what this something is

↓

Work out how it makes the child feel and give the feeling a name

↓

Talk about it

↓

Come up with some choices how you together might deal with it

↓

Try one of the choices

↓

Keep talking

As it is reasonably predictable what sequence of events happens to us throughout life, it might be useful for your child to learn to deal with it early on, particularly in conflict situations.

Based on 'Cycle of Events' in the most useful book for parents, *Happy Families: How to Make One, How to Keep One* by Bill Lucas, 2006

styles how wrong I was and that the way a child is forced to do homework can totally switch off its willingness to learn. I still regret that I found out about different learning styles when my daughter was in her last year at high school and I would never have guessed how she could learn best because her style is so very different from mine. Can you guess what she would have needed to do her homework with more enthusiasm?

forced way
switches off
willingness to learn

her style
very different from mine

She would have worked best in the middle of the living room on the floor, with the cat and the dog close by, with healthy drinks and nibbles, with dim light and the radio going (with the appropriate learning music of course – see Chapter 6) and with me around, in case she needed my help. On top of that she would have needed learning tools she could manipulate to keep her hands busy instead of doodling or chewing pencils.

If the described scenario seems crazy to you, as it did for me when I first heard it, it is true that learning with what we call 'distractions' is the style which works best for many children, particularly when they are more holistic, right-brain dominant. You just have to accept that fact. Research has proven it and we have seen it hundreds of times that children with these style needs (often under-achievers at school) could perform much better, WANT to learn this way and actually do it very successfully. Have your children's learning styles assessed, let them try to study in their own way, set some basic rules (like you can do it your way when you clean up your 'mess' afterwards and when your school performance improves), and watch them succeed.

learning with
'distractions'

holistic, R/B dominant

have children's learning
styles assessed,
set basic rules

watch them succeed

I can guarantee you that not only their attitude towards learning will improve but also the daily battlefield around homework will disappear, and you will have a much more relaxed atmosphere in your own home. Even if it makes you shudder when you watch your child do homework that way, ACCEPT that your child has a different style and learning needs. The best you can do to really help and support is to understand and let your child be the wonderful person he/she is meant to be.

more relaxed atmosphere

accept your child's
different style

Do not confine
your children
to your own learning.
For they have been born
in another time.

Hebrew Proverb

4. Messy rooms – minefields in our family homes

Now we have tackled one area which can cause big problems in a family for years, let's look at another one, equally <u>unpleasant</u> but not with such serious consequences as refusing to do homework. It's <u>messy rooms,</u> for which teenagers are famous. Again we have to ask ourselves, how come that one child is tidy and keeps their room in order, just as the parents want it, and that another child can never be tidy, lives in a 'pigsty', as many desperate parents call their children's living quarters; <u>even if they do tidy up</u>, the <u>mess creeps in immediately</u>, or the mess is shoved under beds or into wardrobes and cupboards, an activity these children have developed mastery in. As if such <u>'bad habits'</u> were not bad enough, they are usually to be found <u>in children</u> who also have <u>problems with doing their homework</u>, whereas their high-achieving siblings often display the welcome skills of being tidy and organized in their rooms. Just as you like it.

unpleasant

messy rooms

even if they tidy up, mess creeps back in

bad habits

in children with homework problems

So, why is it compounded in some children and no matter what we do, nothing seriously works? I remember a time when the mess in our daughter's room started spilling out into the rest of the house. We set a rule which said, whatever you do in your room is none of our business, as long as you keep the mess confined to it. However, that didn't work in the long run, because there came a day when we couldn't open the door and the room was virtually no longer accessible. We were at our wits' end and when I started to tidy up, there arose another fierce conflict because now she couldn't find anything!

Does this sound familiar too? Have you, like me, argued about untidy rooms, complained about the <u>mess in the kitchen or bathroom</u>, despaired over shoes, clothes and school bags flung into a corner or dropped in the middle of the hall? Again, I wish I had known about different learning styles long ago; it would have given me the insight into the profound <u>difference between analytic and holistic</u> human beings (see Chapter 5); it would have explained to me that more left-brain dominant people (like many parents) are tidy, well organized, look after their

messy kitchen/bathroom

difference between analytic and holistic style

AGE (approximate)   DEVELOPMENT

Conception – 15 months   Reptilian Brain
Basic survival needs – food, shelter, security and safety
Sensory development starting with vestibular system, then hearing, tactile, smell, taste and finally
seeing – rich sensory activation
Motor development moving from reflexes to core muscle activation, neck muscles, arms and legs
leading to rolling over, sitting, crawling and walking – motor exploration

15 months – 4 ½ years   Limbic System/Relationship
Understanding of self/others, self/emotions, self/language
Emotional exploration; Language exploration/communication;
Imagination; Gross motor proficiency; Memory development; Social development

4 ½ years – 7 years   Gestalt Hemisphere Elaboration
Whole picture processing/cognition
Outer speech/integrative thought
Image/movement/rhythm/emotion/intuition

7–9 years   Logic Hemisphere Elaboration
Detail and linear processing/cognition
Refinement of elements of language
Linear maths processing
Reading and writing skills development
Technique development – music, art, sports, dance, manual training

8 years   Frontal Lobe Elaboration
Fine motor development – skills refinement
Inner speech – control of social behaviour
Fine motor eye teaming for tracking and foveal focus (2-dimensional focus)

9–12 years   Increase Corpus Callosum Elaboration and Myelination
Whole brain processing

12–16 years   Hormonal Emphasis
Learning about body, self, others, community, and meaningful living through social consciousness

16–21 years   Refining Cognitive Skills
Whole mind/body processing, social interaction, future planning and play with new ideas and
possibilities

21+   Elaboration and Refinement of the Frontal Lobes
Global/systems thinking
High-level formal reasoning
Insight
Refinement of fine motor skills
Refinement of emotions – altruism, love, compassion

From *Smart Moves* by Carla Hannaford (1)

things and keep them in order, whereas the more
right-brain dominant people (like teenage children)
are sloppy, disorganized, don't look after their
things and don't keep them in order. They are
'scatterbrains' and find it very hard to 'get their
act together', they are the risk takers, are impulsive
and most of the time don't see the consequences of
their actions. Whether you like it or not, that's the
way they are and usually they don't change their
basic style very much, although many will learn –
often the hard way – that being organized and tidy
has its advantages. They learn to function in this
manner, but if they don't have to be that way,
they can easily fall back into disorganization
bordering on sloppiness.

R/B dominant teenagers

**'scatterbrains'
impulsive risk takers**

**don't change
basic style very much**

**disorganization
sloppiness**

Once you understand these style features, you can
help your child to become a bit more organized, but
be warned, logical reasoning will not do the trick.
There are some very good books available which
give good advice on how to deal with disobedient
youngsters and you will find these books listed in
Further Reading.

**help child
become more organized
but no logical reasoning**

5. I wish I could bring up my children all over again!

After this host of new insights many of you might
now say this wish with a sigh, as I did. Yet, one
cannot rewrite the past but it's never too late to
apply knowledge of different learning styles, even
to your grown-up children. I realized that, although
I couldn't undo many of the things I had said to my
daughter when it came to learning (some of which
I regret), I can utilize my new-found insights in
all my interactions with her. Despite our distinctly
different styles (remember, she is an only child and
so profoundly different from me in many ways), we
have lots in common and can always capitalize on
these common features, complementing each other.

never too late

lots in common

As we both know our strengths and weaknesses it
has become much easier to communicate, to discuss
things and to get on with each other. Our relationship
has improved dramatically (which is probably also
due to our getting older and wiser) because we now
understand and respect each other for who we are

**know our
strengths and weaknesses**

understand and respect

'All it takes to make a difference is
the courage to stop proving I was
right in being unable to make a
difference ... to stop assigning the
cause for my inability to the
circumstances outside myself and
to be willing to have been that way,
and to see that the fear of being a
failure is a lot less important than
the unique opportunity I have to
make a difference.'

Werner Erhard (1980)

as human beings and not because we are mother and daughter. I am eternally grateful for having found out about learning styles and that it was not too late, although our rift during her late teens was profound and I thought we would never be able to bridge the gap again. But like with my husband, never say never again.

Finally I have also <u>overcome my guilt feelings</u> about the mistakes I made by not understanding her style because at any time I tried my best. Had I known better, I would have acted differently, and I can only advise you to <u>apologize</u> for forcing your style onto your children and get on with your life. <u>Enjoy your children</u> the way they are, stop nagging, help and support them in becoming who they are meant to be, and appreciate every day you can spend with them.

overcome guilt feelings

apologize

enjoy your children

6. Learning styles as new family therapy

These days many people are in <u>rocky marriages</u>, filled with strife and conflict. Less dramatic, but more common, is the situation that after several years of marriage, many people don't like their spouses anymore (see Chapter 10), and this is fertile ground for <u>fighting</u>. But at the same time, both parents are often deeply concerned with the well-being of their children. It seems to be a plain fact – at least statistically – that either <u>separation</u> or fighting in response to an unhappy marriage is likely to <u>harm your children</u> in <u>lasting ways</u>, as Martin Seligman, author of the excellent book, *Learned Optimism*, points out. (2) He has done years of research on <u>pessimism and depression</u>, and re- commends that, if you care about your children, you step back and think twice or three times before you fight. <u>Being angry and fighting</u> are NOT <u>human rights</u>. Fighting is a human choice, and it's your child's well-being, more than yours, that may be at stake. Research shows that the following chain of events is common: parental fighting or separation leads to a <u>marked increase in the child's depression</u>. The depression itself then <u>causes school problems</u> and the child becoming even <u>more pessimistic</u>. School problems combined with this newly minted

rocky marriages

fighting

separation

harms children in lasting ways

pessimism and depression

being angry and fighting are not human rights

increase in child's depression causes school problems, increases pessimism

Until one is committed,
there is hesitancy, the chance to draw back,
always ineffectiveness.
Concerning all acts of initiative (and creation),
there is one elementary truth
the ignorance of which kills countless ideas
and splendid plans:
that the moment one definitely commits oneself,
then Providence moves too.
All sorts of things occur to help one
that would never otherwise have occurred.
A whole stream of events
issues from the decision,
raising in one's favour
all manner of unforeseen incidents
and meetings and material assistance
which no man could have dreamed
would have come his way.

W.H. Murray (1951)

pessimism maintain depression, and a <u>vicious cycle</u> has begun. <u>Depression</u> now becomes a <u>permanent</u> way of life for your child. (3)

vicious cycle
depression becomes
permanent

Long-lasting depression is always one of the vital ingredients <u>leading to suicide</u> and, as recent statistical figures from New Zealand teenagers are on the rise, it is time to consider what else can be done to help families in trouble. Unless the whole situation is already out of hand, and drug abuse, violence and even crime are taking place, we have found that a <u>knowledge</u> of the <u>children's learning</u> and their <u>parents' working styles</u> are an extremely useful tool for <u>family counselling</u>. We have many reports from families where the knowledge about style differences has improved the family climate dramatically, changed the way family members interact, and has brought back the <u>appreciation</u> and <u>love</u> between parents and their children.

leading to suicide

knowledge of
children's learning and
parents' working styles
for family counselling

appreciation and love

In a <u>family coaching session</u> where parents and children bring along their WSA and LSA profiles, style differences are discussed, similarities pointed out and mismatches explained. For many families it is the very first time at such a session that they actually <u>listen and talk to each other</u>, and that their style features are taken seriously because they are printed black on white. It can be very emotional for all family members to clarify misunder-standings and confusions, long-held grudges and false beliefs about each other, and maybe learn to see their nearest and dearest through very different eyes. Such an interpretation of one's own profile can also lead to <u>renewed self-esteem</u> through better self-understanding and <u>more tolerance</u> towards others, as we know there are no good or bad styles.

family coaching session

listen/talk to each other

renewed self-esteem
more tolerance

With <u>soothing music</u> in the background and the skilful <u>help of a family coach</u>, people who before had a communication breakdown begin to talk to each other and find a way to get on in the future. For families with teenagers, career choice is often a point of friction, and a good understanding of the adolescent's style features can often resolve conflicts in this area. Many people told us that such a family coaching session was <u>more constructive</u> and more useful than <u>counselling sessions</u>.

soothing music
help from family coach

more constructive than
counselling sessions

 *LSA-Senior: Parent Version*   Lucie Voller

Profile Summary

Lucie's preferences are her strengths when she can use them in difficult learning situations, and her non-preferences become her weaknesses when she has to use them over longer periods of time. This can lead to frustration, concentration problems, low motivation, and learning difficulties. When Lucie is allowed to learn her way, she will enjoy studying more and her academic performance will improve.

Key elements of her learning style
when Lucie has to learn something NEW and/or DIFFICULT:

Lucie's Preferences: (how she learns best)

BRAIN DOMINANCE: reflective	
SENSORY MODALITIES: visual (external), tactile (touching), kinesthetic (internal)	
PHYSICAL NEEDS: intake, late morning	
ENVIRONMENT: quiet, cool	
SOCIAL: alone	
ATTITUDES: self-starting, non-conforming, high/strong responsibility, self-directed, routine	

Lucie's Non-Preferences: (what she needs to avoid when learning something difficult)

BRAIN DOMINANCE:	Flexibility - see Graph 1
SENSORY MODALITIES:	Flexibility - see Graph 1
PHYSICAL NEEDS: movement needed, no intake, afternoon	
ENVIRONMENT: sound/noise/music, warm	

PHYSICAL NEEDS

MOBILITY:
Whether Lucie can sit still during the learning process, in lectures or while she reads, writes or concentrates, depends on her interest in the topic. If she is interested, she can sit still for longer periods. If she is bored, she can't. Therefore, looking for stimulating learning tasks or study assignments becomes very important to her. However, more often than not, she is quite happy to stay put while she does her homework, concentrates, or works in class.

NEED FOR INTAKE:
Lucie often uses some kind of intake (eating, nibbling, drinking, chewing) when concentrating or learning something new and difficult, but also when she is bored, frustrated or impatient. She finds it hard to go for long periods without something to eat or drink and she might chew her pens, pencils or fingernails instead. Give her frequent opportunities to eat nutritious foods or have drinks of water and healthy snacks during thinking processes, reading, or studying. Please see that her teachers understand her need for intake. Also, watch out how much she eats or drinks because particularly under stress she might not be aware of the amounts she takes in!
(Attention: If she is already smoking, or has tried smoking, she might be in danger of getting addicted to this potentially lethal habit due to her preference for intake!)

TIME OF DAY: early morning
This time of day does not really make any difference to Lucie's concentration or study performance. What she does, why, with whom and whether she is interested in the subject are all more important factors than the being able to study in this time slot of day.

7. LSA Parent version – a guide to your children's true learning needs

Readers will surely remember when they were at school, great fuss was made of the <u>right</u> environment in which <u>to do homework</u>. You know: a quiet spot, a desk or table, how to sit upright, a source of bright light, eat before or after studying and so forth. And we did not dare go against such instructions, often given as harsh prescriptions; we just did it and many suffered.

right
to do homework

From research on LS we know it really is a myth that brighter light is better because generally younger students need less light. Another myth is: homework has to be done at the desk. Some students prefer a more informal setting with soft cushions, or lie on the floor, or stretched out on their bed. And not all children like studying in a quiet area, many need background music for better concentration. However, loud rock music with lyrics is counter-productive (see Chapter 6 for more detailed information about learning music).

The <u>LSA Report</u> will give valuable information about their <u>optimal study environment</u>; for some children this may be a quiet corner, while for others it could be the family room with the music on, with nibbles and water available, papers strewn everywhere, and their pets around. This might seem like a lot of distractions to parents but for many, particularly holistic children, this is just the environment they need. I know it from my experience with my own daughter who I wouldn't allow to learn in HER way with near-disastrous results.

LSA Report
optimal study environment

Therefore I urge all parents: please, please check your children's <u>LSA results BEFORE</u> you expect (or force?) them to <u>do their homework</u> in a certain way, most likely how YOU used to do it. If you have more than one child, you will be well aware that they like doing their homework <u>differently from each other</u>. Let them, as long as they show acceptable results, they should be allowed to <u>work in their own way</u>, even if you cringe, watching them. For more interesting insights about children, parents and their style differences, see also Chapter 11.

LSA results BEFORE
do their homework

differently from each other

work in their own way

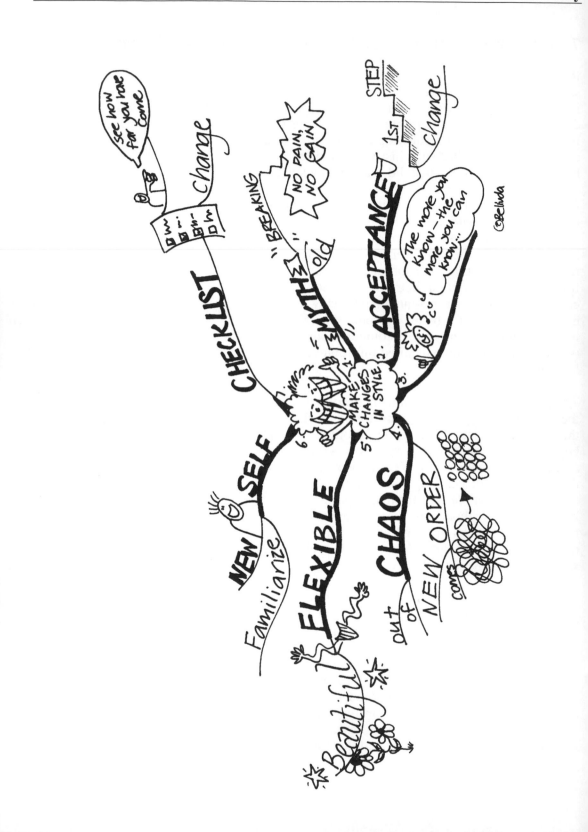

1. Breaking an old myth – no pain, no gain

Thinking back to our schooldays and to any other
<u>formal learning</u> or studying we ever had to do,
it was usually <u>hard, frustrating, stressful</u> and <u>often
boring</u>. This has left many of us with a negative
attitude towards learning, with the uneasy feeling
that <u>learning is painful</u>; we came to believe that
<u>there is no gain without pain</u>. Haven't we heard
this from our parents, teachers and instructors?
After all, they are the experts – they should know!

formal learning
hard, frustrating, stressful
often boring

learning is painful
no gain without pain

Not quite. Because they had a <u>strong belief</u>
in this <u>old myth</u> – it had become their personal
mindset, their own <u>paradigm</u> which kept them
repeating it, making their children's, students'
and their own lives <u>unnecessarily hard</u>. It was
unimaginable to them – and still is for many –
that <u>learning can actually be enjoyable</u> and <u>easy</u>
and have long-lasting, <u>positive results</u>.
The same goes for work – if it's too easy,
let alone enjoyable, it can't be worth much.

strong belief
old myth
paradigm

unnecessarily hard

learning enjoyable and easy
positive results

How then can we <u>do away with these old myths</u>?
As Ronald Gross, in his book *Peak Learning*,
explains, it is possible for anyone who wants
to try, because the <u>principles of 'peak learning'</u>
are based on some fundamental truths about
learning and growing that can liberate us from
over-reliance on schooling.

do away with old myths

principles: 'peak learning'

The main principles are:
a) <u>Adults who take care of their own learning</u>
   often master more things and master them better
   than those who rely on being taught. They tend
   to be <u>more motivated</u>, retain more of what
   they have learned, and make better use of it
   in their private and professional lives.

take care of own learning

more motivated

b) <u>Adults learn in different ways from children</u>.
   They have a different sense of themselves, of their
   time, and of what's worth learning and why. As
   adults we finally realize no one can learn for *me*,
   anymore than someone can eat for me. <u>Education</u>
   is something I must <u>tailor to myself</u>, not something
   I can get <u>ready-made</u> in institutions of learning.

adults learn differently

education
tailored to self,
not ready-made

SAID
is not yet heard,

HEARD
is not yet understood,

UNDERSTOOD
is not yet agreed,

AGREED
is not yet applied,

APPLIED
is not yet implemented.

c) <u>No particular learning style is in itself superior</u> to another. How you learn, as Gross puts it, depends on your temperament, circumstances, needs, tastes or ambition. (1) However, he also says that <u>success in learning</u> depends not on the subject itself or the conditions (how, where and when) of learning, but basically on the <u>learner's engagement</u> – his or her fascination with the subject.

no style is superior

success in learning

learner's engagement

Although I fully agree with the above statements in general, I have to disagree with this last one. Research into learning styles, backed up by our own experience with working styles, shows that for many people, except for the highly flexible, <u>learning to a great extent *does* depend</u> on the <u>how</u>, <u>where</u> and <u>when</u>. It is very important that the <u>conditions of learning</u> are <u>matched with</u> <u>the learner's individual style</u>. Only then will motivation and persistence increase, performance improve and <u>information become knowledge</u> for the learner.

learning depends on
how, where, when
learning conditions
matched with
learner's style
information ~ knowledge

As we have seen, anyone can become a successful or so-called 'peak learner' with ease and no pain. The first and most important step, however, is to <u>know yourself</u>, your true working or learning style and do it *your wa*y when it comes to information intake.

know yourself
do it your way

2. Acceptance: the first step to change

These arguments for becoming more successful, not only in learning or work situations but also possibly in running your life, sound quite plausible you might think, but then ... you have all your <u>past learning experiences</u> – and most of them were <u>not pleasant</u>. You think you know yourself, and you have strong evidence that learning or information intake is really <u>not that easy</u> (you even have written proof for that on your school reports and certificates). As you are a curious person, open to learning new things, you have also assessed your own working style, and studied your profile and report. You are really <u>keen to</u> <u>improve your learning</u> and concentration skills

past learning experiences
not pleasant

not easy

keen to improve learning

My Flow State

Think about work or study situations where everything seemed to go smoothly. You were on a real performance high and the result was better than you expected. To be able to repeat such 'flow states' more often you must become aware of <u>HOW</u> you did things to be able to duplicate these successful strategies in future.

Become aware of the following conditions under which you did the job so well:

1. Physical environment – where were you – inside/outdoors? Was it warm/cool? How about music, other sounds?
2. Time of day – when did you do the work?
3. Your physical needs – did you sit still, move around, eat, drink? Could you take breaks?
4. People – did you work with someone else, a group, or were you alone? How about instructions/guidelines?
5. State of mind – how did you feel – before, during, after the task? Were you eager, excited – even before you started? What kept you going?

Make a list of these important ingredients of your mental 'flow state' and reflect on how you can ensure these are the conditions when you need to do tasks. Your Learning Style Analysis (LSA) Report will give you further suggestions for peak performance.

<u>but</u> you are not quite sure how. The <u>old beliefs</u> about your <u>learning abilities are still very strong</u> and you are not yet quite comfortable with your newly discovered strengths which are your preferences in the profile.

but old beliefs about learning abilities strong

As with anything new, you have to take the first step – to <u>accept your true abilities</u>. Even if you have never realized that you possess such-and-such strengths, accept that you *do* have them. You can <u>trust yourself</u> and your style. <u>Observe</u> how you do things when you are in a '<u>flow state</u>', when <u>everything seems to come easily</u>. Continue practising your abilities and strengths and you might be surprised about the outcome!

accept true abilities

trust yourself, observe flow state, when everything comes easily

To help you in achieving mental peaks more often in your work, your studies or other activities, you'll find some useful exercises opposite. They can be even more useful if you watch how other people reach, and operate in, a 'flow state'; also think about more examples from your own life.

3. The more you know, the more you can know

Whether you experience some drastic changes, some minor changes or no changes at all in your self-perception after you discover your own learning or working style, one thing is for sure: the more <u>you know about yourself</u> and how your brain works, the more you know about your <u>strengths and weaknesses</u> and how you tick, the more you can capitalize on that knowledge. You will be <u>able to live your life your way</u> instead of following other people's advice, even if it's well meant.

know yourself

strengths and weaknesses

live your life your way

The <u>more knowledge</u> you have about the way you <u>take information in</u>, the more you will be able to do it and the <u>easier</u> it will be. It's similar to exercising muscles you have hardly ever used before: in the beginning you might be a little sore, but the more you exercise these muscles, the better you will become, and the better you will feel and perform. With learning ability it goes even further: the more you <u>activate your brain *your way*</u>,

more knowledge about information intake makes it easier

activate brain your way

CHAOS EXERCISE

Sit back and relax.
Think about something that was once a big issue for you,
something which confused you greatly.
Remember how you were desperate for a while
because you didn't know what to do?
Write down what you did to gain clarity and how you felt
when you finally found a solution or saw a way out.

_____

_____

_____

_____

_____

_____

_____

_____

_____

_____

_____

_____

_____

_____

_____

the more it will want to learn, take in information, store and retrieve it. This is the fuel that <u>keeps</u> your <u>motivation going</u>. Diana Beaver, in her book *Lazy Learning*, describes how to 'make the best of the brains you were born with', as the subtitle states, and suggests some very simple but effective structures and strategies to find out how you learn best. (2) Similar exercises can be found on pages 4, 288 and 290.

keep motivation going

With <u>greater self-knowledge</u> and a range of easy, suitable strategies described throughout this book, you will not only be <u>more effective</u> in learning, studying or working, you will also <u>enjoy</u> it more and experience <u>more satisfaction</u> with your results. You might even become addicted to your own learning ability!

greater self-knowledge

more effective

enjoyment, satisfaction

4. Out of chaos comes new order

From what you have read so far about learning and working styles, human diversity, brain functions and information intake, and what you learned from the tests and exercises I invited you to do, you have perhaps gained a very <u>complex picture</u> about yourself and the people you know.

complex picture

You might think, 'I wish I had known all that 20 years ago' or 'Why doesn't everyone know about this?' You might be delighted about what you discovered or not be very pleased at all. Whatever reaction you might have to this wealth of knowledge, you will probably experience <u>mental confusion</u> too.

mental confusion

If I can go by the reactions I have seen in thousands of people exposed to the concept of learning or working styles, you are not alone. Most of them went through a phase of total confusion after accepting human diversity and style as the basis of successful learning, working and interacting. <u>Old beliefs</u>, paradigms and past experiences <u>fight an inner battle with</u> the <u>new knowledge</u>, the unthinkable and the truly unbelievable. However, deep down we might have known intuitively that diversity is the truth.

old beliefs
fight inner battle
with new knowledge

𝔐𝔶 𝔆𝔬𝔪𝔪𝔦𝔱𝔪𝔢𝔫𝔱 𝔱𝔬 𝔆𝔥𝔞𝔫𝔤𝔢:

I herewith decide to become the person I meant to be
so that I can eliminate confusion, doubts, pressures, frustrations
from my life,
stop playing roles and pretending that I am
who I am not,
so that I can enjoy who I truly am and live life
to the fullest in my own right.

Signed this _____ day of _____ 200____.

_____

Your signature

It's hard to know what to do at this stage:
throw out everything you have believed about
yourself, other people and how true learning
works and adopt these somewhat strange new
principles, or try to <u>combine old and useful beliefs</u>
<u>with new insights</u> and leading-edge knowledge.

combine old, useful beliefs with new insights

During this phase many people go back and forth
in their thinking from 'Oh, it can't be true, it's
all a bit over the top, too idealistic,' to 'What if
it's true, what if styles really hold the key to so
many unsolved mysteries?' back to 'I can't be
bothered, I've got so much else to do ... but what
if it could help solve some problems we have
at work, at school, with so-and-so right now?'

This ties in with the <u>chaos theory</u> pioneered by
mathematicians and physical scientists since the
early 1970s and explained by James Gleick in
the best-seller *Chaos: Making a New Science.*
It says that chaos, or the tendency to <u>unpredictable</u>
<u>behaviour</u>, lurks in practically every real-world
system, yet <u>order arises spontaneously</u> in those
systems (3) – so chaos and order occur together.
Furthermore, more often than not, <u>chaos</u> is the
<u>normal operating state</u> of a system! (4)

chaos theory

unpredictable behaviour

order arises spontaneously

chaos is the normal operating state

Given that our brain is an open system, always
in flux, constantly rearranging thought patterns
through sensory input, it is possible that <u>the brain</u>
<u>is designed for chaos</u>, and that this instability
creates purposeful activity and direction. (5)
Once we are <u>through this state of inner chaos</u> –
no one knows how long this will last, one never
knows how and when the breakthrough is going
to happen – we are definitely <u>bound to reach</u> a
<u>higher level of clarity</u>, a new way of thinking,
a <u>new perspective</u>.

brain designed for chaos

through inner chaos

reach higher level of clarity new perspective

Whether it creeps up on you slowly and unnoticed
or whether you have one big, mighty '<u>Aha</u>'
or many small ones, I can assure you, it's a
<u>very pleasant feeling</u> and you might like to
experience it time and again. That's the point
at which you finally get '<u>hooked' on learning</u>.

'Aha'

pleasant feeling

'hooked' on learning

My Strengths and Weaknesses

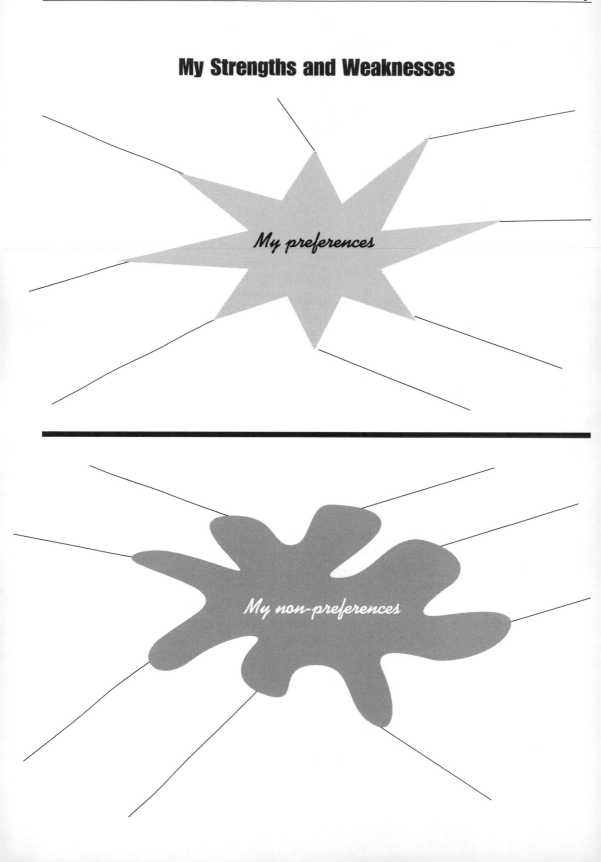

Learning climates of surprise, suspense, even
provocation, slight uncertainty and disorder can,
if properly orchestrated, lead to better, joyful
learning and more satisfying understanding.

**joyful learning and
satisfying understanding**

When people reach this new stage of awareness,
something else might occur in their brains,
impacting on their information processing ability
and learning skills: they discover they are capable
of things they thought they could never do,
their learning abilities broaden and their
self-esteem increases.

new awareness

**learning abilities broaden
self-esteem increases**

5. Focus on strengths and manage weaknesses

One of the most damaging, unwritten rules many
families, schools, companies and organizations
follow is: 'Let's fix what's wrong and let the OK
things take care of themselves.' As so accurately
described in the book *Play To Your Strengths*, such
systems are set up to catch people's weaknesses
rather than build on their strengths:

damaging, unwritten rules

fix what's wrong

- business managers spend most of their time
  working with their weakest performers, trying
  to eliminate their mistakes;
- almost all social work is focused on problems
  instead of helping people to become really
  self-sufficient;
- parents usually point out their own children's
  shortcomings, and teachers always concentrate
  on their students' lowest marks rather than
  on their highest. (6)

**managers
work with
weakest performers
social work focuses
on problems**

**teachers concentrate
on students' lowest marks**

We tend to focus our energies on fixing weaknesses
while ignoring strengths because we have been
conditioned to believe that fixing weaknesses will
make everything all right, strengths can take care of
themselves, success is the opposite of failure, and
practice makes perfect.

**fixing weaknesses
ignoring strengths**

What happens when we follow these myths is
that fixing weaknesses will only ever achieve
average results; excellence is developed solely
by focusing on strengths.

**by following myths ~
only average results;
excellence develops by
focusing on strengths**

THE BEST PREDICTOR

OF FUTURE SUCCESS

IS PRIOR SUCCESS.

Interesting dialogue:

Young woman:
  Pardon me sir. Can you tell me how to get to Carnegie Hall?

Old man: Practice, practice, practice.

Apart from arts and sports, personal strengths are not considered as important areas of professional development. So many people never discover their real talents and only achieve <u>mediocre performance</u> because they focus on their weaknesses and <u>neglect their strengths</u>.

mediocre performance

neglect strengths

The <u>study of failure</u> can give very misleading information about what needs to be improved. It is also a widespread <u>false belief</u> that if we can <u>identify weaknesses</u> we are then able to <u>turn them into strengths</u>.

study of failure

false belief
identify weaknesses
turn them into strengths

One of the most damaging beliefs, for adults and particularly for young people while they are still impressionable, is the saying 'If so-and-so can do it, you can do it.' The assumption that 'anyone can do anything' assumes that <u>all people are clones</u>, possessing <u>identical abilities</u>, totally <u>disregarding human diversity</u>. As common sense and research into style differences tell us, we are all different, equipped with a <u>unique combination of strengths</u>. The saying should be rephrased into: "If someone can do it, those with the same strengths can do it."

all people are clones
identical abilities
disregard human diversity

unique combination of strengths

So far it has become quite clear that for achieving any success at all it is essential to focus on one's strengths. But how can we <u>manage our weaknesses</u>?

how to manage weaknesses

Again, Clifton and Nelson give great advice which fits perfectly into my notion of diversity and can be applied by interpreting the Working Style Analysis for adults and the Learning Style Analysis for students of primary and secondary schools:

- learn how to find out how good people can be by <u>identifying their strengths</u> rather than their weaknesses;

identify strengths

- learn how to stop wasting time <u>working on your weaknesses</u>;

stop working on weaknesses

- learn how to double and triple your productivity or effectiveness by <u>exercising your strengths</u>. (7)

exercise strengths

As we'll see later, there is <u>no magic formula</u> for dealing with weaknesses. They can be removed but they cannot be transformed into strengths. The goal, therefore, is to manage our weaknesses

no magic formula

MY
FLEXIBILITY

See results from your LSA or WSA profile and write down/draw
the elements in which you are flexible.

How to get questionnaires and computer-generated WSA/LSA profiles – see Appendix II

so our true strengths can be freed up to develop
and become so powerful that they ultimately
make our weaknesses irrelevant.

**true strengths freed up
make
weaknesses irrelevant**

This is an attitude good, loving parents as well as
brilliant, caring teachers seem to understand
intuitively; but the majority of teachers, particularly
in our high schools, seem only to be focused on
weaknesses therefore making their own and many
students' learning life miserable. It's time to heed
the message and act on it.

With these new mental skills another phenomenon
occurs: their flexibility strengthens and they
experience perhaps that ...

flexibility strengthens

6. Flexible is beautiful

In the process of understanding diversity we have
learned that human beings are uniquely different
from each other in their preferences and needs,
unearthed the profound differences between
holistics and analytics, and also discovered
the importance of the biological aspects of a
person's learning or working style profile.

**humans are
uniquely different**

**holistics and analytics
biological aspects**

Now we must add on one last but probably the
most important aspect to make the picture complete:
human flexibility. When looking at any Working
Style Profile, you can see one's preferences
(people usually have between three and fifteen
strong preferences); non-preferences that can
become weaknesses when continually used
instead of one's preferences; and question marks
indicating inconsistencies or contradictions about
certain aspects. The bulk of the information,
however, usually shows your overall flexibility.

**most important is
flexibility
style preferences**

non-preferences

**question marks indicate
inconsistency/contradiction**

overall flexibility

Although it is very important to be aware of
all your strengths and non-preferences, it is
probably even more important to know
your flexible areas because combined they can
become a personal strength in itself, and are
often the only feature which will help you
survive difficult situations.

**important to know
flexible areas,
become a strength**

 **LSA-Senior: Student Version**   Freddie Flexible

Graph 1. Natural / Biological Elements

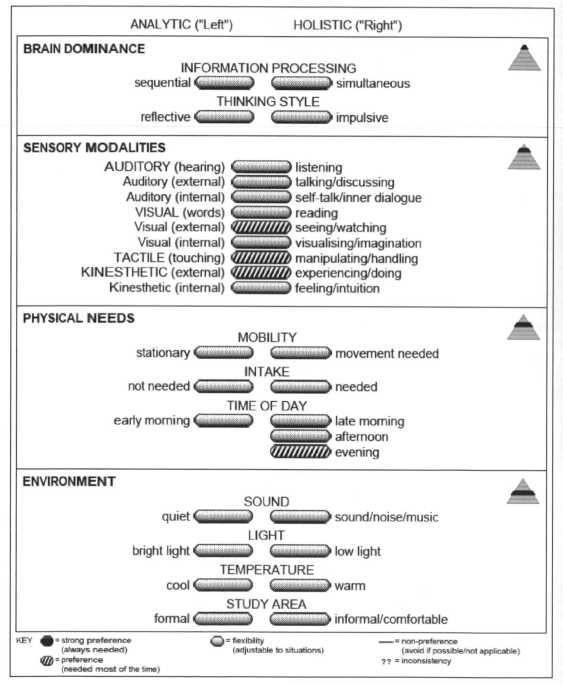

ANALYTIC ("Left")   HOLISTIC ("Right")

BRAIN DOMINANCE

INFORMATION PROCESSING
sequential ▢▢▢ ▢▢▢ simultaneous

THINKING STYLE
reflective ▢▢▢ ▢▢▢ impulsive

SENSORY MODALITIES

AUDITORY (hearing) ▢▢▢ listening
Auditory (external) ▢▢▢ talking/discussing
Auditory (internal) ▢▢▢ self-talk/inner dialogue
VISUAL (words) ▢▢▢ reading
Visual (external) ▨▨▨ seeing/watching
Visual (internal) ▢▢▢ visualising/imagination
TACTILE (touching) ▨▨▨ manipulating/handling
KINESTHETIC (external) ▨▨▨ experiencing/doing
Kinesthetic (internal) ▢▢▢ feeling/intuition

PHYSICAL NEEDS

MOBILITY
stationary ▢▢▢ ▢▢▢ movement needed

INTAKE
not needed ▢▢▢ ▢▢▢ needed

TIME OF DAY
early morning ▢▢▢ ▢▢▢ late morning
                ▢▢▢ afternoon
                ▨▨▨ evening

ENVIRONMENT

SOUND
quiet ▢▢▢ ▢▢▢ sound/noise/music

LIGHT
bright light ▢▢▢ ▢▢▢ low light

TEMPERATURE
cool ▢▢▢ ▢▢▢ warm

STUDY AREA
formal ▢▢▢ ▢▢▢ informal/comfortable

KEY ● = strong preference   ◯ = flexibility   — = non-preference
        (always needed)   (adjustable to situations)   (avoid if possible/not applicable)
     ▨ = preference   ?? = inconsistency
        (needed most of the time)

Considering our fast-changing world, the changing shape of work, as Gordon Dryden and Jeannette Vos describe it so succinctly in their excellent book *The Learning Revolution*, and the estimation that people in the workforce of the future will be changing their profession, not only their jobs, up to five times during their working life, it will be more necessary than ever to be flexible and adaptable.

changing shape of work

**changing professions
up to five times**

flexible and adaptable

Self-knowledge and flexibility will be the two most important qualities – for employees and managers as well as for people who want to be successful in training, teaching and learning. The same goes for anyone who wants more than just to survive, who wants to thrive in the times ahead and live a rich, fulfilled life.

self-knowledge, flexibility

Highly flexible people (like those in the sample profile shown on page 300/302) have the ability to use both left- and/or right-brain processing skills equally well and can, according to the requirements of the situation, respond easily, either the analytic or the holistic way. They can effortlessly adjust to different conditions in their environment and have hardly any strong needs or preferences. They are appreciated for being all-rounders and are usually very easy-going, accommodating, and most of the time not overly ambitious.

highly flexible people

left/right-brain skills

**analytical or holistic
adjust effortlessly**

At work these people are generally the appreciated all-rounders, colleagues who are most of the time willing to do anything and are always prepared to help anyone.

**at work
all-rounders**

People with no preferences at all, just flexibilities, usually display average performance and will hardly ever become leaders. Unless something triggers their interest or motivation deeply, they are usually content with their roles for quite a long time.

**no preferences
average performance**

content with their roles

Strong flexibility in the sensory areas (visual, auditory, tactile, kinesthetic) means that such people need information intake and learning through all their senses. Doing it through one or two modalities only is not quite enough for

sensory flexibility

through all senses

LSA-Adult

My Flexibilities

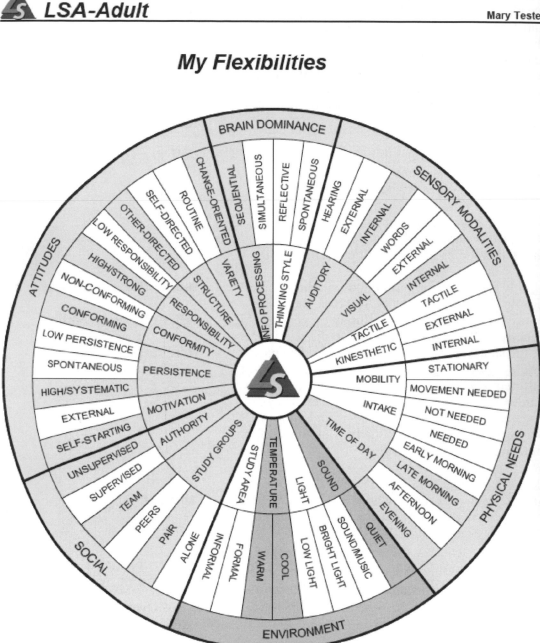

Flexibilities (shaded in the pie chart) allow you to adjust to changing situations naturally and adaptabilities are influenced by the situation and usually come with effort.

their brain. They need a <u>multisensory approach</u>.
That's why <u>creative, accelerated learning methods</u>,
taking into account all the senses, seem to be
particularly useful for anyone with high flexibility
in their perceptual areas.

**multisensory approach
creative, accelerated
learning methods**

Being <u>flexible</u> in one's <u>thinking style</u> means that
these people can be either <u>quick</u> and <u>impulsive</u> in
their thinking or they can <u>slow down</u> and <u>reflect</u>
on things before they make decisions. The true
advantage is they can adjust their thinking style
easily to match the diversity of situations or
problems. This gives them a <u>greater capacity</u> to
<u>understand</u> what's going on and enables them
to <u>respond more appropriately</u>. Given the great
complexity of human life these days in our
Western societies – privately and professionally –
it is almost a <u>necessity to be highly flexible</u>, at least
in our thinking style, because <u>mental rigidity</u>
(either strongly analytical or holistic, left- or right-
brain style) will <u>not be sufficient</u> to cope with
our <u>fast-changing world</u>. The future belongs
to flexible thinkers!

**flexible thinking style
quick and impulsive
slow down and reflect**

**greater capacity of
understanding
respond appropriately**

**necessity to be flexible
mental rigidity**

**not sufficient for
fast-changing world**

So, how can you become more flexible if you
have been using more or less only one kind of
thinking style for many years? The good news is
that <u>mental flexibility</u> can be <u>learned</u> like any
other skill. <u>Through practice</u> every human being
can become more flexible in their thinking style.
The exercise on page 304 will help you become more
flexible in areas of your choice.

**mental flexibility – learned
through practice**

In his book *The Right Brain Manager*, Harry Alder
takes a clear stand against the way in which
<u>Western culture</u> generally values most highly
those skills which reflect <u>left-brain dominance</u>.
Such skills as <u>logical or mathematical ability</u> and
<u>sequential or analytical reasoning</u> are focused on
throughout higher education and professional
training and are vital to all scientific methods.
The <u>abilities located in the right brain</u>, however,
tend to be <u>neglected, even suppressed</u>, because
the imaginative powers of the right brain are not
valued highly. Such an <u>imbalance</u> is bound
to affect a person's <u>overall abilities</u> and may be
the cause of <u>losing the intuitive powers</u> of the
creative part of the brain. (8)

**Western culture
left-brain dominance
logical/mathematical ability
sequential/analytical skills**

**right-brain abilities
neglected, suppressed**

**imbalance
overall abilities
losing intuitive powers**

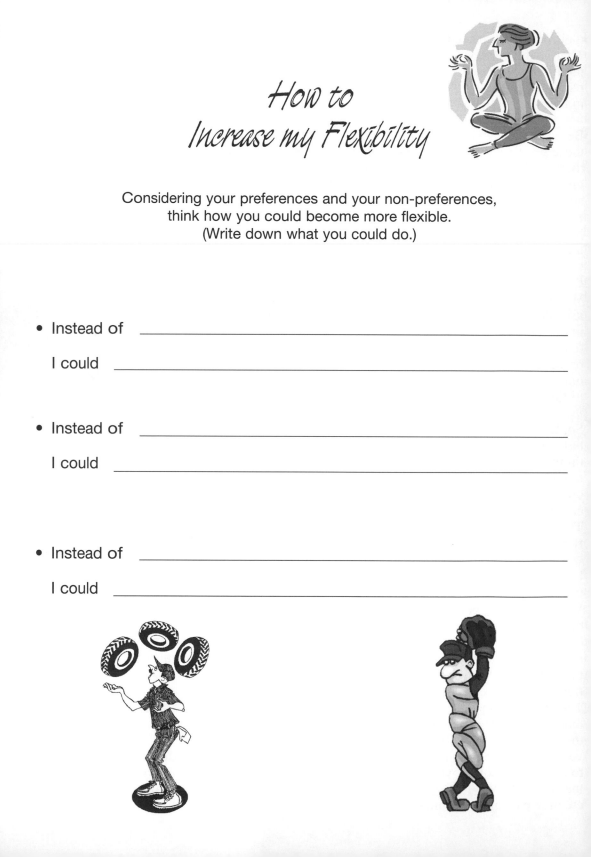

How to Increase my Flexibility

Considering your preferences and your non-preferences,
think how you could become more flexible.
(Write down what you could do.)

- Instead of _____

  I could _____

- Instead of _____

  I could _____

- Instead of _____

  I could _____

People have been trained through formal education into being more analytic, using predominantly logical thinking; it would <u>help analytics</u> to <u>use their intuition more often</u> and enhance their right-brain thinking skills. <u>Holistics</u>, on the other hand, who often have a hard time in our left-brain dominated society, could <u>practise logical thinking</u> and use their left-brain, analytical skills more often. This way, not only their <u>flexibility would increase</u>, but also their <u>brain power would be enhanced</u>.

help analytics
use intuition more often
holistics

practise logical thinking

flexibility increased
brain power enhanced

If you want to begin your own '<u>flexibility training</u>' I invite you to try out the suggested exercises on the opposite page. Not only are they fun, they will also give you an insight into your existing <u>thought patterns</u>, some of which you have been building up over a lifetime. The more often you <u>repeat certain mental patterns</u>, the more they are likely to <u>become</u> 'habits'; many of them may even have manifested themselves as <u>bad habits</u>! The only way <u>to get rid of these</u> is to <u>become aware</u> of them in the first place, observe how they no longer serve you, and then consciously get rid of them until you have <u>developed new patterns</u> which are more appropriate or which make you more flexible, or even more 'likeable'.

flexibility training

thought patterns

repeat mental patterns
become 'habits'
bad habits
to get rid of by
becoming aware

developing new patterns

7. Know who you want to become and go for it!

The more you know yourself, the more you know who you are, the more you will be able to become who you are truly meant to be. Some years ago, when I heard statements like these, I could not see any meaning in them and found them rather weird. They sounded odd and my well-trained analytical mind rejected them. I had been an academic for such a long time that I had <u>somehow forgotten</u> that there is <u>more to life than logic</u>, well-founded arguments, <u>reasoning</u> and belief systems which categorically stated that what doesn't make sense can't possibly exist.

forgotten
more to life than logic
reasoning

However, I had always felt there was <u>something missing</u> from my very successful academic life as well as my private life. I really did not know what it was until my <u>awareness grew</u> and I learned about things I had never learned at school, during

something missing

awareness grew

HOW THEY HANDLE

TIME

Left-Brain Processors Strong Analytic Thinkers	Right-Brain Processors Strong Holistic Thinkers

Left-Brain Processors
Strong Analytic Thinkers

- highly organized
- overly punctual
- plan their time
- like to use time planners
- keep diaries/journals
- love To-Do lists
- want daily routine
- plan activities in advance
- get upset when time
  schedules are disrupted
- live within 'real' time frames
- prefer morning hours

Right-Brain Processors
Strong Holistic Thinkers

- disorganized
- difficulty being on time
- tend to lose track of time
- find time planners very stressful
- only keep diaries if they have to
- hate To-Do lists
- find routine limiting
- do things spontaneously
- have problems following
  time schedules
- live with 'diffused' time concept
- prefer late afternoon/evening

Based on observations, experience and reports from people

my training as a teacher or at university, even
studying psychology. I learned fascinating facts
about the human brain and how it works, how
learning processes influence us in whatever we do,
and that brain patterns are <u>powerful mechanisms</u>
which either limit us or further us in our
<u>personal development</u>.

brain patterns
powerful mechanisms
in personal development

Deeper insight into diversity and <u>personal growth</u>
came when I began to attend seminars and started
reading books about personal growth. Slowly
I began to understand that we can truly determine
who we want to be and how we can actually
<u>shape our own future</u> by developing our
<u>untapped brain power</u> and applying strategies
to <u>use our mental strengths</u> much more effectively.

personal growth

shape own future
untapped brain power
use mental strengths

Among the hundreds of books on <u>self-development</u>
(and there are many excellent ones on the market), I
found the books and tapes by Anthony Robbins,
Unlimited Power and *Awaken the Giant Within*, some
of the most useful. All his recommendations, theories
and practical exercises are based on <u>how the brain</u>
<u>works</u> and how our brain patterns influence our
development in life. 'Properly run,' he states in his
remarkable book *Unlimited Power*, 'your brain can
make your life greater than any dream you've ever
had before.' (9)

self-development

how the brain works

The ultimate <u>success formula</u> he advocates is very
simple: <u>know your outcome, take action</u>, know what
results you are getting, and have the <u>flexibility to</u>
<u>change</u> until you are successful. Robbins' books are
full of success stories and I know many people who
are constantly following this formula with great results.
I, myself, have been using this formula for the past
four years with great success, especially in my business.
But only by combining it with thorough
<u>self-knowledge</u>, by understanding, experiencing and
accepting my own and other people's uniqueness
could I fully appreciate why this approach works so
well. It all depends on how you <u>use your brain power</u>
and what you do with what you have got.

success formula
know outcome, take action
flexibility to change

self-knowledge

use your brain power

People who never ask themselves in what direction
they are presently going, (or if they follow their
current direction, where they will be in five or

RISK

- To laugh is to risk appearing a fool.
- To weep is to risk appearing sentimental.
- To reach out for another is to risk involvement.
- To expose feelings is to risk exposing your true self.
- To place your ideas, your dreams, before the crowd is
  to risk their loss.
- To love is to risk not being loved in return.
- To live is to risk dying.
- To hope is to risk despair.
- To try is to risk failure.

But risks must be taken because the greatest
hazard in life is to risk nothing.
The person who risks nothing, does nothing,
has nothing, is nothing.
He may avoid suffering and sorrow, but
he simply cannot learn, feel, change, grow, love, ... live.
Chained by his certitudes, he is a slave:
he has forfeited freedom.
Only a person who risks is free.

Anonymous

ten years' time, and is this where they want to go)
tend to miss out on a lot in life and will not be able
to shape their own future. If, however, they begin   **shape their own future**
to ask questions, learn more about themselves,
their style, their needs, their preferences, and
accept and appreciate diversity, they will find   **appreciate diversity**
that life gets easier, efforts are more worthwhile   **life gets easier**
and they will become masters of their own destiny.   **masters of own destiny**

8. Get familiar with your new self

If, by any chance, through reading the book or
doing your WSA profile, you have found out
that the style you have been displaying and using
up to now is not really your true style (you may   **not your true style**
have discovered that you are much more holistic,
right-brain dominant than you had thought or
allowed yourself to be, or that you have more
analytic style features than you believed you had),
rest assured. You are in the company of numerous
people – intelligent, successful human beings who
have lived all their lives without really knowing   **without knowing**
what their true preferences are, like myself.   **their true preferences**

Since I discovered my true self and became clearer   **clearer about**
about my strengths and weaknesses, I have been   **strengths and weaknesses**
utilizing my style features differently and have
gained a new awareness about myself and other   **new awareness**
people. Even if your reaction to some of the results
in your profile might be: 'But that's not me' or
'That's not how I do it', think again, because such
a reaction could be a sign of not having used your   **not using your true style**
true style, and the cost is probably stress, exhaustion,
frustration and dissatisfaction. Therefore trust your
profile if the results are valid, experiment with your   **experiment with flexibility**
flexibilities and practise your new-found strengths.   **practise your strengths**
In the beginning it might be a bit awkward, you
might even experience a slight slump in your
performance or efficiency because you are now   **changing**
changing old routines and habits, but trust your own   **old routines and habits**
abilities, they will give you greater ease and more
success in whatever you do in future. Believe me,
your true self is the best you can have – everything   **your true self –**
else is pretence and costs a lot more energy.   **the best you can have**

One surprising aspect of your new 'You' might be the fact that you are actually less analytic than you thought or that you are a 'learned' analytic which means you have been conditioned to function, think, learn or work analytically, although by nature you are more holistic, feeling-oriented. This can lead to frustration or great integration in your head, but recognized and accepted it is a special skill you can use to great advantage. For more on that matter see pages 244–5.

learned analytic

frustration or integration special skill

9. Walk your talk – dance your story – celebrate your glory!

Years ago I had a cooking apron with the following words printed on it: 'What you see is what you get'. I found it an amusing saying, nothing more. Later, when I had learned more about diversity, style differences and how people learn to play roles until they don't know any longer who they really are, suddenly, in the light of human diversity and brain functioning, this sentence took on a deeper meaning. I imagined how it would be if we could all be ourselves at all times, if we could only stop pretending that we are something or someone we are not, if we could most of the time 'walk our talk'.

style differences how people play roles

could be ourselves stop pretending

walk our talk

The more I thought about role playing and observed masked behaviour, the more I began to ask why. Why are we doing this? Why can't we be who we are? And then it dawned on me: most people don't know who they are, because they never really bothered to find out, they never dared to discover their real self, their own unique style. They were living their lives mostly by other people's standards and expectations, using up all their mental and physical energy to play these roles, never knowing why they were so exhausted, stressed, frustrated, confused, and burnt out.

masked behaviour

people don't know who they are real self – unique style

With the use of style analysis instruments, people suddenly gain deep insights into themselves, their own needs and preferences, and their own uniqueness. They learn what makes them tick and realize why they and others do things.

style instruments deep insights

In many conversations with people who had their styles assessed with our instruments, I have

Sit back and relax and think about yourself. Think about all the things that you don't like about yourself, things you would like to change or improve. Draw or write them down in the left-hand column. After two minutes switch your mind over to things you like about yourself, things you are proud of or you have been successful in. Write or draw these in the right-hand column. Compare the two lists and now you have an indication where you need to start your change process.

What I don't like about myself	What I like about myself

discovered the <u>power of self-knowledge</u>. Those
with low self-esteem and very uncertain beliefs
about themselves gained the most from their
new insights. Getting their profiles, interpreting
them and learning that there is nothing 'good'
or 'bad' about styles, they finally began to
<u>believe in themselves</u>, and to see their past
failures and their whole self in a different light.

Equipped with these new insights they could now
be true to themselves and <u>help themselves</u> in their
own way. They saw who they were, what <u>qualities</u>
they had, that it is OK to be who they really are,
and that they are <u>good enough</u>. By learning more
about themselves and appreciating their unique
qualities, people also learned that they <u>don't have
to take themselves and life so seriously</u>, that they
can experience what one movie title describes as
'the (un)bearable <u>lightness of being</u>' and not only
'walk their talk' but also '<u>dance' their unique story</u>.

We know that life is never plain sailing, that there
will always be ups and downs, but with greater
self-knowledge and better understanding of
human diversity it is much easier to cope with
whatever happens, keep one's integrity, remain
true to oneself and <u>celebrate one's own greatness</u>.

Even if people have a lot of negative beliefs about
themselves, they can consciously <u>change their
brain pattern</u> (with know-how and patience) to
produce a more <u>positive self-image</u>, which in turn
leads to <u>greater understanding</u> and tolerance
as well as to <u>more brain power</u>.

For those of you who are keen to begin the change
process now, the exercise on the opposite page
is a good starting point; with repeated use you
will notice how your negative beliefs will slowly
but surely be replaced by positive ones. Once
you have acknowledged your negative beliefs,
your brain will help you to get rid of them,
especially when you keep practising and stay
focused on the positive ones.

If people can <u>appreciate and cherish</u> their and
others' <u>uniqueness</u>, they are also more capable of

power of self-knowledge

believe in themselves

help themselves
qualities

good enough

don't have to
take themselves & life
seriously
lightness of being
dance their story

celebrate own greatness

change brain patterns

positive self-image
greater understanding
more brain power

appreciate and cherish
uniqueness

If a child lives
with approval,
he learns to live
with himself.

Dorothy Law Nolte (1998)

It is a great sign
of mediocrity
to praise always
moderately.

Vauvenargues

recognizing strengths, sharing successes, and
appreciating achievements. When people are ready
for that, they will be strong enough to take praise
and be able to celebrate their glory. Everyone

celebrate their glory

wants recognition and it is virtually impossible

recognition

ever to give too much praise for achievement,

praise

especially to children. Knowing how powerful
positive reinforcement is, it is really sad to see

positive reinforcement

how overlooked praise is in most areas of life,
in our families, in business and in education.

Clifton and Nelson have devoted a whole
chapter to celebration in their interesting book

celebration

Play to Your Strengths. There they describe
many examples of significant improvement
of productivity when recognition for someone's

productivity improvement

work is received, and they state: 'In the largest
sense, people are attracted to that which
is celebrated, and people do what they are
celebrated for.' (11)

As every educational institution has their own
styles of celebrating, you need to understand your

styles of celebrating

own need for recognition and must find ways

need for recognition

to fulfill it. Consider the following questions,
answer them honestly and see how you can
celebrate your personal strengths:

celebrate strengths

1. Are you getting enough recognition in your
    current work/school (home) environment?
2. What kinds of recognition can you expect
    over the next two or three years at work,
    at your studies (or at home)?
3. How could you get more?
4. If you are not getting the recognition you
    know you deserve, what can you do?

If you think you don't need any rewards, or that's
not your sort of thing, rethink your attitude. As
many studies have shown, personal rewards are

personal rewards

an important part of building personal strengths;

building strengths

they stimulate your brain to better performance
and can come in many forms. One should never
forget that young people and old need to
celebrate their uniqueness, their achievements.

celebrate uniqueness

What is Success?

To laugh often and love much;
To win the respect of intelligent persons
and the affection of children;
To earn the approval of honest critics
and endure the betrayal of false friends;
To appreciate beauty; to find the best in others;
To give of one's self without the slightest
thought of return;
To have accomplished a task, whether
by a healthy child, a rescued soul, a garden patch,
or a redeemed social condition;
To have played and laughed with
enthusiasm, and sung with exaltation;
To know that even one life has breathed
easier because you have lived;
This is to have succeeded.

10. See how far you have come – a checklist for change

Now that you have hopefully found a whole new world of possibilities opening up for you, answer the questions on the <u>learning attitudes</u> checklist again in the 'How I Feel About Learning' post-test on page 340. <u>Compare</u> how you scored before you began reading this book with how you have scored now. Has <u>anything changed</u>?

learning attitudes

compare

anything changed?

Have you scored higher? If not, ask yourself if you actually wanted to change your attitudes towards learning and working and why not. <u>Reflect</u> on what might be the reason for your unchanged mindset and consider if it is useful for you to continue in the same way. If your answer is 'Yes', that's good, but if your answer is 'No', maybe you could go over certain chapters of the book again, complete some exercises, talk to people or read some more books. It could be the beginning of a great discovery.

reflect

If something HAS changed, you are on your way to becoming a <u>skilled brain user</u>, a more effective and <u>satisfied learner</u>. That will definitely help you in whatever you do – it might even help you to finally live the life you have always wanted.

skilled brain user
satisfied learner

Congratulations!

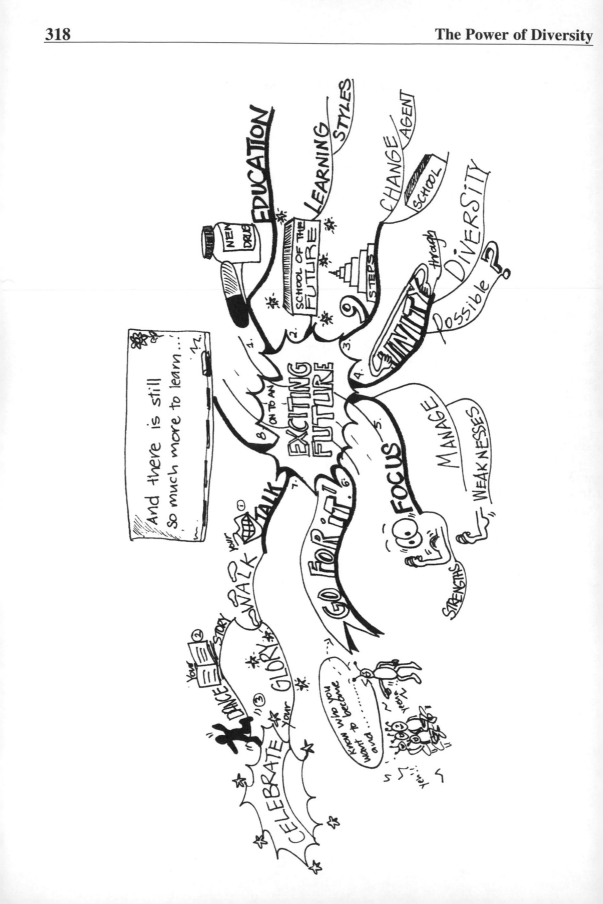

1. LS and creative learning – the new drugs of education

'If students receive an <u>ecstatic high from successful learning</u> in a pleasant, fun, socially comfortable and caring environment, then drugs have no allure,' wrote Lyelle Palmer, professor of education and director of the office of accelerative learning at Winona State University, back in 1990. (1) Over ten years later, as creative, accelerated, student-centred learning and teaching methods are spreading around the world, new paradigms in education and <u>new standards of classroom practice</u> are producing results in achievement far beyond the old norms of any subject matter, age group or social setting.

**ecstatic high from
successful learning**

**new standards
of classroom practice**

These new methods, <u>based on learning styles</u> and a better understanding of <u>how the brain works</u>, have re-inspired teachers, re-energized students and given parents new hope.

**based on learning styles
how the brain works**

Many components of this new approach are not new at all – they have been researched and used for many years. What is <u>new is the system,</u> the total package in which they are now being used, taking into account the <u>sequence of preparation and presentation</u> of curriculum content, and the <u>holistic view</u> of matching students' needs and teaching styles in a positive, <u>emotionally supportive</u> learning environment.

new system

**sequence of preparation
and presentation
holistic view**

emotionally supportive

This new way of teaching is in <u>stark contrast</u> to <u>traditional educational settings</u> where much of the time is spent on complaining, finding negative aspects and pointing out mistakes; where students' individual needs are not considered really important or even valid; and <u>negative expectations</u> prevail on either side.

**stark contrast
traditional education**

negative expectations

Under such conditions the energies of teachers and students alike are depleted very quickly, and then the climate is one of <u>resignation</u>, <u>boredom</u>, complaint, <u>frustration</u> and <u>hopelessness</u>.
The resulting attitude of all concerned is one of '<u>getting by</u>', not only at school but often in life.

**resignation, boredom,
frustration, hopelessness**

getting by

The Three Learning Zones

> *Think about your own schooling or training —*
> *when and how frequently have you been in each zone?*

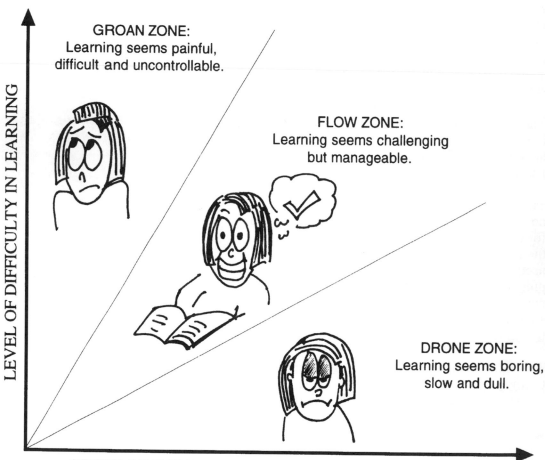

GROAN ZONE:
Learning seems painful,
difficult and uncontrollable.

FLOW ZONE:
Learning seems challenging
but manageable.

DRONE ZONE:
Learning seems boring,
slow and dull.

LEVEL OF DIFFICULTY IN LEARNING

SCOPE OF YOUR ABILITY – Skills, Attitudes, Strategies

Based on an idea from *Peak Learning* by Ronald Gross, 1991

As explained throughout the book, when <u>styles</u> <u>are matched</u>, methods are truly <u>student-centred</u> and brain processing is understood, teachers become energized and inspired, and students experience a <u>positive learning environment</u>, remarkable <u>creativity</u> and <u>retention rate</u> as well as self-discipline, joy, <u>high</u> responsibility and <u>motivation for learning</u>.

matched styles
student-centred methods

positive environment
creativity and retention

high learning motivation

Learning under such favourable conditions is brain-friendly, fast and easy. Students quickly develop a <u>positive self-image</u>, show relaxed attentiveness during classes and display an <u>eagerness for learning</u> – they want more, more, more.

positive self-image

eagerness for learning

Even if teachers (particularly in high schools) may find it hard to believe, <u>learners</u> under such favourable conditions can really <u>get 'high'</u> <u>on their own abilities</u>, experience learning as an exciting adventure, and can actually get <u>addicted to learning</u>. This 'natural high' produced by these new educational strategies has <u>far-reaching implications</u>: drug use and alcohol abuse, which have reached frightening proportions among the younger age groups in New Zealand and in many other countries, can be stopped when students begin to feel good about themselves and experience learning success and higher self-esteem.

learners
get 'high'
on own abilities

addicted to learning

far-reaching implications

When this is achieved, their need for <u>killing</u> <u>emotional pain through drugs disappears</u>.

killing emotional pain
through drugs disappears

Although I accept that this particular social problem is much more complex, it is also true that we as educators can do a lot to help students who have experienced nothing but rejection, negative expectations, underachievement, frustration and desperation combined with low self-esteem during their years of schooling, and make them <u>feel better about themselves</u>.

feel better about selves

When we accept these students are not 'thick, lazy, slow or stupid', as often labelled by their teachers, and also <u>not learning disabled</u>, as often described by psychologists, when we appreciate they are just '<u>learning different</u>' and provide them

not learning disabled

learning different

Learning Styles implementation
around the world

At completion of this updated, third edition of this book, there are now too many schools around the world who have partially or fully implemented the Learning Styles concept based on our software and each month more are being added to the list.

Therefore I have gone through my records and below is a list of countries where I either have conducted LS training and/or this concept has been introduced (often without my initial knowledge). The list is not quite in historical order, but close enough. It all started back in 1992 when I began to conduct professional development seminars for teachers in New Zealand and it is continuing to this day in September 2007:

New Zealand
Sweden (with Swedish software)
Finland (with Finnish software)
Australia
United Kingdom
Cyprus
Switzerland
United States of America
Denmark (with Danish software)
Norway (with Norwegian software)
Canada
Peoples' Republic of China (in Mandarin)
Singapore
Chile (with Spanish software)
South Africa (partly in Afrikaans)
The Caribbean
Slovenia
Austria (with German software)
Turkey (with Turkish software)
Dubai
Sweden (with Swedish software and POD book)
Finland (with Finnish software and POD book)
Switzerland (with English software)
Norway (with Norwegian software and POD book)
Indonesian (POD book published 2007)

The question is, which countries will be next?

with opportunities for successful learning, we
will have done more for them and their future life
than just trying to ensure they – and their school –
achieve better grades.

There is plenty of evidence that these holistic
methods produce a <u>high level of productivity</u>
and <u>caring</u>, <u>independence</u> and deep <u>respect for</u>
<u>human diversity</u>. Considering our fast-changing
world, these are certainly the attitudes we need
to develop in our children to enable them to take
<u>personal responsibility</u> for their own learning and
for making <u>positive choices in life</u>. Instead of
becoming helpless victims, they have abundant
opportunities to choose success for themselves.

**high level of productivity,
caring, independence
respect for human diversity**

**personal responsibility
positive choices in life**

2. The 'School of the Future' based on learning styles

When I began conducting <u>in-service training</u>
<u>programmes</u> for schools I became acutely aware
that single seminars and workshops sometimes
achieved personal changes for individual teachers
but could definitely not bring about a change
for the whole learning culture of their institution.
Out of that consideration grew a programme
which has been extremely successful here in
<u>New Zealand and overseas</u> and which is still
growing. The programme is called 'School of
the Future based on Learning Styles and Quality'
and is based on the notion that for any <u>change in</u>
<u>education</u>, if it is <u>to be successful</u>, there have
to be <u>three vital ingredients</u>:

**in-service
training programmes**

New Zealand and overseas

**changes in education
to be successful
three ingredients**

1. *A Basic Philosophy* which says that students
   possess unique learning style preferences and
   that <u>educators must adopt</u> a <u>new view of education</u>,
   recognizing and valuing the uniqueness of each
   human being, and accepting that both teachers
   and students have distinctly different abilities
   to absorb and retain new information.

basic philosophy

**educators must adopt
new view of education**

2. *A Model* which helps educators to identify and
   administer assessment instruments, providing a
   <u>suitable framework</u> for capitalizing on individual
   differences in students' learning abilities.

a model

suitable framework

Educational change is like
being on a rotten boat,
with a mutinous crew,
sailing into uncharted waters.

Only the person not rowing
has

3. *The Transformation* – after having adopted and identified a suitable model, the challenge then is to establish practical guidelines for transforming a rigid teacher-centred traditional school and classroom situation into an exciting, child-centred learning environment suitable for any age group. To accomplish this, the school needs to invest time and resources to train their existing staff in learning styles and leading-edge teaching methods. Educational leaders, principals, teachers and parents need to agree on and implement policies which support such change programmes. (2)

the transformation

practical guidelines

**child-centred
learning environment**

train existing staff

Dryden and Vos, in the second edition of their book *The Learning Revolution*, give a detailed description for planning tomorrow's schools and how to transform a nation's education system by recommending the following 12-step programme:

12-step programme

1. *Schools as lifelong, year-round community resource centres*
   It can fulfil the role of an information resource centre, regarding education as a whole-of-life process involving families.
2. *Ask your customers first*
   Entire communities can be involved in planning a new school and where it has been done, results are inspiring.
3. *Guarantee customer satisfaction*
   Like with successful businesses, schools should be based on building and keeping satisfied customers – their students and parents.
4. *Cater to all intelligence traits and learning styles*
   With the most important single innovation – multiple intelligences and learning styles – school dropout rates could be greatly reduced.
5. *Use the world's best teaching techniques*
   Changes in education will only be successful with a major emphasis on teacher training and continual retraining, and one of the keys are accelerated, integrative learning techniques.
6. *Invest in your key resources – teachers*
   The world's most thoroughly researched educational breakthroughs are not being modelled at universities and teacher training colleges, and tomorrow's teachers are not being trained in these methods.
7. *Make everyone a teacher as well as a student*
   Many problems of staff 'burnout' could be solved by involving parents, grand-parents and the community in the teaching process – and students too.
8. *Plan a four-part curriculum*
   It consists of personal growth, life skills, learning-to-learn programmes and content, and is as important in continuing education as in childhood and during teenage years.

The **AIDA** Principle

Awareness – see, hear (about learning styles)

Information – read (about practising schools)

Decision – OK to go ahead – plan implementation

Action – start programme (on a school-wide basis)

9. *Change the assessment system*
   There are numerous efforts worldwide to change this key principle of school reform; the most important ones are doing away with traditional teaching and testing, involvement of the whole person, self-assessment and critical thinking.
10. *Use tomorrow's technology*
   Interactive computer–satellite–video–television and electronic games technology provide the catalyst that will finally force a much-needed change in the teacher's role – from information to transformation.
11. *Use the entire community as a resource*
   Many successful change models underscore the common sense of moving schooling away from the traditional classroom.
12. *For everyone: the right to choose*
   As the world has not only become one giant electronic, automobile, fast food and financial services market but also a major one-world educational market, the days of school monopoly on education are rapidly coming to an end. (3)

If you as a reader are a principal, administrator or politician dealing with educational matters, the above mentioned facts and philosophies should give you enough food for thought so that you hopefully in all earnest begin to contemplate how you can instigate change in the educational institution you are responsible for or involved with. The following process will help you in carrying out this task with the best possible preparation for hitches and glitches on the way.

principal, administrator, politician

instigate change

3. Nine steps to being a change agent in your school

Years ago, when I visited Linda MacRae-Campbell at Antioch University in Seattle, she gave me an article which describes 'how to do what must be done' when you want to start a revolution at your school. I have recommended this process to many schools over the years, and it has never failed to produce results. Individuals willing to serve as instigators of change will encounter formidable resistance as they work at the forefront, but with strategies and coordination these 'change agents' can successfully topple the entrenched traditions.

individuals
instigators of change

strategies and coordination

Step One: Identify a need for reform within the school
A starting point for many schools will be writing a new mission statement that specifies the school's philosophy, goals and values, and addresses serious concerns such as underachievement, discipline problems, dropout rates, high stress among teaching staff, lack of parental involvement and other problem areas.

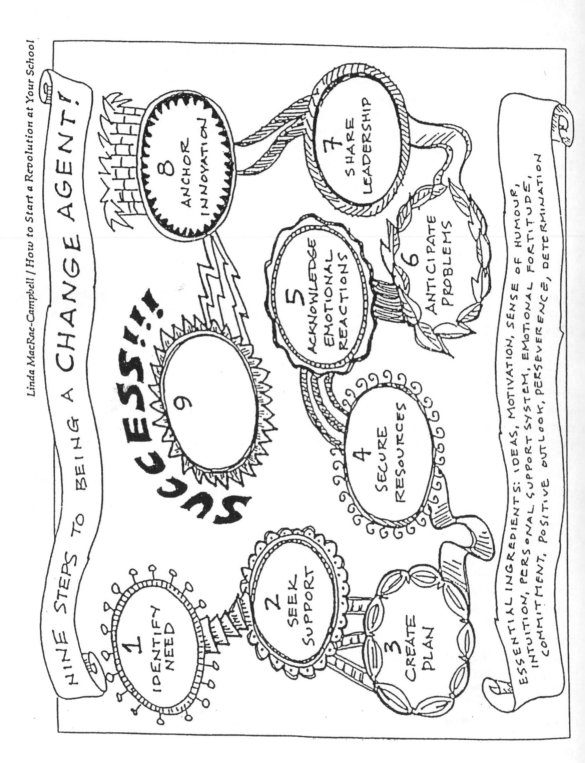

Linda MacRae-Campbell / How to Start a Revolution at Your School

Step Two: Seek supporters for change

The number of people who must be convinced of a new concept or approach is approximately 15–20 per cent of a school's population; strong advocates for the change project need to be identified from both within and outside the school, and their support actively sought.

Step Three: Create and communicate an action plan for the change

It's wise to begin with small projects that will succeed within the first few months. The projects should be well organized and co-ordinated to reduce the open scepticism abundant among traditional school staffs. For major restructuring efforts, plan a minimum of 3–5 years.

Step Four: Secure the needed resources

Identify and secure human resources as well as material needs. These might include consultants, training programmes, financial resources and definitely additional time for the staff involved.

Step Five: Acknowledge the emotional reactions

As a change agent you must anticipate personal reactions to change; a typical emotional cycle has been identified through research, and includes five stages:
1. uninformed optimism
2. informed pessimism
3. hopeful realism
4. informed optimism
5. rewarding completion. The 'Implementation Dip' is another phenomenon encountered in restructuring and means a frustrating decline in performance or work quality is experienced for a while.

Step Six: Anticipate problems, identify problem-solving skills

Predictable problems during any restructuring process are attitude and emotional issues, lack of coordination or communication, lack of resources, and unanticipated crises. Active problem-solving methods are extremely important for the project(s) to be successful.

Step Seven: Share the leadership

For widespread change to become firmly implanted, it is necessary to share the control of the project and work collaboratively with others.

Step Eight: Anchor innovation very quickly to classroom practice

For new classroom practices to be implemented, a combination of support and pressure is required, and change efforts that are quickly linked to the classroom are perceived as relevant and important; ongoing staff development is necessary.

Step Nine: Embed the innovation into organizational practice

Once implemented, measured and refined, innovations become part of school life and restructuring efforts become embedded in the school's philosophy, budget, policies and administration. Never forget to celebrate the progress! (4)

For teachers starting out on this road and undertaking the burden of change and the risks involved, they need support.

It's not enough to have an abstract statement that this is the target. You have to understand what it looks like when you have achieved that target, what something which is halfway looks like and why it's only halfway there.

Quotes from Paul Black, emeritus professor of education, King's College London in the accompanying booklet to the DVD: "Partners for Learning", an initiative by Birmingham City Council, 2006

4. New leaders in education understand learning diversity

Forbury Primary School in Dunedin in the south of
New Zealand had experienced significant difficulties
over several years; had been governed by a
Commissioner for over a year and by March 2001
the school roll had fallen by 52.3 per cent. Despite efforts
to turn the school around, there was no improvement
of the dire situation and closure of the school or
merging it with neighbouring primary school were
options being considered by the Ministry of Education.

When I was approached by the Commissioner he
conveyed to me that a 'radical, innovative' approach   **radical innovative**
was needed to rescue this troubled school. Although   **troubled school**
it was the first time that I agreed to take on such a
complex and difficult project and I wanted to prove   **complex difficult project**
what researchers of LS in Canada and the USA had
reported many years ago: through LS it is possible to   **turn a failing school**
turn a failing school around and this is what we did!   **around**

The Forbury Project is described in full in Chapter 23
in my book *Learning Styles in Action* together with
several other LS school projects in Australia.

Without a strong school leader who truly understood   **strong school leader**
the importance of the diversity concept this huge   **diversity concept**
success would not have been possible and I commend
the **principal, Ms Janice Tofia** on her vision for
Forbury and her leadership strength. I loved working
with their staff and admire their commitment and   **commitment**
enthusiasm for this project.   **enthusiasm**

Most of all I was impressed by the willingness of all
concerned to be open to scrutiny as part of this   **open to scrutiny**
development, by their readiness to trust me, to change   **readiness to trust**
their thinking about learning and teaching, and finally   **trust their thinking**
to put a considerable amount of extra time and work   **extra time and work**
into personal as well as professional development.   **professional development**
And that over a period of nearly 3 years!

Last but not least, I was impressed by their acceptance
of being advised, observed and judged on every step
of the way – all for the well-being of their students   **well-being of their**
and often for their own sanity.   **students**

The school is doing very well now, has increased
student numbers and does not need my help any
longer which makes me very happy.

PRINCIPLES FOR RESTRUCTURING

based on VISION, PIONEERING SPIRIT and PEOPLE NEEDS

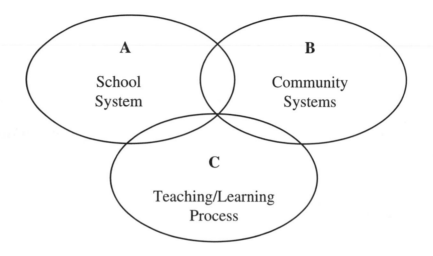

They need to:

A. include the organizational restructuring
   of the school system itself

B. be related to changes and needs in the
   community and society

C. focus on the restructuring of the
   teaching/learning process.

5. The myth of individualized learning in mass education

The only way of educating <u>large numbers</u> of people has historically been by gathering them in <u>groups</u> (in classrooms of up to 30, 40 students, in lecture theatres with up to 500 or more seats, in church or political congregations of up to several thousand people) and having usually ONE person (often a gifted orator) instructing, informing, enlightening, reprimanding, sometimes even entertaining them. To some degree, the audience was allowed to participate, but generally people were <u>passive recipients</u> of whatever wisdom was disseminated.

large numbers
groups

passive recipients

This model has been wholeheartedly embraced by education systems because it is <u>easy to control</u> and <u>economical</u> too: one teacher for 200 to 2000 or more students per week! It was mass education for the industrial age, but really effective it was not, as only those who could benefit from such <u>verbal instructions</u>, lectures and <u>frontal teaching</u> would actually <u>remember</u> what was taught/read out to them. And that was the <u>minority</u>, particularly in schools. The majority who couldn't 'get' the information that way, remained <u>poorly educated</u> – intentionally perhaps?

easy to control
economical

verbal instructions
frontal teaching
remember
minority

poorly educated

When <u>achievement levels</u> of students began to <u>drop</u> dangerously, pedagogical researchers came up with the brilliant idea of <u>student-centred teaching</u> and <u>individualized learning</u>. Theoretical papers were written, conferences organized, and politicians could use education once more for their own ends. In all that furore it was convenienty forgotten to give instruction manuals to <u>classroom teachers</u> and tell them HOW one could <u>focus on individuals</u> and do that in large groups.

achievement levels drop

student-centred teaching
individualized learning

classroom teachers
focus on individuals

The concept looks good on paper and reads well in theory, but for classroom teachers it was <u>not practical</u> because <u>individualization</u> is possible with very few students and to a certain extent workable in primary schools, but <u>impossible</u> to implement <u>in high schools</u> and large classes.

not practical
individualization

impossible in high schools

So this concept quietly faded away in most countries, remaining a myth to this day and <u>frontal teaching</u> with <u>lectures</u>, lots of reading and <u>rote learning</u> are still the most often used instructional methods in secondary and tertiary schools – of course with a bit of team work and modern technology thrown in for good measure.

frontal teaching
lectures
rote learning

I am your teacher and I will:

> Support you

> Encourage you

> Challenge you

> Listen to you

> Be honest with you

> Respect you

> Learn from you

> Trust you

> Laugh with you

> Provide you with the most effective
  teaching methods I know

BUT I WILL NOT:

Do everything for you.

6. From student-centred teaching to personalized learning

Although the main theme in this book is human
diversity and how our learning, our work, actually our
whole life can benefit from an understanding of style
diversity, it is now necessary to define the term
'personalized learning' in this context. Let me use a
definition given by the then UK Education minister,   **definition**
David Miliband, at an education conference in 2004:
'Decisive progress in educational standards occurs
where every child matters; careful attention is paid to
their individual learning styles, motivations and needs.'

Despite scepticism of academic researchers towards
the LS concept, there is no other way for teachers to
accommodate diverse LS needs of students but to   **accommodate diverse**
assess them, understand them how they interact with   **LS needs**
other factors and how they change during schooling   **assess**
years. If we seriously want to understand HOW our   **change**
students learn, we need to begin with getting to know
their idiosyncrasies in information intake, particularly **idiosyncrasies**
when learning content is perceived as new   **information intake**
and/or difficult.

However, such knowledge about individual LS helps   **individual LS helps**
students and their parents tremendously, but as
important as it is, does not help teachers to deliver
the curriculum to large classes (see also page 000).
Something else is necessary to 'personalize' teaching
and learning: the results from the **LSA Group Profiles** **results**
of a whole class. (For explanations see Chapter 4,   **LSA Group Profiles**
Part 7.)

It has never been possible before to see at one glance
which learning preferences a particular group of   **learning preferences**
students has, how flexible group members are, and   **group**
how they can't learn well; in other words, what effects **flexible**
their learning positively and negatively – not just as
individuals but as a group which has to spend time
together often under stressful conditions.

Group profiles reveal which learning environment   **learning environment**
is most conducive to a certain group's learning, how
students can be subgrouped to work and learn   **students can be**
together according to their preferences and how far they **subgrouped**
can be stretched in their flexibilities. They also show who **stretched**
needs different treatment, special attention and how   **flexibilities**
students can help each other. With this information   **special attention**
teachers can teach to collective individuality within   **collective individuality**
groups and personalize their instructions accordingly.

In Birmingham the components of personalised learning are:

leadership and management

effective teaching and learning

curriculum enrichment and choice

organisation for personalisation

beyond the school

targeted support for schools with concerns

7. Unity through diversity – it IS possible!

During my years of studying every possible
aspect of this new discipline, by learning from
the masters in their field as well as from my own
teaching experience in formal education settings
and in business training, I have experienced:
* so many diverse and yet parallel movements,
* so many different schools of thoughts,
* so many unique and yet similar avenues to the
  one common goal – <u>to help people learn better</u>.

help people learn better

<u>Many fine scholars</u> in this field <u>have researched</u>
phenomena, gained most useful insights into
the mystery of human learning and have created
<u>methods, techniques and tools</u> to enhance learning.

many scholars researched

methods, techniques, tools

Alas, many scholars are only capable or willing
to see *their own approach*. Unless they collaborate
with other specialists, they only theoretically accept
the other specialists in their field and hardly ever
look outside their own discipline. Most academic
researchers find it very 'unscientific' to blend
different techniques or tools, often <u>refusing</u> even
to discuss possibilities of <u>combining their own</u>
<u>with other experts' methods</u>.

only see own approach

refuse
combining own with other
experts' methods

Thus the developmental process is slowed down
and they deprive themselves and others of greater
possible successes. Therefore the conclusion has
to be: it is not really important who invented what,
when and where, and whose ideas, programmes or
approaches are the best. The <u>most important is what</u>
<u>serves the learner</u>. What can help them best in
coming to terms with difficulties during the learning
process? Which programmes or techniques will <u>match</u>
<u>someone's unique style</u>? How <u>successful and satisfied</u>
have learners been during the learning process? How
much have they gained and grown personally?
Was there <u>fun and enjoyment</u>, or boredom, stress
and frustration? And finally, is the learned
<u>information retained and useful to the learner</u>?

most important
what serves the learner

match unique style
successful, satisfied

fun and enjoyment

information retained,
useful to learner

As learning has become such a frustrating activity
for so many people, it is no longer enough only to
<u>acknowledge</u> (sometimes grudgingly) one another's

acknowledge

Brain Functions

MENTAL STATE	COGNITION	PRIMARY & SECONDARY BRAIN AREAS	SENSE OF TIME
calm	abstract	Neo-cortex Sub-cortex	extended future sense
arousal	concrete	Sub-cortex Limbic System	days hours
alarm	emotional	Limbic System Midbrain	hours minutes
fear (flight/flight)	reactive	Midbrain Brain Stem	minutes seconds
terror	reflective (survival)	Brain Stem Autonomic Nervous System	loss of sense of time

Dr Robin Fourcourt

contributions in the fields of education, brain research, sociology, psychology, cognitive science, management and business training.

It is high time that <u>specialists join forces</u> to create the synergy necessary for helping individuals, educational institutions, small businesses and large corporations as well as communities around the world in <u>coping with change</u>, capitalizing heavily on diversity, and finding more satisfactory ways of learning, working, training, studying, communicating, interacting and effective information intake.

specialists join forces

cope with change

Unless these leading forces in their different fields manage to create <u>unity through diversity</u> by recognizing and accepting that they all somehow work for the same cause – to further the development of the human race by <u>enhancing our knowledge</u> about the most powerful force in human beings – the <u>brain's unlimited ability to learn</u> – valuable insights will remain undiscovered, people will continue to struggle and many good ideas will be lost for ever.

unity through diversity

enhance knowledge

brain's unlimited ability to learn

8. It's the difference that makes the difference

In the context of learning styles, being different means having one of the <u>many possible style combinations</u> and stretches across the full brain processing scale (the entire 'brain dominance spectrum', as Ned Herrmann calls it). If this assumption is true and the scale has universal applicability, each <u>uniquely different</u> person in this world with a completed style analysis is indeed <u>normal</u>. By understanding their own profiles, their left-right brain dominance and the true meaning of human diversity, people can now come to terms with <u>why they are the way they are</u>. As a result of having their own learning or working style assessed, we see many people finally coming to terms with who they are and feeling OK about themselves, <u>appreciating</u> their own <u>uniqueness</u> often for the first time in their life.

many possible style combinations

uniquely different

normal

why they are the way they are

appreciating uniqueness

In their new book *Mavericks at Work* the authors Taylor and LaBarre go a step further and advocate that for companies to succeed in the 'new economy' they need more unconventional, off-the-wall thinkers – real <u>mavericks</u> in the positive sense of the word.

mavericks

HOW I FEEL ABOUT LEARNING

Post-test

Please respond to these statements by ticking the appropriate box –
do it fast, without analysing.

		True	False
1.	If I really want to learn something, I have to do a lot of studying and repetition	☐	☐
2.	Learning is something very interesting and pleasant for me	☐	☐
3.	I think I have a good memory	☐	☐
4.	Learning is hard work most of the time	☐	☐
5.	I think I've always been a good learner	☐	☐
6.	I wish I could concentrate better	☐	☐
7.	I don't think I'm very intelligent	☐	☐
8.	Often I think 'If only I didn't forget everything so quickly'	☐	☐
9.	If I can learn something new, I get the feeling of deep satisfaction and contentment	☐	☐
10.	If I think back to my time at school, I think 'Oh no! I'm glad that's over!'	☐	☐
11.	I think learning is very hard for me	☐	☐
12.	I know I learn quickly	☐	☐
13.	Learning has hardly ever been fun for me	☐	☐
14.	Learning gives me satisfaction, happiness and contentment	☐	☐
15.	I can't imagine that I'll ever be able to master a difficult subject (e.g. a foreign language, mathematics) easily	☐	☐
16.	Foreign languages have always been my favourite subject	☐	☐

For scoring see page 352

They argue that more orderly and respectable workers who mainly <u>reinforce the status quo</u> (analytic, logical, left-brain dominant people in LS terminology), are certainly not the source of innovative thinking and fresh ideas. I can only agree as I have seen countless times in businesses and education institutions that change can only be brought about by <u>risk-takers</u> who <u>think differently</u> and are open to new ideas, actually seeking them out, often under considerable difficulties.

reinforce the status quo

risk-takers
think differently

But there is <u>one more difference</u>, that makes the difference: it is finally no longer 'politically incorrect' to say that there is a difference <u>between men and women</u> when it comes to thinking, brain functions, information processing. Many neuroscientists have known that for a long time but in our eagerness to create <u>equality</u>, we have been guilty of <u>confusing it with sameness</u>. Male and female brains are wired differently and schools need to acknowledge that by using a wider spectrum of teaching methods based on these natural (style) differences.

one more difference

between men and women

equality
confusing it with
sameness

The message of hope behind all these insights is that <u>differences are not only normal</u>, they are <u>also positive</u> and enable people to live more creatively, appreciating and using diversity to make change easier to handle. When we learn to appreciate style differences more – in ourselves and others – we are capable of making better choices in education, our professions and personal lives.

differences are not only
normal – also positive

Above all, <u>accepting and acknowledging diversity</u> in our families, relationships, schools, companies, and organizations can lead to top performances, greater creativity and tremendous productivity gains as well as to <u>new values and attitudes</u> in human beings, something we need more than anything else right now.

accepting diversity

new values & attitudes

To remind the reader how diversity can become normal (the new 'norm'), throughout the book there are many examples from people in education who <u>dare to be different</u>, dare to take risks, dare to go against traditional beliefs about teaching and learning, and dare to <u>accept</u> and <u>welcome</u> <u>diversity in their classrooms</u>.

dare to be different

accept/welcome diversity
in classrooms

He
who knows much about others
may be learned,
but he
who understands himself
is more intelligent.

He
who controls others
may be powerful,
but he
who masters himself
is mightier still.

Lao-tsu 604 BC-531 BC

9. Never-ending learning is the name of the game

'The more you know the more you can know' is
another statement that is best understood in light
of our unlimited brain capacity and lifelong learning
ability. In the past I believed that my memory was
not that great, but once I began to apply these
new brain-based methods to my own learning,   **new learning methods**
I was amazed how much more information I could
absorb, retain and access whenever necessary.
I also found, together with my new-found self-
knowledge, it was much easier to understand
difficult concepts (although I knew I had a 'high IQ'
and during my schooling was considered 'very
intelligent', I still had my doubts).

The amount of information I have taken in over
the past few years in the field of creative learning
and human diversity is much much greater than
everything I had ever learned during my 21 years
of formal education – from primary school to
university. It might sound boastful, but my memory   **greatly improved memory**
has improved dramatically, I feel younger and   **more energetic**
more energetic, enjoy life more, I do more and   **enjoy life more**
accomplish more. (I even learned to play golf,
something I never thought I could master!) I also
know more and am capable of passing on information
better, faster and more effectively.

All these changes are still quite new to me and it
took a while to get used to this new 'Me'. For
a long time, while I was observing these often
dramatic changes in my abilities, I kept asking   **changes in my abilities**
myself 'Why?', 'How come?', 'What's happening
in my head?', etc. In hindsight the answers
seem very simple: I began using my preferences   **using my preferences**
more consciously, surrounded myself with people
who complemented me in my style, created
learning environments which matched my style
and learned to manage my weaknesses. In short,   **manage my weaknesses**
I dared to do things 'My Way' without limiting   **do things 'My Way'**
others in my environment to do things 'their way'.

But most importantly, by using my brain according
to my strengths and unique style, I also increased   **increased my flexibility**
my flexibility, my tolerance for diversity, and my   **tolerance for diversity**
love for human beings in general. Over the years,
I have seen similar developments in virtually

To deal with any situation successfully

you need to know

YOURSELF

and how to handle your weaknesses;

you also need to know

YOUR STYLE

and how to utilize your strengths.

B. Prashnig

everyone who has embraced diversity and adopted
<u>new attitudes</u> towards themselves, their own
learning abilities, their work and other
human beings in general.

new attitudes

However, the <u>greatest changes</u> I have experienced
so far have been in my <u>personal life</u>: in my
<u>transformed relationships</u> with my husband, as
described in Chapter 10, and the vastly improved
relationship with my daughter, as described in
Chapter 5. I have even worked with her for a while
when she rejoined our company and we both love it.
Again, I never thought this would be possible,
but as experienced before, never say never.

greatest changes
personal life
transformed relationships

Because I am a very private person, it was not easy
for me to reveal these deeply <u>personal experiences</u>.
However, I had to do it for everyone who is going
through hard times with their loved ones themselves,
and still struggles to find better ways of getting on.
I also had to do it for the simple reason that we need
to fully <u>understand human diversity</u>.

personal experiences

understand diversity

It is obvious that, by utilizing new scientific insights
and brain-friendly teaching techniques, by acquiring
self-knowledge and becoming more flexible, and
by dealing with our nearest and dearest in different
ways, we are not only capable of learning, doing
and knowing more, but we can also seemingly
<u>become better people</u> on our lifelong journey, able
to help ourselves and others to live, learn and grow –
particularly our children.

becoming better people

Since the second edition of this book I have visited
many schools in many countries and worked with
many wonderful educators. What excites me most, is
that my old home country Austria is now taking on
the diversity concept and I feel privileged and grateful
for being part of this no longer quiet but profound
<u>shift in thinking</u> about learning and teaching <u>on a
global scale</u>. I have seen incredible changes in
previous 'hopeless' learning situations, countless
projects being instigated and witnessed even more
long-term, <u>sustainable changes</u> in schoools.

shift in thinking
on a global scale

sustainable changes

And that gives me great <u>hope for the future</u>.

hope for the future

In possession of
more developed minds,
people will be able to find
within themselves
the elements needed
to build a new society.

Luis Machado

Afterthoughts to this third edition of *The Power of Diversity* by Hofrat Dr Günter Schmid, Principal of two combined secondary schools in Vienna, Austria

An internet search on 'learning theories' is an awe-inspiring experience indeed. The sheer wealth of names and titles is so imposing that it may make even the most committed reader shrink from plunging into yet another publication on the subject and, for convenience's sake, adhere to cherished old beliefs instead. After all, are we not all experts in the field? Have we not all been learners at some point in our lives? Some of us may even be active teachers, who by definition know all about the craft anyway – or so we think. And those who are not, have experienced what it is like to be the object (or victim, as the case may be) of teaching to such an extent that they may well feel they cannot be bothered with further literature on the subject.

On the other hand, not many former students were lucky enough to have been actively involved in a learning process as subjects in the full sense of the word, i.e. as the ones who actually organize and manage their own education. Therefore, any author who does not confine himself or herself to dealing with the phenomenon of learning in an abstract way, i.e. as an object of theoretical research, but focuses rather on the practical situation of the individual learner, indeed deserves our wholehearted attention.

Barbara Prashnig is not a researcher by nature, although she does rely on the results of empirical research. As a practising teacher, she endured the duration of a classical teaching career from primary school to high school. But being a 'special case', as pointed out above, she soon realized that fulfilling the role of an authentic 'pedagogue' in the original sense of the word meant more than simply dealing out information and knowledge for learners to 'consume'. She was also conscious of the fact that the traditional system did not provide for any alternative approach. Finding herself unable to accept the conditions that this system was imposing on her as a teacher, she decided, instead of lamenting it, to actively address it. As the preliminary results of her reforms bore fruit, she embarked upon a career as a teacher trainer and, in due course, as a university lecturer – not with a view to personal professional promotion but because she was determined to improve the situation of learners and teachers alike.

The degree of her success was reflected in the numerous compelling reports of learners, teachers and head teachers in the first edition of this volume (published in 1998). In his preface to the first edition Gordon Dryden wrote that he 'love[s] this book [as] it delivers a vital message of hope that is desperately needed by millions of students and parents around the world'. I for my part would add: 'It is above all a "must" for teachers, no matter to which pedagogical "school" they adhere.' For the 'traditionally minded', highly committed, but often frustrated teacher, this book may be somewhat of an eye-opener; it is capable of providing a stimulus for self-development and may thus prepare the ground for a quick remedy to alleviate the teacher's (and possibly the learners') suffering. The inveterate 'conservative' teacher may at least be given pause for thought. And for those already on their way into the twenty-first century, this volume will contribute to confirming and reinforcing views already held (albeit often subconsciously) and will provide the impetus for further development.

I believe....

your life can be changed in a matter of hours
by people who don't even know you.

I believe....

that our background and circumstances
may have influenced who we are,
but we are responsible for who we become.

I believe....

either you control your attitude
or it controls you.

I believe....

The impossible is what nobody can do
until somebody DOES it.

It is my firm belief that 'being a good teacher' (however one may choose to define this) is much more dependent on a certain pedagogical attitude than on factual knowledge or even methodological competence. Knowledge was looked upon as the ultimate goal of education until the middle of the twentieth century. The dominant approach to teaching was content-oriented; what counted was quantity (of teaching content and the resulting knowledge) rather than quality (of the learning experience). In the final decades of the twentieth century (the pedagogical revolution started at different times in different parts of the world) the focus of attention was gradually shifted from the product of teaching to the process of learning. It was the 'golden age' of methodology (or rather: methodologies). While this was certainly an important step forward, the 'revolution' was only half-cooked. It was still the teacher who was regarded as the key figure in this process. It fell to him or her to find suitable strategies to deal with the groups of learners of which he or she was in charge. Learners were still considered to be 'objects' (victims?) in this process.

It was not until the 1990s that the focus was finally shifted from the teaching to the learning end of this continuum. Methods such as Suggestopedia, Superlearning or NLP, to name but a few, have since helped many a highly motivated learner to achieve better results at a faster rate.

The basic problem, however, remained unsolved. For not all learners are highly motivated and prepared to actively look for more promising learning techniques. What is needed, therefore, is yet another paradigm shift: having proceeded from an object-based approach (focusing on contents to be taught/learned, goals to be achieved) to a process-oriented approach as described above, we now need to demarcate the subject of the learning process, the learner him/herself, as the ultimate priority.

But is a learner-centric focus not a 'holy cow' of modern pedagogics anyway? Would anyone dare to argue against the tenet that schools are meant for learners rather than for teachers in the same way as hospitals are meant for the sick rather than for doctors?

Obviously, this catchy formula of a 'learner-centric focus' requires a closer definition. As we understand it, it goes far beyond just focusing on the learner and on his/her role as an object of teaching. It means taking them 100 per cent seriously as a person and accepting them with all their likes and preferences. This goes far beyond that which is traditionally understood by the term and requires a very specific attitude on the part of the teacher. It can be achieved only on the basis of a deep sense of respect for the learner's entire personality, of a close understanding of how he or she functions as a human being, on the intellectual as well as the emotional or even physical planes.

What is needed to promote such a 'holistic' approach is not so much training on various theories of methodology as awareness-raising. For a good teacher it is not enough to 'differentiate' (however this may be achieved in the individual learning situation), as 'differentiation' only affects the teacher's own lesson planning and classroom management. Even that which is currently looked upon as the 'alpha and omega' of good teaching, viz. individualization, is not in itself sufficient. It is certainly a very important, if not the most important principle in the teaching–learning continuum, as it proceeds on the correct assumption that each learner is a unique individual who should be supplied

While you are alive,
You are unique.

Only corpses are
All alike,
Alive persons are unique.

They are never similar –
They cannot be.

Life never follows
Any repetitive course.

Osho

with materials and tasks that suit his or her specific interests and special gifts and will thus motivate them to learn rather than to simply be taught. But this is extremely difficult for the teacher to put into practice, unless the necessary information about each individual learner´s specific needs and learning styles is available or easily accessible.

To sum up: each learner has a natural right to be fully accepted as the person he or she actually is: not condescendingly, in the sense of being 'pardoned' for their deficiencies, but with full respect for their unique personality. To enable the learner to develop this unique personality by actively planning and managing their own education rather than just 'consuming' information – however attractively this may be presented – is the first and foremost task of a good teacher. The ideal of the 'individualization' of the learning process as the ultimate goal of teaching should actually be replaced by the concept of 'personalization'.

In order to achieve this, the teacher must:

(a) be willing to cater to the specific needs of each individual learner; and

(b) gain the deepest possible insight into these needs by trying to empathize with each learner and by identifying their personal learning styles.

The former requirement is a matter of attitude on the teacher's part. As for the latter, Barbara Prashnig has developed a tool that does this part of the job for the teacher. The LSA (learning style analysis) has meanwhile been successfully tested around the globe and has met with universal approval, as witnessed by the numerous contributions to the first edition as well as a number of new submissions in this volume. The most important supplement to the first edition that this volume offers is a professional development tool for teachers, the TSA (Teaching Style Analysis). While there can be no doubt that the learner remains the central figure in the pedagogical process, it is also very helpful for the teacher to be fully aware of his or her own teaching style. For whenever this turns out to be incompatible with the learner's learning style (an all too familiar scenario in so-called 'problem classes'), a quick remedy may be at hand, i.e. if the teacher can bring him/herself to adapt their own teaching style to individual learning situations, rather than to expect his students to do so.

By way of conclusion, I am not intent on belittling the merits of preceding pedagogical reforms. It is clearly important to deal very seriously with questions of methodology and to develop ever more efficient teaching and learning strategies. It is more important still to understand the phenomenon of learning, preferably on the basis of a sound comprehension of how the human brain works (brain research). It is absolutely essential to accept the fact that each learner is a unique individual and to organize one's teaching accordingly (individualization). Barbara Prashnig's book seeks not to contradict any of these principles, on the contrary: as the situation of the individual learner (and of the 'suffering' teacher, for that matter) will improve as individual learning styles are better understood (and teaching styles adapted), it can be seen as the 'missing link' between all preceding useful contributions to pedagogical theory and the actual, measurable benefit for the learner (and teacher).

How I Feel About Learning

<u>SCORING</u>: Circle your results for each statement.

Quest.	True	False	Quest.	True	False
1	-2	+2	9	+2	-1
2	+1	-1	10	-1	0
3	+1	-2	11	-2	+2
4	-1	+1	12	+2	0
5	+1	0	13	-1	+1
6	-1	0	14	+1	-1
7	-1	+1	15	-2	+1
8	-1	+1	16	+2	0

Please add up all the + and − figures. Subtract the minus result from the plus result. You will either have a zero, a plus or minus end result.

<u>RESULTS</u>

+9 to +19 points: You have a high learning motivation and a very positive attitude towards learning. Learning in general is fun for you and you always gain a lot from learning situations.

+8 to -8 points: Your learning attitude is average, neither very positive nor really negative. By working through this book you have (had) the opportunity to gain a totally new learning experience. This will definitely change your attitude towards learning into a more positive direction.

-9 to -17 points: You have a rather negative attitude towards learning. Maybe you should ask yourself the following questions and try to answer them honestly:

1. Can I really prove that I am a poor learner? Maybe I have just adopted one teacher's negative remarks from the past?
2. Can I really prove that I have a poor memory – in general or only when I am learning difficult content?
3. Is there really any proof that I cannot concentrate?
4. Is learning always a drag for me? Maybe the reason for that lies in the methods used.
5. What was the reason for why learning has been little fun for me in the past? Perhaps my learning style has never been taken into account?

Before I conclude my attempts to open your minds to the joys of human diversity and its effects on our daily lives, privately and professionally, I would like to thank you sincerely for reading the book and taking an interest in a topic which has grown ever closer to my heart over the past few years.

Depending where you are on your path to discovering, accepting and appreciating diversity, particularly in learning, teaching and life situations, this book will either have provoked your thoughts, stimulated your interest, given you some answers or new perspectives or generated more questions than answers. When any of the above happens, we know that your brain is learning, and usually learning fast, and that is good for you, because only by stimulation and new input is it possible to develop your mental capacities.

No matter who you are or where you are in your development right now, I hope this book has inspired you to take action, to *do* something to help yourself and others to learn, teach, study, work, concentrate and communicate better. Hopefully it will also help you to achieve your goals, to develop your full potential and to be the best you can. You deserve it! I am sure you will agree with me: to master any situation successfully you need to know yourself, your style, your strengths and weaknesses.

This book is a more specific 'How to' guide to deeper self-knowledge, to better learning and teaching methods, and to managing yourself, your children and your life more satisfactorily with the help of learning, teaching and working styles.

If the revelations or the exercises in this book have helped you to come to terms with some nagging questions or doubts you might have had about your own style or your learning abilities, I do hope that each chapter has given you some insights, some 'Ahas!', some comfort even, so that you can say: 'Now I understand!'

I also want you to know that you are not alone in your struggle to make sense of other people, your children or even yourself. Thousands of people around the world have the same difficulty in understanding themselves, are often puzzled by their own and other people's reactions to learning, teaching or life situations, and wonder (like I did for years) what's going on inside their heads and how they could come to terms with what makes them tick.

If you are a teacher, I hope I have not offended you. If you are a parent, I hope I have shown you some ways to support your children in learning. And if you are a person who wants to learn, I hope I have given you plenty of food for thought.

As I am always looking for better and more exciting ways to help people help themselves, I would be delighted to hear from readers who have already used our TSA, LSA or WSA instruments and the diversity approach in their school, family or workplace. Your feedback, your ideas for improvement, your creative applications and/or your general experiences with this new tool would be greatly appreciated. Please write to me; you can find our website address in Appendix II.

Chapter 1

1. Dunn, Rita and Dunn, Kenneth. *Teaching Secondary Students Through Their Individual Learning Styles: Practical Approaches for Grades 7–12.* Boston: Allyn and Bacon, 1993. p. 2.

Chapter 2

1. Dellinger, Susan. *Psycho-Geometrics: How to Use Geometric Psychology to Influence People.* Englewood Cliffs, NJ: Prentice Hall, 1989. pp. 1–12.
2. Dunn, Rita and Dunn, Kenneth. *Teaching Secondary Students Through Their Individual Learning Styles: Practical Approaches for Grades 7–12.* Boston: Allyn and Bacon, 1993. p. 25.
3. Grinder, Michael. *Righting the Educational Conveyor Belt.* Portland, OR: Metamorphous Press, 1991. pp. 16–17, 19–21.
4. McCarthy, Bernice. *The 4MAT System: Teaching to Learning Styles with Left/Right Mode Techniques.* Barrington, IL: Excel Inc, 1987. pp. 35, 48–50.
5. Dunn, Rita and Dunn, Kenneth. *Teaching Elementary Students Through Their Individual Learning Styles: Practical Approaches for Grades 3–6.* Boston: Allyn and Bacon, 1992. pp. 3–5, 488.
6. Herrmann, Ned. *The Creative Brain.* Lake Lure: Brain Books, The Ned Herrmann Group, 1989. pp. 162, 218.
7. Butler, Kathleen. *Learning and Teaching in Style: In Theory and Practice.* Australia: Hawker Brownlow Education, 1986. pp. 14–16.

Chapter 3

1. Barker, Joel A. *Future Edge: Discovering the New Paradigms of Success.* New York: William Morrow & Co., 1992. p. 32.
2. —. pp. 205–206.
3. Caine, Renate M. and Rosengren, Tennes M. 'What's happening in students' brains may redefine teaching'. *Educational Leadership,* May 1990, p. 49.
4. Campbell, Don. *The Mozart Effect™: Tapping the Power of Music to Heal the Body, Strengthen the Mind, and Unlock the Creative Spirit.* Rydalmere, NSW: Hodder & Stoughton, 1997. p. 147.

Chapter 4

1. Prashnig, Barbara. *Diversity is our Strength: The Learning Revolution in Action, a Guide to Better Living, Learning and Working.* Auckland: Profile Books, 1996. pp. 22, 109–131.

Chapter 5

1. Dunn, Rita. 'Teaching underachievers through their learning style strengths'. *A Review of Articles and Books,* Part I, Winter 1990, 51.
2. Elgin, Suzette Haden. *Try to Feel It My Way: New Help for Touch Dominant People and Those Who Care About Them.* New York: John Wiley & Sons, 1996. page x, preface.

3. *A Review of Articles and Books*. Part I. Learning Styles Network, School of Education and Human Services, Jamaica, NY: St John's University, 1992. Various articles, pp. 64, 68, 164.
4. Treffinger, Donald J. 'Programming for giftedness and talent development', in the workbook for the 16th Annual Leadership Institute, St John's University, Jamaica, NY, 1993, p. 166.
5. Zenhausern, Robert. *Hemispheric Dominance Test*. Used with permission and based on an extract given to the author in New York (1993).
6. Treffinger, Donald J. 'Programming for giftedness and talent development', in the workbook for the 16th Annual Leadership Institute, St John's University, Jamaica, NY, 1993, p. 164.
7. Dunn, R., Beaudry, J. and Klavas, A. 'Survey of research on learning styles'. *Educational Leadership*, March 1989, 50–1.

Chapter 6

1. *Annotated Bibliography*. Learning Styles Network, Centre for the Study of Learning and Teaching Styles, Jamaica, NY: St John's University, 1991.
2. Milgram, R., Dunn, R. and Price, G. (eds) *Teaching and Counseling Gifted and Talented Adolescents: An International Learning Style Perspective*. Westport, CT: Praeger, 1993. p. 10.
3. —. p. 18.
4. Klivington, Kenneth A. *The Science of Mind*. Cambridge, MA: The MIT Press, 1989. p. 176.
5. Gold, Lonny. *Suggestopedia: Activating the Student's Reserve Capacities*. Paris: Trajectoires Associées, 1985. pp. 2–3.
6. Schuster, Donald. *How to Learn Quickly – An Introduction to Fast and Easy Learning*. Ames, IA: Iowa State University, 1987. p. 1.
7. Lozanov, Georgi and Gateva, Evelina: *The Foreign Language Teacher's Suggestopedic Manual*. New York: Gordon and Breach, 1988. pp. 64–6, 133, 214–226.
8. Webb, Terry W. and Webb, Douglas: *Accelerated Learning with Music – A Trainer's Manual*. Denton, TX: Accelerated Learning Systems, 1991. p. 51.
9. Rauscher, F., Shaw, G. and Ky, K. 'Listening to Mozart enhances spatial-temporal reasoning: towards a neurophysiological basis'. *Neuroscience Letters* 185, 1995, 44–7.
10. Weinberger, Norman. 'Announcing a free information source in music', University of California, Irvine, CA. email: mbi@mila.ps.uci.edu

Chapter 7

1. Dunn, Rita and Dunn, Kenneth. 'Dispelling outmoded beliefs about student learning'. *Educational Leadership*, March 1987, 55–60.
2. Paine, John, Turner, Phillip and Pryke, Robert. *Total Quality in Education*. Sydney: Ashton Scholastic, 1992. p. 8.

3. Glasser, William. *The Quality School, Managing Students without Coercion.* New York: Harper Perennial, 1992. pp. 1–2.
4. —. *The Quality School Teacher.* New York: Harper Perennial, 1993. pp. 22–5.
5. Chamberlain, V., Hopper, B. and Jack, B. *Starting Out MI Way: A Guide to Multiple Intelligences in the Primary School.* Bolton: D2, 1996. p. 7.
6. Gardner, Howard. *Multiple Intelligences: The Theory in Practice.* New York: Basic Books, 1993. p. 36.
7. Armstrong, Thomas. *Seven Kinds of Smart – Identifying and Developing Your Many Intelligences.* New York: A Plume Book, 1993. pp. 18–23.
8. Salovey, Peter and Meyer, John D. 'Emotional intelligence'. *Imagination, Cognition and Personality,* Vol. 9, 1990, 185–211.
9. Goleman, Daniel. *Emotional Intelligence: Why It Can Matter More Than IQ.* London: Bloomsbury Publishing, 1996. p. 233.
10. Coles, Robert. *The Moral Intelligence of Children.* London: Bloomsbury Publishing, 1997. p. 5.

Chapter 8
1. Marston, William Moulton. *The Emotions of Normal People.* Minneapolis, MN: Persona Press, 1979. pp. 12–14.
2. EFL – *Excellence for Learning* (Administrator Version – computer-generated report) Software. Scottsdale, AZ: Target Training International, 1991.
3. Robbins, Anthony. *Awaken the Giant Within.* New York: Summit Books, 1991. p. 97.

Chapter 9
1. Glasser, William. *The Quality School Teacher.* New York: Harper Perennial, 1993. p. 19.

Chapter 10
1. Ornstein, Robert. *The Roots of the Self: Unraveling the Mystery of Who We Are.* New York: Harper San Francisco, 1993. pp. 131–2.
2. Moir, Anne and Jessel, David. *BrainSex – The Real Difference Between Men and Women.* London: Mandarin, 1989. p. 111.
3. Evatt, Cris. *He & She: 60 Significant Differences Between Men and Women.* Berkeley, CA: Conari Press, 1992. p. 48.
4. Tannen, Deborah. *That's Not What I Meant: How Conversational Style Makes or Breaks your Relations with Others.* London: Virago Press, 1992. pp. 109, 110.
5. Moir, Anne and Jessel, David. *BrainSex – The Real Difference Between Men and Women.* London: Mandarin, 1989. p. 111.
6. Jensen, Eric. *The Learning Brain.* Del Mar, CA: Turning Point for Teachers, 1994. pp. 296–7.

Chapter 11
1. Hannaford, Carla. *Smart Moves: Why Learning is Not All in Your Head.* Arlington, VA: Great Ocean Publishers, 1995. pp. 82–3.
2. Seligman, Martin. *Learned Optimism.* Sydney: Random House, 1994. p. 147.
3. —. p. 148.

Chapter 12
1. Gross, Ronald. *Peak Learning: A Master Course in Learning How to Learn.* Los Angeles: Tarcher, 1991. pp. 9–10.
2. Beaver, Diana. *Lazy Learning: Making the Most of the Brains You Were Born With.* Shaftesbury: Element, 1994. p. 135.
3. Gleick, James. *Chaos: Making a New Science.* New York: Penguin, 1988. p. 8.
4. Legge, John. *Chaos Theory and Business Planning: How Great Effects Come from Small Causes.* Melbourne: Schwartz and Wilkinson, 1990. p. 122.
5. Jensen, Eric. *The Learning Brain.* Del Mar, CA: Turning Point for Teachers 1994. p. 90.
6. Clifton, Donald, O. and Nelson, Paula. *Play to Your Strengths.* London: Piatkus, 1994. p. 7.
7. —. *Play to Your Strengths.* London: Piatkus, 1994. p. 133.
8. Alder, Harry. *The Right Brain Manager: How to Harness the Power of your Mind to Achieve Personal and Business Success.* London: Piatkus, 1993. pp. 15–16.
9. Robbins, Anthony. *Unlimited Power.* London: Simon and Schuster, 1988. p. 348.
10. Wohlman, Gary. A quote frequently used during his workshop *Mastering Presentation Skills.* Mill Valley, CA (since 1993).
11. Clifton, Donald, O. and Nelson, Paula. *Play to Your Strengths.* London: Piatkus, 1994. p. 28.

Chapter 13
1. Palmer, Lyelle, L. 'Education's ecstasy explosion: the joyful experience of super-accelerative learning and teaching'. *Holistic Education Review*, Fall 1990, 47–51.
2. Ingham, Joanne. 'Learning styles: challenging and transforming education'. *Innotech Journal,* Vol. XVI No. 1, January–June 1992, 37–44.
3. Dryden, Gordon and Vos, Jeannette. *The Learning Revolution: Your 21st Century, Passport for Families, Students, Teachers, Managers, Trainers.* Fully revised 2nd edition. Auckland: The Learning Web Co., 1997. pp. 431–55.
4. MacRae-Campbell, Linda. 'How to start a revolution at your school'. *In Context,* Vol. 27, 1990, 56–9.

Armstrong, Thomas. *Multiple Intelligences in the Classroom*. Alexandria, VA: Association for Supervision and Curriculum Development, 1994.

—. *The Myth of the A.D.D. Child: 50 Ways to Improve Your Child's Behaviour and Attention Span Without Drugs, Labels or Coercion*. New American Library, 1997.

Barrett, Susan L. *It's All in Your Head: A Guide to Understanding Your Brain and Boosting Your Brain Power*. Minneapolis: Free Spirit Publishing Inc., 1992.

Bartlett, David and Davis, Ann. *Partners in Learning*. Booklet and DVD. Birmingham: Television Junction, Birmingham City Council, 2006.

Birkenbihl, Vera F. *Stroh im Kopf: Vom Gehirn-Besitzer zum Gehirn-Beutzer*. Heidelberg: MVG Verlag, 2006.

Bonnstetter, Bill J., Suiter, Judy and Widrick, Randy Jay. *The Universal Language – DISC: A Reference Manual*. Scottsdale, AZ: Target Training International, 1993.

Bramson, Robert M. *Coping with Difficult People: Learn the Six Basic Steps that Allow you to Cope with just About Anyone*. Melbourne: The Business Library, 1981.

Brewer, Chris and Campbell, Don. *Rhythms of Learning*. Sydney: Hawker Brownlow Education, 1992.

Burns, Stephanie. *Great Lies We Live By*. Ultimo, Australia: Bramley Press, 1993.

Buzan, Tony with Buzan, Barry. *The Mind Map Book: Radiant Thinking. The Major Evolution in Human Thought*. London: BBC Enterprises, 1993.

Caine, Geoffrey, Nummela-Caine, Renate and Crowel, Sam. *Mindshifts*. Tucson, AZ: Zephyr Press, 1994.

Campbell, Don G. *Introduction to the Musical Brain*. 2nd ed. St Louis, MO: MMB Music Inc., 1992.

—. *The Roar of Silence: Healing Powers of Breath, Tone and Music*. Wheaton, IL: The Theosophical Publishing House, 1989.

Capelli, Glen. *Born to Learn. Advanced Learning Strategies*. Englewood: Jones Education Network, 1995 (Study Guide and video tapes).

Cherry, Clare, Godwin, Douglas and Staples, Jessie. *Is the Left Brain Always Right?* Belmont, CA: Fearon Teacher Aids, 1989.

Csikszentmihalyi, Mihaly. *Flow: The Psychology of Optimal Experience*. San Francisco: Harper Perennial, 1990.

Claxton, Guy. *Wise Up: The Challenge of Lifelong Learning*. London and New York: Bloomsbury, 1999.

—. *Building Learning Power*. Bristol, UK: TLO Limited, 2002.

Creating the Future: Perspectives on Educational Change. Compiled and edited by Dee Dickinson. Aston Clinton, Bucks: Accelerated Learning Systems, 1991.

Cummings, Rhoda W. *The School Survival Guide for Kids with LD** [*Learning Differences]. Minneapolis, MN: Free Spirit Publishing, 1991.

Cutter, Rebecca. *When Opposites Attract: Right Brain/Left Brain Relationships and How to Make Them Work*. New York: Dutton, 1994.

Dare to be Yourself: Knowing Who You Are – You and Others – Learning to Like Yourself – Conquering Your Fears – Going for Change. Edited by Jane Lang. Amsterdam: Time-Life Books, 1995.

Dennison, Paul E. *Brain Gym: Simple Activities for Whole Brain Learning*. Ventura, CA: Edu-Kinesthetics, Inc., 1986.

De Porter, Bobbi. *Quantum Learning*. London: Piatkus, 1993.

Diamond, Marian. *Enriching Heredity*. New York: Macmillan, 1988.

Dickinson, Dee. *New Horizons for Learning: Creating an Educational Network*. Seattle: New Horizons for Learning, 1990.

Dudink, Ad and Clifford, Pamela. *The Brain Pack*. Datchet, Berkshire: Van der Meer Publishing, 1997.

Dunn, Rita and Dunn, Kenneth. *Teaching Students Through Their Individual Learning Styles: A Practical Approach*. Reston, VA: Reston Publishing Co., 1978.

Dunn, Rita and Griggs, Shirley A. *Learning Styles: A Quiet Revolution in American Secondary Schools*. Reston, VA: National Association of Secondary School Principals, 1988.

Faber, Adele and Mazlish, Elaine. *How To Talk So Kids Will Listen & Listen So Kids Will Talk*. New York: Avon Books, 1982.

Feuerstein, Reuven. *Instrumental Enrichment*. Baltimore, MD: University Park Press, 1980.

Fleetham, Mike. *Multiple Intelligences*. London: Network Continuum Education, 2007.

FUNdamentals. Edited and published by Accelerated Learning Systems, Aylesbury, 1996.

Gardner, Howard. *Frames of Mind*. New York: Basic Books, 1983.

—. *The Unschooled Mind*. New York: Basic Books, 1991.

Gee, J.P. *What Video Games Have to Teach Us About Learning and Literacy*. New York: Palgrave Macmillan, 2003.

Gilchrist, Robert. *Effective Schools: Three Studies of Excellence*. Bloomington, IN: National Educational Service, 1989.

Glass, Lillian. *He Says, She Says: Closing the Communication Gap Between the Sexes*. Sydney: Bantam Books, 1993.

Gordon, Noah. *Magical Classroom: Creating Effective, Brain-Friendly Environments for Learning*. Tucson, AZ: Zephyr Press, 1997.

Gray, John. *Men are from Mars, Women are from Venus: A Practical Guide for Improving Communication and Getting What You Want in Your Relationships*. London: Thorsons, 1993.

Greenfield, Susan. *The Human Brain: A Guided Tour*. London: Weidenfeld and Nicolson, 1997.

Griggs, Shirley A. *Learning Styles Counseling*. ERIC Counseling and Personnel Services Clearinghouse, Ann Arbor: The University of Michigan, 1991.

Grinder, Michael. *ENVoY: Your Personal Guide to Classroom Management*. Washington: Michael Grinder, 1993.

Hannaford, Carla. *The Dominance Factor: How Knowing Your Dominant Eye, Ear, Brain, Hand and Foot Can Improve Your Learning*. Arlington, VA: Great Ocean Publishers, 1997.

—. *Smart Moves: Why Learning Is Not All In Your Head*. Arlington, VA: Great Ocean Publishers, 1995.

Healy, Jane M. *Endangered Minds*. New York: Simon & Schuster, 1990.

Heitkämper, Peter. *Mehr Lust auf Schule: Ein Handbuch für innovativen und gehirngerechten Unterricht*. Paderborn: Jungfermann, 1995.

Hutchinson, Michael. *Mega Brain Power – Transform Your Life with Mind Machines and Brain Nutrients*. New York: Hyperion, 1994.

—. *Brain-Based Learning and Teaching*. Del Mar, CA: Turning Point for Teachers, 1995.

Iggulden, Conn and Hal. *The Dangerous Book for Boys*. New York and UK: Harper Collins, 2006.

Jensen, Eric P. *Brain Compatible Strategies*. Del Mar, CA: Turning Point Publishing, 1997.

—. *Completing the Puzzle: A Brain-Based Approach to Learning*. Del Mar, CA: Turning Point for Teachers, 1996.

—. *Super-Teaching*. Del Mar, CA: Turning Point for Teachers, 1988.

Kline, Peter and Martel, Laurence D. *School Success*. Arlington, VA: Learning Matters Inc., 1992.

Kühn, Lotte. *Das Lehrerhasserbuch: Eine Mutter rechnet ab*. München: Knaur Taschenbuch Verlag, 2005.

—. *Elternsprechtag. Wie Schlimm ist Schule wirklich?Was Eltern, Schüler und Lehrer täglich erleben*. München: Knauer Taschenbuch Verlag, 2006.

Lang, Binny and Lang, Chris. *Your Future Success: A Student's Guide to Effective Study*. Melbourne: Ashwood House, 1990.

Lazear, David. *Seven Ways of Knowing: Teaching for Multiple Intelligences*. Sydney: Hawker Brownlow Education, 1990.

Lucas, Bill with Dr Stephen Briers. *Happy Families: How to Make One – How to Keep One*. Harlow, Essex: BBC Active, 2006.

MacGregor, Sandy. *Piece of Mind*. Lindfield, Australia: Creative Accelerated Learning Methods, 1993.

McPhee, Doug. *Limitless Learning: Making Powerful Learning an Everyday Event*. Tucson, AZ: Zephyr Press, 1996.

Maples, Tim. *Accelerated Learning: Effective Knowledge Acquisition*. Nelson, New Zealand: Inova Publications, 1994.

Margulies, Nancy. *The Magic Seven: Tools for Building your Multiple Intelligences*. Tucson, AZ: Zephyr Press, 1995.

—. *Mapping Inner Space: Learning and Teaching Mind Mapping*. Tucson, AZ: Zephyr Press, 1991.

Mellander, K. *Power-Learning*. Landsberg: MVG Verlag, 2001.

Merritt, Stephanie. *Mind, Music and Imagery: Unlocking the Treasures of Your Mind. 38 Activities With Music To Stimulate Creativity And Transform Your Life*. Santa Rosa, CA: Aslan Publishing, 1996.

Mukerjea, Dilip. *Brainfinity*. Singapore: Oxford University Press, 1997.

—. *Superbrain: Train Your Brain and Unleash the Genius Within*. Singapore: Heinemann Southeast Asia, 1996.

New Directions in Education: Selections from the Holistic Education Review. Edited by Ron Miller. Brandon, VT: Holistic Education Press, 1991.

Nicholson, John. *Men and Women: How Different are They?* Oxford: Oxford University Press, 1993.

Nummela-Caine, Renate and Caine, Geoffrey. *Making Connections: Teaching and the Human Brain*. Menlo Park, CA: Addison-Wesley Publishing Co., 1994.

O'Hara, Brendan. *The Children's Song Book*. Rye, Victoria: The F# Music Company Pty., 1991.

Ornstein, Robert. E. *The Roots of the Self: Unraveling the Mystery of Who We Are.* New York: Harper San Francisco, 1993.

Patterson, Marilyn, N. *Every Body Can Learn: Engaging the Bodily-Kinesthetic Intelligence in the Everyday Classroom.* Tucson, AZ: Zephyr Press, 1997.

Prashnig, Barbara. *Learning Styles in Action.* London: Network Continuum Education, 2007.

—. *Learning Styles and Personalized Teaching.* London: Network Continuum Education, 2007.

Ritt, Thomas C., Jr. *Understanding Yourself and then Others.* Tequesta, FL: People Concepts, 1980.

Robbins, Anthony. *Awaken the Giant Within,* New York: Summit Books, 1991.

—. *Giant Steps. Small Changes to Make a Big Difference: 365 Daily Lessons in Self-Mastery.* Simon & Schuster, New York, 1994.

Rodriguez, E. and Bellanca, J. *What Is It About Me You Can't Teach? An Instructional Guide for Today's Educator.* Sydney: Skylight, 1997.

Rose, Colin and Goll, Louise. *Accelerate Your Learning. A World of Opportunity in Your Hands. Introduction. Action Handbook. Six Super Skills.* Aylesbury: Accelerated Learning Systems, 1992.

Segal, Jeanne. *Raising Your Emotional Intelligence: A Practical Guide.* New York: Henry Holt and Company, 1997.

Smith, Shirley with Neller, S. *Set Yourself Free.* Sydney: Bantam Books, 1990.

Spitzer, Manfred. *Lernen: Die Entdeckung des Selbstverständlichen.* Book and DVD. Hamburg: Archiv der Zukunft, 2006.

—. *Lernen: Gehirnforschung und die Schule des Lernens.* Berlin-Heidelberg: Springer-Verlag, 2007.

Stockwell, Tony. *Accelerated Learning in Theory and Practice.* Triesen, Liechtenstein: EFFECT: European Foundation for Education, 1992.

Sylwester, Robert. *A Celebration of Neurons: An Educator's Guide to the Human Brain.* Alexandria, VA: Association for Supervision and Curriculum Development, 1995.

Tannen, Deborah. *You Just Don't Understand: Women and Men in Conversation.* New York: William Morrow Company, 1990.

Taylor, William and LaBarre, Polly. *Mavericks at Work. Why the Most Original Minds in Business Win.* New York: Harper Collins, 2006.

Van der Kley, Martin. *Disruptive Children – How to Manage their Behaviour.* New Zealand: Macprint Printing, Christchurch, 1992.

Veen, Wim and Vrakking, Ben. *Homo Zappiens, Growing Up in a Digital Age.* London: Network Continuum Education, 2006.

Wade, John. *Super Study. Mount Waverly,* Australia: Dellasta Pty, 1994.

Ward, Christine, and Daley, Jan. *Learning to Learn: Strategies for Accelerating Learning and Boosting Performance.* Christchurch, New Zealand: published by the authors, 1993.

Was für Schulen! Gute Schule in Deutschland. Im Auftrag der Robert Bosch & Heidehof Stiftung. Herausgegeben von P. Fauser, M. Prenzl, M. Schratz. Seelze-Velber: Klett-Kallmeyer, 2007.

Wege zur Begabungsförderung – Symposion Sir Karl Popper Schule. (4–6.10.2004) Edited and published by Dr Günter Schmid, Vienna: Wiedner Gymnasium, 2005.

Weiss, Daniel E. *The Great Divide: How Males and Females Really Differ*. New York: Poseidon Press, 1991.

Whitmore, Diana. *The Joy of Learning: A Guide to Psychosynthesis in Education*. Crucible, Wellingborough: The Aquarian Press, 1990.

Winebrenner, Susan. *Teaching Kids With Learning Difficulties in the Regular Classroom: Strategies and Techniques Every Teacher Can Use to Challenge and Motivate Struggling Students*. Minneapolis, MN: Free Spirit Publishing, 1996.

Wujek, T. *Salto Mentale. Fitneß Für den Kopf*. Kreuzlingen: Ariston, 1998.

Articles

'A remedy for underachievement'. *Programme designed by Paul Butler. Out Of The Box Consultancy*. (2001) handout www.geocities.com

'Das Zappelphilipp-Syndrom: Wann sind Kinder psychisch krank?' *Special Report, Der Spiegel Nr. 29*. (15.7.2002), 123–38.

'How a child's mind develops: fertile minds'. *Special Report, Time Magazine*. February 3, 1997, 34–42.

'Integrative learning: discovering "genius" in every child'. *Innotech Journal*. Volume XVI, No. 1 (January–June 1992): all articles.

'Overcoming dyslexia: what new brain science reveals – and what parents can do'. *Time Magazine*. July 28, 2003, 50–7.

'The Mozart Effect'. *Quality Life Magazine*. February/March 1998, pp. 20–2.

'Suggestopedia: the inner dimension of change'. Lonny Gold in *Conference Proceedings, International SEAL Conference, 31.3.–3.4.2005*, Liverpool, UK, 53–5.

www.authentichappiness.org (Martin Seligman's website about personal strengths)
www.archiv-der-zukunft.de (videos and books about successful schools)
www.ascd.org (professional development, books)
www.allianceforchildhood.net (young children's education)
www.bill-lucas.com (general learning information)
www.buildinglearningpower.co.uk (learning strategies)
www.brainstore.co.uk (making learning fun)
www.brainexpo.com (brain-based learning and teaching)
www.brainconnection.com (brain science and learning)
www.C4lifelonglearning.co.za (learning and working styles)
www.cdipage.com (parenting information and child development)
www.clubztutoring.com (home tutoring services)
www.criticalskills.co.uk (advice for real-life learning)
www.deutscher-schulpreis.de (case studies of exemplary schools)
http://education.college.hmco.com/students (exceptional children)
www.education-otherwise.org (home schooling)
www.ericec.org (myths about gifted students)
www.esteemplus.com (personal and professional growth)
www.eurydice.org (information on education in Europe)
www.findarticles.com (underachievers)
www.fishpond.co.nz (book information LS)
www.funwork.cl (learning techniques)
www.funteaching.it (professional development)
www.hoagiesgifted.org (gifted underachievers)
www.howtolearn.com (learning, reading, LS)
www.interdys.org (information about dyslexia)
www.kidsource.com (gifted underachieving)
www.k-l-s.co.uk (Kaleidoscope Learning Solutions)
www.learningnetwork.ac.nz (general education information)
www.ldpride.net (learning styles)
www.mavericksatwork.com (interesting views about the future of business)
www.mckergow.com (research on music and learning)
www.narva-bel.de (full-spectrum lighting)
www.networkcontinuum.co.uk (resource books for teachers)
www.newcityschool.org (a world-leading MI school)
www.playtoyourstrengths.com (how to maximize one's talents)
www.positivelymad.co.uk (effective teaching and learning)
www.pz.harvard.edu (Howard Gardner's Project Zero and Spectrum research)
www.skyscapes.biz (panels for diffusing light)
www.smartkids.co.uk (self-correcting learning tools)
www.songsforteaching.com (music and learning)
www.tlgworks.com (The Learning Game, Scotland)
www.themindgym.com (learning enhancing exercises)
www.thinkingclassroom.co.uk (for discussing MI with Mike Fleetham)
www.treeof.com (fun learning tools)
www.21learn.org (21st Century Learning Initiative)

How to Order CLS Software

For orders worldwide:

www.creativelearningcentre.com
or:
www.clc.co.nz

Creative Learning System's Personal Assessment Software is easy to use, and available for individual or group use, online from our websites above. At the time of print of this book the software was available in eight different languages: English, German, Swedish, Finnish, Norwegian, Danish, Spanish, and Turkish; others are being added continually.

Online profiles
Upon registering on one of our websites, visitors can access their own secure web pages by creating a personal web account, using their personal username and password. From that web account they are able to purchase profile credits, complete questionnaires, send access codes to other users and generate their own personal profiles. These can be viewed on screen, printed and downloaded as a PDF file and stored at their own computer for further use.

Group profiles are free of charge and can be created as soon as five individual personal profiles or any kind of product are stored in one web account. Any combination of individuals can be used according to the group members and more profile credits can be purchased online and added to the existing web account.

Our Style Analysis software is currently available in the following versions:

Learning Style Analysis™ for students of all ages including student, teacher and parent versions

Teaching Style Analysis™ for practising educators

Working Style Analysis™ for people in the workplace including employee and manager versions

Training Style Analysis™ for corporate trainers

Offers the Following Training Programmes:

✍ 'Introduction to Learning Styles' for classroom teachers and educators

✍ 'Diploma in Holistic Education' – a seven-module professional development programme

✍ The 'School of the Future based on Quality and Learning/Teaching Styles' – a management seminar for principals

✍ The 'School of the Future' – an INSET programme for schools

✍ 'International WSA Certification' for managers and trainers

✍ 'DISC' – Managing for Success intensive training

✍ 'Your Way – My Way' – a partner programme based on styles.

For content and dates of our programmes please check our website:

www.creativelearningcentre.com

For information about our new international

Prashnig Style Solutions Partner Programme

please visit:
http://www.creativelearningcentre.com/partners/license-information.html
and for downloading an Application Form:
http://www.creativelearningcentre.com/partners/license-application.html

please visit our website:
www.prashnigstyles.com